Cycling Proficiency
the road to recovery

Written and illustrated by
Alice Lushington

*This book is dedicated to Tom: the only fella
to ever truly embrace hurricane Alice with grace
and patience. I love you to smithereens.
Thank you for all the laughs.*

Cycling Proficiency
the road to recovery

Alice Lushington

ISBN 978-1-903110-92-8

First published in this edition 2022 by Wrecking Ball Press

Book design: humandesign.co.uk

Printed and bound in Great Britain by Clays Ltd, Elcograf S.p.A.

Supported using public funding by
ARTS COUNCIL
ENGLAND
LOTTERY FUNDED

CONTENT

Prologue

How stupid. How utterly, utterly stupid. I told Dad I didn't want to do this stupid cycling proficiency thing, but would he listen? Hannah's Dad didn't make *her* do it so why did *my* Dad have to be such a selfish git? Hours and hours and hours and *hours* in the cold, trying to follow instructions I'd forgotten to listen to – I was thinking about my twig collection. The whole thing was completely pointless. Anyway, I hope Dad feels really, really bad.And God! It was awful. One by one: Greg, Beatrix, Callum, Max, Thomas – 'Thanks Mrs Edmonds!' – other Thomas, Cameron, Lucy, Miles, all gawping at their new triangle badges, twinkling on top of their English books. I peer over Charlotte's shoulder to see hers, perfectly red, green and gold, tucked inside a Ziplock bag. I can't wait! More for the bag, really: me and Tara were going to stash icing sugar in it and pretend to be druggies. I kick my feet into the carpet as Mrs Edmonds kneels beside me, smelling of sweets and antique shops, empty handed. 'Alice,' she whispers, 'Can I talk to you outside?' The only one. The only one in the whole history of the school's cycling proficiency to ever fail. Whatever. I'll probably never cycle again.

1

Leaving home

'Fresh morning.' This was the name of the alarm I had optimistically chosen last night. But at the cold, dark, premature hour of 5.30am, with ears as flimsy and delicate as value ham, I find the title completely offensive. 'Brutal morning' might've sufficed. And what a horrible alarm too. So determinedly shrill! So wilfully perverse! Tearing me away from yet another erotic dream (always about furniture). Peeling *away* the duvet is abo*ut* as painful as peeling off a layer of skin; the day is just too ra*w*.

Could I just... not go? Call the whole thing off and go to France another day? Ugh, I feel sick. Bloody thing. Oh, piss off. Just PISS. OFF.

A flick and a rumble sound from downstairs. Tea. Dad. I thump the screen of my phone until my alarm finally stops, roll onto the floor – THUD – and drag myself on my elbows over to the light switch.

'Argh,' I groan.

Whoever thought upgrading to super-bright bulbs was a good idea? Bet it was Mum.

Once the searing pain in my eyeballs eases and my pupils have shrunk into tight little dots, I wriggle into my permanent outfit for... however long this whole shebang will take. Months, perhaps. My ensemble features: a green cropped-top that, scooping down far too low and finishing much too short, looks like a tiny fabric castle (I call it my 'Lara Croft' top); a lacy-racy bra bought in Marks and Sparks for the bargain price of £1 (because *you never know*); a pair of mum's socks swiped with stealth from the airing cupboard; my trusty, age-14 shorts and finally Dad's XL high-vis vest. Also, like any good cyclist, I've gone commando.

What next? I stagger into the bathroom and assess the abomination staring back at me in a mirror speckled with spearmint spittle (we are six enthusiastic brushers). Dammit! My pasty complexion does nothing for my purple eye-bags, unplucked eyebrows and dirt-flick freckles. Is that a wrinkle? Surely not. At least my hair, which last night was in ringlets and this morning is in zigzags, does a little something to distract from the graphics of my *visage*. I shake my fingers through the zeds then douse my eyes in lashings of black makeup. Thank heavens for eyeliner. I salute into the mirror and tip-toe downstairs.

'How's it going sport?' whispers Dad, dropping a steaming teabag into the bin. I've always been more of a catapultier myself, as the dried-up, brown tears wriggling down the side of the bin so suggest.

'Great! Cheers, that's lovely. Hey Dad, thanks for joining me for today. Ah! I'm so excited!'

'Hey, my absolute pleasure.' Dad hands me our ugliest of Poundland mugs: one naff mug for one naff mug. 'Get that down ya.'

You can tell a lot about a family based on their mugs. None of ours match – doesn't that just scream 'working class' – and I could count on one hand how many of them we'd actually bought. In our house, mugs just seem to spawn.

'Thanks Dad,' I say.

Ah, Dad and me: we've always had a special kind of friendship. Blossoming from a childhood of pasta-Saturdays, fishing trips (fuelled by sausage rolls and Tango), London visits (featuring sausage rolls and Tango), and delivery days (again, more sausage rolls and Tango). Not a lot has changed since then. Apart from the addition of a few almost-mature conversations sprinkled in here and there amid a plethora of stupid jokes, terrible puns and crass impersonations. And of course, these days, a veggie sausage roll substitute.

With a belly full of hot tea, I kiss the soft fluff of my bunny's forehead – 'Bye Bobby' – and ready my panniers. Passport? Yep. Toilet roll? Yep. Pocket French dictionary? Yep. Eyeliner? Yep. Bikini? Yep. Adult baby-grow? Hell yeah! I look over at my Frisbee and pink stilettos. *No, Alice.*

Panniers full, I fasten them onto my bike affectionately christened as *The Insect*. One of our many freebies, given to someone who gave it to Dad, who gave it to me. An Evans Cycles, whose black, scrawny frame the clumsy side of elegant much resembles a praying mantis.

I give Dad a thumbs-up and say, 'Alright, let's go!'

He returns a sharp nod.

We wheel our bikes past the communal trampoline and squirm between the political arena of parked cars, keeping our excitable whoops as whispers so to not wake up the Longs, or Dave, or Kerry, or – God forbid – Albert.

It begins. Tara's old house, the smoking corner, my old primary school, the blowjob wall, the tree I climbed and hid inside when I smoked too much weed. The piece of tarmac I had my very first kiss on, the woods I had once planned to make my permanent home when I ran away from school, the swings I swung on tentatively as a child and dangerously as an adolescent. Home shrinks away behind us.

17 miles later, Dad and I reach the Downs: swelling undulations of green, rippling far into the distance. Amidst them, an unfortunate blotch of grey mould sits next to the sea.

'Look!' says Dad. 'There's Newhaven!'

So down we plummet over the bumpy fields towards what I could only describe as a kind of urban abscess.

Naturally, Dad has bought the wrong ticket, much to the grief of the ticket lady who sighs, pursues a 10-minute tip-tapping session on a keyboard, requests a £38 sacrifice, and prints a new one. With all that admin done we plonk ourselves in the waiting lounge and retrieve Mum's potato cakes. I smile at the cheerful punctuation of peas and sweetcorn, then assess the room. Can you really call a dingy box only a line of blue chairs and a dodgy coffee machine away from complete vacancy a 'lounge'? I have my reservations. It's austereness and general sense of impending doom remind me of hospital, and I cannot eat breakfast.

Prompted by a screeching whistle, people begin shuffling their way outside.

'Shit,' hisses Dad, scalding his hands with coffee.

We roll aboard, me following behind Dad who is still cursing the coffee he'd just bought from the vending machine.

Window seats bagsied, we nestle ourselves with overpriced

cups of tea which judder and slosh as the ferry sets sail. Me and Dad exchange a look of frenzied excitement and watch Newhaven recede out of view.

Ten minutes in and Dad's conversational responses have turned limp as last night's too-many-beers-on-the-sofa have finally caught up with him. So I considerately leave him, tea in one hand newspaper in another, to nurse his hangover in peace. Besides, surely one of the best things about ferry trips is the nauseating walk around the nauseating shop? The rocking motion needn't be there: the garishness, claustrophobic Feng Shui, sacrilegious price tags and suicidal misery of its keeper are sickening enough. A 'make your own baguette' kit catches my eye. Novel, yes. Though, when you think about it, £10 for a handful of flour and some yeast is a bit of a con. Still, I'm tempted. And yep, I feel quite sick.

Slowly, my nausea unwinds as does Dad's hangover. It takes us two hours, facilitated by a relay-style sipping of multiple caffeinated beverages. Then lunch: couscous and beetroot for me, chips for dad.

'It was actually really interesting because they had all these different kinds of boxes and all these different ways of folding them,' he says, folding his arms and leaning back from his finished lunch.

'I so admire your enthusiasm Dad,' I say, still poking at my couscous. 'But I think this new job is going to be *even* better than the cardboard box factory.'

'It's kinda nerve-wracking, I've never done a job like this before.'

'You'll be great. I just know it. Care work is just made for you,' I say.

Dad's old job (pre-care, pre-cardboard box) as a courier was great. So the day the franchise went bust and he had to sell the van and work in the dusty brown depths of a cardboard box factory, was a sad day indeed. I thumb the coarse plastic of my high-vis vest, and reminisce.

'Dad?' an 11-year-old me asks over the groan of the van's engine, swinging my feet, sipping my Tango and thumbing a glossy magazine. It was a close call between Top of the Pops and Art Attack: Top of the Pops came with a tube of lip gloss but the latter ultimately won, thanks to its page about how to build a rocket out of toilet roll tubes and crayons.

'Yes?' he answers.

'Have you ever thought about killing yourself?' I ask.

'Alice...' Dad scratches his stubble and looks out of the window. 'I'll tell you about that when you are a little older.'

I look at him, then back down at the magazine.

'Okay,' I chirp.

How funny.

Hey presto: it's France!

'Hey, Alice? We're supposed to be on the right,' says Dad, as I spin the wrong way around a roundabout.

Lefts and rights are not my thing and this is much of the reason I failed my cycling proficiency those ten years ago. But thankfully after a few miles of weaving through Dieppe, the *Avenue Vert* paves the remaining 55 miles to Gournay-en-Bray. Clear and direct, not a single leaf or twig daring to spoil its liquid-smooth surface, the bike path proves leagues above some of the questionable attempts I've happened across in England. Through forests, caged alongside motorways, over rocks, within the head-scratching mazes of industrial estates: these are all places an English cyclist might find him or herself should she or he follow a 'bike route'.

Normandy is charming in a kind of modern-medieval, sterile sort of way: all chestnut-brown beams the cute side of gothic and neatly contained foliage. Don't get me wrong, it's gorgeous. Though I can't help but feel a bit of ruffle, perhaps an overgrown shrub or a patch of un-mowed grass, might've made it that bit friendlier. Maybe that has more to do with a permanently bedraggled, un-mowed me.

'Look!' Dad points to a chateau. White, ostentatious and inhumanely immaculate, it reminds me of a Barbie castle I once saw in an Argos catalogue. 'Can I take a picture of you in front of it?' he asks.

I roll my eyes but oblige. I ain't no Barbie, unless she'd been run over and then given to a dog as a snack.

71 miles later, after sailing past chateaus, brasseries, beamed

houses and corn fields, all the while remembering this *cycling on the right* malarkey (I've invented a rhyme for this: stick on the right and you'll be alright, or cycle on the left and there won't be much left... of you'), we arrive outside our Warmshowers host in Gournay-en-Bray. Warmshowers is essentially an online network of cyclists, opening their homes to fellow pedallers. Essentially couch surfing on two wheels. God bless the 21st century.

'Welcome!' Veronique kisses our cheeks.

Joel, her husband, puts down a piping bag bloated with icing and follows suit.

'We kiss a lut in France,' he excuses.

Inside their house, a cat swaggers about, completely aware of his good fortune and refusing to be petted by the common likes of myself. How does an animal that bathes itself with saliva look so much prettier and tidier than me, I wonder to myself as we scale the stairs.

'Zis iz your room. Iz okay?' asks Veronique, her voice echoing.

There are two beds in the room, bookshelves, a lamp, views across the cornfields. But these things might as well have not been there at all: my focus is set on that porcelain throne, set in the middle of the room. Uh-oh. Please, God, tell me the French don't eat curry. I look at Dad, and send subliminal messages to his intestines: *don't you dare.*

'Would you like zum wine?' asks Veronique, so perfumed and so French the pressure of these two extremes crushes her eyes into a squint.

Gushes of belly-aching crimson land in our glasses and I spend the evening sipping the acid-reflux 'delicacy', willing for Jesus to turn it into water. He does not.

Meanwhile, a dinner spread of bread, soup, roasted peppers, preserved peaches and pongy cheese is splayed across the table. Dad and I tuck in with eager eyes and polite fingers, being careful to achieve the right balance of courtesy and enthusiasm. I cringe at the wine, *what a waste of calories,* then look at Dad whose eyebrows are arched and whose glass is tipped in my direction. I discreetly top his up full.

'An tomorroh,' asks Joel, ironing cheese onto a hunk of bread, 'where you go?'

'Um, À demain?' I start. Joel and Veronique nod. 'À demain, je vais à Paris, mais mon Père,' I point at a wide-eyed, soup-slurping Dad. 'Il alles a la...chez-moi.'

Veronique's eyes widen, somehow understanding my wonky French.

Joel flops a pile of preserved peaches onto my plate. 'You will need zis for tomorroh,' he smiles.

Only a few hours of closed eyelids stand between me and my 22nd year now. I scrub my eyes with a makeup wipe and wonder, as tiny pink veins collect in my watery eyes, what the consequence of all this mascara and crayon might be as I age. Will my eyelids peel downward like a bloodhound?

'Night Dad,' I whisper.

'Night,' he whispers back.

I dump my head, dizzy from a 71 mile transatlantic adventure, onto the pillow.

2

Bon anniversaire à moi

A scratching noise pulls me away from a shard of sleep. I keep my eyes shut and smile into the duvet, pulled just up to my nose.

'How'd you sleep, kiddo?' Dad whispers.

'Great!' I lie.

Dad's snores lasted the entire night. And not in a steady, cosy, forgivable stream but in thunderous seizures, like he'd just remembered to breathe and choked on the sensation.

'Brilliant! Happy birthday.' He hands me my only card, written entirely in capitals, the words 'GO GET EM' in biro still shining a little wet.

'Aw, thanks Dad.'

'No problem sport. Hey,' he lowers his voice, 'd'you think they'll give us breakfast?'

Right on cue a scuttling of footsteps sounds from underneath us.

The footsteps belong to Veronique who swiftly flavours our morning with a spread of jam, cheese, pastries, bread and one fibrous slab, shamed to the bottom of the bread basket. I select the ugly duckling, relieved.

'Zere we goh,' says Veronique, setting two cups of 'tea' ahead of us (way too floral for a 'builder' and not strong enough for 'breakfast').

'Merci!' I say, pulling it to my lips.

'Merci!' Dad agrees, burying his face in a croissant.

He tears through the selection with all the zeal of a mouse left alone with a crumb of cheese, and I can't help but feel hot with anxious envy as I nervously nibble at my roughage. *Another* pastry? I stifle a laugh, as it flutters into flakes that cling to the tiny prongs of his stubble.

Meanwhile 'Happy Birthday' texts agitate my phone. Another year away from jelly shoes and little boxes of raisins, another year closer to fatigue and death: thanks for reminding me. Anyway,

I feel unreasonably pissed off now, so I pat my thighs and sigh excessively until my ceaseless huffing finds me and Dad out in the fresh morning air. Joel lunges towards me with pursed lips and I remind myself to slacken my shoulders and not be so damned English. Veronique follows suit. The French must get so many colds.

And now for the last of the goodbye admin.

'Thanks for joining me Dad. Gosh, you're always such good fun. I'll see you... later?'

'I guess so! Ah, good luck Alice. I wish I was joining you. You've done so well to get this far. You know, after all you've been through.'

I wish he hadn't said that.

'Bye Dad... Thanks...'

We hug (awkwardly, because I have guilt-induced rigor mortis) then pedal off in opposite directions.

'I'm going on a long bike ride.' T his was my exit-speech at the hotel. Once they'd finished laughing at me, I handed in my notice – no loss to them, I was a rubbish waitress – and here I am, what feels like seconds later, squawking 'bonjour' at fellow cyclists. I even try 'salut' a couple of times, but I blush because it's obvious I'm trying and failing to look cool. Funny, isn't it? Try to look hot in low cut tops and short-shorts and you end up cold, try to look cool and your face sets on fire. Or maybe that's just me: a creature of hot pink cheeks and cold blue feet. I went to my GP about it once and he couldn't stop laughing. *'Some people are just different,'* he'd said, too hysterical to even glance at my purple toes.

'Bonjour!' I call to a couple of pulled-over cyclists.

'Hello!' says the man, looking up from his map, surprised. 'We're lookin' for a shortcot.'

Images of dog-eared slippers, vast cups of tea, and lovingly masticated sofas flash though my head.

'Oh hi! You're from Yorkshire!' I say.

'Yeah. I'm Andy un this is Sue.' Andy points to a gentle lady, blonde on the cusp of grey.

'Yu can join us if yu like,' she says, 'If yer goin' to Paris, we'll be goin' tut same direction.'

'Groovy!' I return.

Andy's receding hairline peels back a little further and a great grin warms his face. Off we go, chopping up the air with our pale English legs.

'Ure so yung. How uld are yeh anyway?' asks Andy, cycling at a pace that contradicts his beige trousers.

'Twenty-two, as of today,' I say.

'Nuh waye! T's me Sixtieth Buthday tudae!' he says.

'And we're doin' sixty miles for Andy's sixtieth,' adds Sue.

'Well, blimey! *Bon anniversaire* Andy!'

'An' to you too,' he says 'It's great tut meet yuh. I can't believe yu don't 'ave a boyfriend, yu suh interestin'.'

'Our boy Michael is single...' Sue raises an insinuating eyebrow. 'Maybe we'll aff to put yuh buth in totch.'

I laugh and change the subject. Alice is a lone wolf, an independent disaster. No boy is invited into my hurricane, it is simply too dangerous.

Lunchtime: the word though unspoken sits heavy in the atmosphere, which is suddenly devoid of people and open shops. A loud rattle of the last falling shutter, then silence. Though if you listen carefully enough, you can hear the gentle and slightly sinister sawing noise of knife to baguette from behind closed doors. 'Déjeuner' is no joke to the French but rather a threat, akin to a zombie apocalypse.

With our bellies growling in the stiff silence, we bench our bums in Bray-et-Lû. Andy lifts out a couple of golden baguettes fresher than untrodden snow, handing the smaller one to Sue: a stroke of pink, a scrape of yellow and ruffles of green in their centre, they crackle and flake. In perfect contrast I peel the lid off my tin of lentils, – '*if you were hungry, you'd eat it*' a mother's wisdom has become a rule – tip my head backwards, and wait for the congealed grey matter to hit my tongue.

'Ere,' Andy waggles a spork at me, but tightens his grip as I reach out for it. 'I'm gunna need that back thugh, t's part of a collection.'

Sue rolls her eyes at him and pours swamp water – ahem, sorry, *green tea* – into three cups.

'I didn't 'ave much room when packing and t'were either the

fancy tea cops or me raincoat. But they're while nice like,' she says.

Right on cue the sky ruptures, diluting my too-salty lentils and cooling down the too-hot tea. 'Water resistant' the inner label of my coat claims. HA! Don't make me chortle, I've seen more water resistance in a single sheet of toilet roll. If it wasn't for the jazzy stars pasted all over it, I'd have peeled it off right there and then. But I suffer through, stiff-limbed but cheerfully fashioned. Anyway, rain is great. So often cursed, falsely accused, under-appreciated, we forget how it saturates emerald fields, makes cosy tip-tapping noises on roofs and sets the scene for eating buttery crumpets.

In the same all at once way it had started, the rattling downpour abruptly quietens. Inspiring the grateful tweeting of birds as we resume, gliding among the endless waves of yellow cornfields, wobbling through villages whose cobbled roads glitter and steam under a post-rain sunshine. Chaussy, Maudétour-en-Vexin, Gadancourt, Avernes, Wy-dit-Joli-Village: their cottages are precisely just the right degree wonky and their streets seasoned by a single chicken, clucking nervously, wondering what the hell she's supposed to be doing. Apparently, we are en route for the metropolis of Paris though this has yet to seem feasible.

'Our average speed is op by 0.2 miles per hour!' yells Andy, charging furiously ahead, his beige trousers and pink head becoming an 'i' shape in the distance. His speed announcements recede to nothing and me and Sue look at one another with rolling eyes.

'Jost let 'im go on. He's jus showin uff,' she says.

We catch up with him a while later in Vigny with his arms folded, pretending to look indifferent. But his reek of self-satisfaction and sweat gives him away.

'This is uhs,' says Sue. 'Good lock with the rest of yuh journey. Yuh aven't got far av yuh?'

'Naaah!' I lie.

'Com ere!' Sue pulls me into a motherly hug. 'Good lock. Yuh gunna 'ave a great time.'

Andy nods stiffly behind her.

'Thanks, so much. You guys have been brilliant fun.' I pull away and hop onto the saddle. 'Phew, okay. Wish me luck–'

'Wait!' Andy hesitates, goes pinker with adrenaline and unzips his utensil collection. 'A buthday present,' he says, handing me one special, green spork.

It happened in a single turn, I'm sure of it. What happened to the swaying cypress trees, closed shops and self-conscious chickens? There's a different kind of bird in this city, she's called Julia Roberts and her scrawny frame frequents bus shelters, smiling, the words 'la vie est belle' captioned next to her perfumed self. Everybody ignores her.

Denser and denser, as severe and synthetic as neat orange squash, the metropolis unfolds: a dystopia of peeling advertisements, high-rises, hustle, neon lights and blaring horns. Red lights don't count for nothing round here, the roundabouts are basically free-for-alls and don't even get me started on these murderous hooligans on electric scooters. Scooters belong in the 90s to pre-teens, not to briefcase wielding suits, apparently too elite to walk and hell-bent on knocking over pedestrians. Somebody needs to tell them, this is *not* Grand Theft Auto.

Eight miles to go; the rain returns and it's getting dark. Red city lights glaze the puddles, and the yellow beams of taxis sparkle in the falling rain.

'I'm in Paris, PARIS I TELL YOU!' I yell, squinting through the downpour.

85 miles spent and looking a bit like Alice Cooper I push the button to Marie's block of flats with a wet, shivering finger.

'Aleece!' she beams.

Marie is as pretty as her name suggests: a slim figure with cork-screw spirals of black hair that finish just above her shoulders, surely destined for squirrel-befriending, spontaneous song and pie baking. Then there's me: I look like a rat that's been flushed down the toilet.

'Ench-chanté! I'm s-s-s-so h-happy t-t-to s-s-see you,' I stutter.

'Oh gosh Aleece!' Marie puts her hand on my arm, 'you muz be so culd. Zon't worry, I make you dinni and you can az a warm showugh.'

Despite my disgusting state, Marie gives me an honest hug and invites me and The Insect into her flat where two girls lounge around looking excessively pretty.

'Ello!' says the first of Marie's flatmates, stroking a cat. Her chocolate bob flicks slightly inwards, pointing towards her perfect, dainty face.

'Enchanté,' I try, weakly, dripping all over the floor like a rotating lump of meat in a kebab shop.

'Iz okeh Aleece, we can speak Engleesh,' says Marie.

'Ello zere,' says another pretty French thing.

My skin feels like an unfair wardrobe choice. A hot shower irons away every goose bump. Then dinner.

'You no like it?' asks Marie.

'Je suis désolé. Je suis vegan,' I say.

'You can juz pick out de feta.'

I begin surgically removing the feta, banishing it to the raised edge of my bowl, fraught. The clatter of utensils on plates, the sound of Marie chewing, the contracting walls of the kitchen, I haven't felt this way since– I don't want to think about it.

'What do you do Marie?'

'I wurk with uld peepol, in psychology' – must be a French thing – 'and I study. Anne says you study. What you study?'

I'd met Anne (Marie's sister) only a fortnight ago, bent into a curious shape, wild black ringlets thrashing in the winds of Falmouth beach. *'Hey zere! Do you wunt to join me for yoga and meditation?'* she'd asked as I was discreetly subtracting seaweed from my unmentionables (I guess I couldn't bear the lecture theatre that day). Me and Anne sealed a friendship and after I'd told her about this cycling idea she said, *'Acourse! you can stay wiz my sistuh if you eza goh to Pari'.*

'Yes... I do Art,' I reply.

'Oh cool!' says Marie.

'What do you study?' is my least favourite question. It makes my belly shrink. Because I can hear it, I can hear the laughing judgements beating in their heads when I tell them, *Art, I do Art.* Such a stupid word, pretending it doesn't rhyme with fart.

'Do you wunt to come to Pierre's burzday party tomorroh? We

go in zee afternoon zen you can stay ere anutter night, if you wunt?'

'I would absolutely *love* that. Really?'

Marie nods.

I smile at the reject-pile of white left on my plate. I'd forgotten all about the cheese sacrilege which I suppose wasn't such big a deal, in hindsight. Exhaustion and hunger can make everything seem like the end of the world. Of all people, I should know this.

A reeling sensation urges me awake – that old feeling – drawing me towards the heady smell of fresh bread in an anxious daze. Hunger is so embarrassing.

'Bon matin,' Marie chirps, shuffling about the kitchen. 'Tu as bien dormi?'

'Bon matin! Oui, comme un...Like a baby!'

'Comme un *bébé*. Ere, you can eat zis, ' Marie sets a baguette on the table. 'Parisian bread, my gush. Iz ze best in ze world.'

I tear a piece and apply peanut butter. And my gosh, it tastes so delicious that I feel instantly panicked and just ever so slightly aroused. Best stick to wholemeal. Dry wholemeal.

'We go see Pierre, yez? We go to de markette first. Iz okeh?'

'Oui.'

We walk away from the quiet of Marie's neighbourhood and, following the full-bodied scent of fromage, join a herd of berets, funnelling towards the market.

Cheese, meat, fish, pastries, wine, brown paper bags and jams (oh so many jams!) as far as the eye can see. The street is swelling with music, thanks to a man with a moustache hefty enough to polish shoes with who is kneading buoyant tunes out of an accordion. Ladies weave under and over one another to pluck patisserie samples from trays, men exchange kisses, vendors roar pleasantries at their customers, willing them to buy cheese. And oh, the cheese! As big and leathery as tyres, it's a wonder the pongy demons aren't galloping.

Stopped in the thick of it all (Marie wants to buy a pot plant for Pierre), my eyes fall on a ring of men playing cards, their rears spilling over tiny stools. One of them shouts something and they all – in perfect synchronisation – raise a shell to their lips and jerk back their heads, leaving the fate of the squirming oysters to their gullets. Without meaning to sound obtuse, France is very French.

Finally, we reach the tail end of the market and I buy jam. No, not gold, jam. Although its sacrilegious price tag might have you believe otherwise. Pierre better be fucking grateful.

Hurrying behind her perfect clip-clop I try to keep up with Marie, but because my legs are used to gyrating and not swinging like pendulums, my gait is wonky and unpredictable. I stumble, crash into a lamppost but recover my position just in time for Marie to present me to her friends.

'Salut! C'est Aleece!' she says.

A bunch of new faces smile wildly at me, under the tatty shelter outside the bar. The bar is scruffy and sticky and smells like spilt booze so I'd have felt quite at home, if only Marie's friends weren't quite so damn gorgeous. Especially Pierre.

'Bonjour! Je suis désolé! Je suis anglaise!' I flap, panicked by their gorgeous faces.

Their faces crack open and throaty laughter fills the atmosphere. What a relief.

Party time! Tabouleh, punch, kisses and chatter swallow up the hours. An Italian guy called Nico talks to me for a while in immaculate English, but I'm not quite sure what he's saying: the punch is making my ears woozy and I can't stop looking at Pierre. Then the worst happens. A cake glowing with lit candles appears from the dark depths of the bar. Silence. The singing begins, sudden and jarring, corrupting the easy-going atmosphere of five seconds ago.

'*Joyeux anniversaire!*'

Oh god.

'*Joyeux anniversaire!*'

Poor Pierre.

The cake-walk is agonisingly slow, the singing too loud, the attention unfairly concentrated at the ageing victim and yet the whole shebang doesn't seem a torture to anybody. Maybe the need to be slightly invisible is a British thing.

'Ey!' everybody shouts, as Pierre blows out his candles.

Deep breath – sweet, musky, nostalgia blooms in my nostrils –

and here goes. 'Pierre?' I ask.

'Oui?' His eyes widen, sparkling like spring dew. I actually love Pierre. If only his pregnant wife wasn't so pregnant and wifey.

'Bon anniversaire.' I hand over the jam.

'ALEECE!' Pierre gasps. He gives me a kiss on the cheek so forceful, my dimple deepens. 'Zank you Aleece! Zat is so kind. I will zink of you when I have zis with my breakfast tomorroh morning!'

I laugh, blush, fidget and in an effort to blush less, blush more. Then I sneak more punch.

Time speeds up as the punch sinks deeper into my cells. My inhibitions lapse, bad French tumbles off my tongue.

'Do you mean zat?' says Guillaume, a timid and nimbly creature. Even his hair is too shy to grow any longer than a couple of apologetic centimetres.

'Oui. Je pense les français est très jolie,' I repeat.

'Ah! You really zink zat ze French are beautifol? Merci! Et très bien, tu parles bien français,' he says, orchestrating his speech with his left hand. The other stays firmly in his pocket (why *do* men do this?).

'Ha! Tu est très drôle. Tu habite ici? Dans Paris?' I ask.

'Yez, juz around ze cornugh. You should come stay wit me!"

'Oui?'

'Yez. Ere, take my numbere. I work in zee day, but you can come tomorroh eveneeng. If you wunt?'

Apparently not fully rinsed from yesterday's downpour, the sky erupts.

'SACREBLEU!' I yell. For some reason, this makes everyone laugh.

'The most romantic city in the world' they'll have you believe. So why is everyone so pissed off? Parisians swoosh about, too busy to smile, too fashionable to wear fun clothes. Amidst these currents of muted coats, you might spot an exotic print or outrageous top bobbing about. Don't get your hopes up: these are tourists. Where are the lovers and laughers and painters and poets? I uncrumple my list, curated by Guillaume yesterday. Aha! Watch out *Pari*, there's a freckled beast on two wheels about to culture the shit out of you.

Well, what a complete *dommage*. The Louvre? Interdit. Musée d'Orsay? Interdit. Arc de Triomphe? So 'interdit' they've circled it with a roundabout more perilous than the Bermuda Triangle. Not so much 'give way' as 'OUTTA THE WAY', drivers spin around it, surviving the infinity of ambiguous lanes by way of angry honking. Having no horn to blare, I scream my way around, wondering how on earth to get to that damn Arc. But never mind! I've still the Eiffel Tower left on my list which may indeed be 'Interdit', but hell, they can't stop me looking at it. I sit in its gardens with my wholemeal croissant – so wrong but so right – and a cuppa.

'Bon anniversaire de MOI!' I call, shaking my 350 calorie treat into brown confetti. Twenty-two! I never thought I'd make it. Now to see Guillaume: uncultured, but at least pastried.

'Hey Aleece! Did you av a good day exploring Pari?' he asks, helmet in arm, suited and groomed, smelling of bank notes and expensive aftershave.

'Yeah! Although everything was INTERDIT. What's with all the hunky men with machine guns?'

'Oh. Well, we az a problem wit de terroristes, so zere is a lut of security in ze city. Ere, come, an welcome to my ome. I'm sorry for zee lift, iz very smol.'

Guillaume is not kidding, in fact my pastry-speckled jumper and his crisp white shirt stand no more than a foot apart. I stare at his tie for the longest ten seconds of my life. PING: Guillaume's apartment. Our footsteps clip-clop on the marble, echoing.

'Woah...My goodness...' I whisper.

Guillaume laughs, 'Yez, iz nice. I'm very lucky. Ere, come see zis.' He leads me towards his balcony, opens the doors, 'See?'

We gaze out at a relief of tall apartments, elegant and finessed, with long windows and ruffly flowers arranged neatly on balconies. At peasant level, Paris is all noise, dusty bars, McDonalds, suspicion, cigarette butts: everything a rat would see. But up at this hoity-toity height Paris is classier than a hold-the-cream-double-shot-oat-latte-to-go. Even the light pollution has an ethereal charm, the noise of distant traffic mistakable for wind. A familiar figure haunts the horizon.

'The Eiffel Tower!' I gasp, pointing like an idiot.

'Ha. Yez. Pretty special, noh?'

'Oui, very.'

Mopeds growl gently, ripping a pleasant texture into the air.

'Do you wunt to goh out?' asks Guillaume.

'Yeah!'

'Cool. I go get changed and you can az a showugh'

Cool? Don't you know Guillaume, that cool wasn't cool since the 90s? Though, kudos, you have redeemed yourself for stocking such good quality razors. You'd be amazed the abrasive trash other people make do with. And yes, I'm sorry to say (plot twist, I'm not), if you've let me use your shower, or even your toilet, I'll have sampled your razors too. In my justification, the planet is well enough stocked with them and I always, always, pick out the Alice-carpet afterwards. Such a good house guest, me.

'Lez go!' says a more casual looking Guillaume.

'Oui!' I reply, wet but in exactly the same clothes as before.

Guillaume takes me to a bar, buys me a rum cocktail and we drink outside, chatting about this and that, the odd French lesson percolating. Gosh, look at Guillaume, so gorgeously French, so unlawfully charming. Are English girls charming? I carry this question into the best toilet in the world, coated wall to wall in fluorescent graffiti and spinning disco lights. I tuck my ears between my knees and giggle. I'm in Paris! And drunk.

Then we go for pizza (Guillaume's idea). I squirm helplessly, a worm caught on fire, and try to find somewhere to put my eyes.

'Alice, this is your second warning. That's a behaviour.'

'Alice, you're running out of time. If you don't finish dinner in five minutes, you will have to take the Jevity.'

'Alice, you have to wear shoes in the dining room. You know this. Where are your shoes? That's your third warning. I'm afraid you're *being moved into the upstairs dining room.'*

Memories swash around my head like old plastic bags in a river, unwilling to biodegrade. Alcohol! Do your fucking job and lower my inhibitions, please.

'You are brave travelling like zis.'

Shit, has he been talking this whole time?

'Especially alon as a girl. I remembugh when I travel alon, I get mugged an I af to wulk around Africa in juz my pants. Iz more complicated as a girl. Ey, you struggling wiz zat?'

'Oui. Can I take it away, have it for petit-déjeuner tomorrow?'

'Zat is a gud idea Aleece. Ey, Aleece, how you like Pari?'

Paris is pants. What kind of city makes you pay to have a glass of water, then pay again when it comes out as wee? Not like Ratatouille at all.

'Paris is nice! Do you like living here?'

'Oui.' he says, eyes darkening with conviction. 'I love Pari. Iz alive an exciting, an my friends are ere, an we have museums, places to wulk. I love it.'

Guillaume is right. I like Paris too. Yes, I'm sure I do. Absolutely.

With all that booze and starch pillowing my head, I sleep like a tranquilized sloth and awaken chirpy and limber. I breeze through Paris, crossing the Seine over a bridge, doused with padlocks: pink, blue, gold, silver, green. On closer inspection – a car honks at me 'OH FUCK OFF!' – on closer inspection, I see each padlock has a pair of names written in Sharpie, some with little messages. Oh! How sweet! I love, love. Then Notre Dame, which I make a special effort to stop for because it only burnt down last Thursday (ish). Only, no it hasn't. Apart from some scaffolding and a gigantic blanket, most of it looks fine. I'd imagined a pile of ash, plumes of smoke, Parisians fallen to their knees, howling with anguish. Nope, the most dramatic thing here is the crunched brows of a couple trying to photograph it.

'C'EST TRISTE!' I shout at them.

They scorn at me and shuffle away. And I decide, not giving a Notre damn, to leave Paris behind.

Paris quickly falls behind me, making way for picnic spot after picnic spot. Guillaume had sent me off with a baguette, about the size and girth of my forearm. I don't eat baguettes. At home Mum buys them: footlong, always three. One for Billy, Louis and Joel. Sometimes there's a fourth (if Tesco has them on offer). Every now and then when I'm home from uni, inspired by my brother's enthusiastic stuffing (butter, olives, salami, at least two types of cheese, and mayonnaise) I might tear off the heel of the spare one and pretend to join in. This time I had my very own. I dump my ass under a tree, away from all eyes, fill the baguette with mushroom pâté and eat it. The whole damn thing. My bones fill with something denied and my muscles, wound tight around them, let go. I melt my way to Pithiviers wondering, for just how many years had this baguette-shaped hole been waiting.

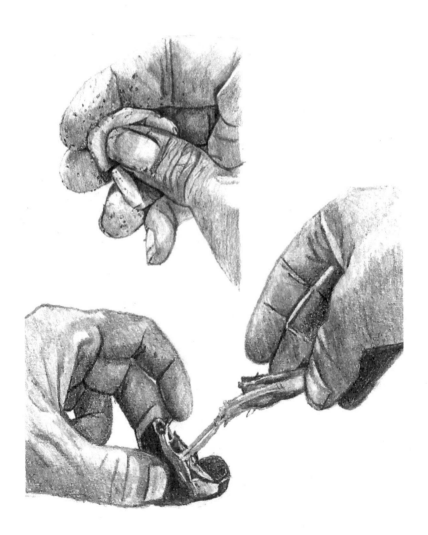

3

Hungry

'WOAH!'

Orléans: a fairy-tale city of golden sandstone, Victorian (probably Victorian) lampposts, tiny boutique shops that at the ripe hour of 11am have yet to open, and about four people clip-clopping slowly, importantly, down the pavement. I have my suspicions they're holograms.

'JESUS!'

One of the four non-people throws me a disgusted look. But how could I not *'woah'*, how could I not *'Jesus'*, with such a cathedral to my left? Notre Dame ain't got nothing on this beast: so heavily carved, so excessively finessed, it's a wonder it doesn't collapse under its own porousness. Even the Trams are g–

A blur of gold and blue spins in my eyes. Grey concrete jumps at me with a painful SMACK.

'ÇA VA?' yells a voice.

'Um… Ow,' I groan, tangled under cogs and bars, blood pouring down my leg.

The following sixty seconds happen in a formula one pit stop flash of different hands. A girl no older than fourteen, squats beside me with a first aid kit, sterilises and binds my knee in white cotton, while a man hovers above me, clamps The Insect's bent front wheel between his legs and yanks the handlebars true and then a blonde woman sprints towards me, yelling about the baton of cookies rattling in her hands. So there, The Insect and I are fixed and good to go. Bloody hell, no wonder France don't have an NHS.

After all that blood and thump, fate kindly unravels 'La Loire à vélo' in front of me: a 550-mile, river-side treat, as flat as a pancake, as straight as Nigel Farage. Look! No hands! My knee stings back at me. Best not, Alice.

It takes about an hour for the novelty of my tough-girl injury to wear off, undermined by each ligament-snipping strike of my knee. And no, there is no way of cycling with straight legs, I tried it. To cheer myself up I start yelling at random people: 'bonjour' and 'salut' and 'QUE BELLE TEMPS!'

'O, HEY!' replies a Marmite-brown creature.

I pull in, intrigued by his Dutch accent (and admittedly, his collar bones).

'You are an English gorl?' says the human Twiglet, voice muffled by bread. 'Wot are you doing here?'

Jesus, his baguette has more girth than his arm.

'Dunno, really,' I say. Felt like a little adventure, s'pose. What about you?'

'Hm,' he rubs his chin, 'I cycle away from my home in the Netherlands seven years ago and I never went back. I hate normal life.'

Seven years! I wouldn't have believed him, if not for his excessive tan, rusted-to-dust bike and emaciated body. You know, I used to be thin too... once.

'That's amazing! But if you don't mind me asking, what do you do for money?'

'I rob banks,' he says.

I laugh but the Dutchman just stares at me, completely sober.

'Ahem. Ur, bye then!' I pedal off, slightly confused and just a little jealous of his vast thigh gap.

The sun is softening, and I have made it to Blois, to Paul's house. I knock thrice and a shy, balding figure appears, opening the door as though peeling off a plaster: slow and wincing.

'Hi, C'est Paul,' He says, eyes shifting about nervously. 'Veux-tu une douche?'

'Oh, um.' – bit rude, isn't it? To offer a girl a shower as an opening line – 'Oui?'

'It's full of sheet.'

'Oh?'

'Zere was a bird... Ee go mentul.'

No kidding. Paul's bathtub, more squit than porcelain, is about as gory as my knee. Thwap: my waterlogged bandage lands in the tub, revealing a swollen fury of gashes. I bounce back downstairs and announce, 'Look! J'ai un petit accident!'

Paul cringes, then laughs. 'Yez, I see zat.'

We chat for hours, eating potatoes dusted with cumin, until there is no light left except for the synthetic glow of Paul's laptop. Paul takes off his trousers excusing himself that it is just too hot. Ah, that's okay: it's gotten so dark that we can't see each other's faces, let alone his – Alice! Stop looking at the damn crotch, he'll get the wrong idea!

'You can sleep in my bed if you wunt?' says Paul.

Amazing. He can't speak English, except for 'full of shit' and 'sleep in my bed'. But maybe that just says it all.

'No, merci,' I laugh gently. 'I think I'll go to bed now.'

New day, new jam. Rhubarb flavour, courtesy of Paul's now-dead mother. Ghost jam, how utterly delicious! And how liberating to bail on this whole anti-sugar bandwagon we've got going on in England. All those taxes, headlines, close-up shots of spilling bellies tromping down high streets had of course made my weekly food shop twice as complicated. Yet here, my blood has become so thick with jam since Francing it, I'm basically a tart now. And have I died of obesity, or developed diabetes? Have my teeth rotted down to grains of pilau rice? No. Shove that up your aspartame UK government.

'Au revoir Aleece!' Paul hollers. 'I'm sorry I did nut feed you any strawberries!'

God bless these strange French men.

With a flick of the thumbs The Insect's gears clunk, our efforts harmonising as though his cogs and my legs were of the same body. We zip alongside the Loire River, me singing, The Insect making a noise like the after-pong of a tennis ball as it hits the exact centre of a racket: clean and resonating. Chailles, Chaumont-sur-Loire, Chargé, Amboise, Montlouis-sur-Loire, flitter by. I stick out my left leg and kick a fluffy blanket of seedlings into a flurry of summer snow. Where's an Activia sponsorship when you need it? Here I am, living my best yogurt advert life: active, merry, weather blessed and (thanks to a pedal-powered metabolism) regular.

Lunchtime rolls around and I gratefully moan my way through a naughty but cruciferous sprout baguette that I'm not even going to count (though, if I were to, it'd be about 430, which is fine). All washed down with some forbidden water from a fountain slashed with warning signs. The taste of chlorine and instant cold sweats are undeniable, but I just keep gulping. My stomach has taken far worse and insofar, no explosive repercussions.

60 miles spent, a little sunburnt but stomach contents intact, I veer off from the river and arrive at the house of the 'Big Unfriendly Giant', christened as such because I've forgotten his actual name and also, he's built like a gorilla giving a piggyback to another gorilla. Never have I received an 'Enchanté' as devoid of its meaning as the B.U.G's and never have I been snarled at with such a look that I was a steaming turd. Still, he lets me into his house made entirely of mud, straw and rocks.

Impressively, his wife is almost as humongous, though her presence is kitchen-based and made smaller by her glasses. She points a very slight smile at me, then resumes her duties with a meat cleaver. To complete the set, the all-podge product of these two tromps in and gives me a flower and a kiss. I can't quite work out whether she's about six, or just a very enormous three-year-old.

'You Vegan. Well, ziz is oll I can feed to you,' the B.U.G. interrupts, putting a stinging nettle in my flower-free hand. 'Fold it tight an it no sting.'

He's right: bitter and horrible, but no sting.

The B.U.G's next Warmshowers guests arrive sparkling and Swiss, the perfect, nuclear family: one girl, one boy, one husband, one wife. Clean, polite, with perfect French accents and unblemished complexions. In contrast there stands a collaged me: a red wound, some purple bruises, white skin, browner skin, burnt skin, a few oil stains, and a curious lilac rash on my knuckles I've been meaning to worry about.

The B.U.G takes to the Swiss entourage immediately, roaring with heartfelt welcome, wrapping each of them in sturdy hugs.

'DINNI!' he bellows cheerfully as his wife plonks a bucket, a cauldron, a vat of soup on the table. He then glares at me and says, 'Dinnere iz ready.'

Thick green sludge lands in our bowls, all but mine.

'AH!' roars the beast. 'Zis not vegan. HA! I poot cream. I poot Butter. I poot egg. I poot beef. You wunt?'

'Um, no. Merci,' I mumble.

Thus the evening progresses carnivorously. After the anti-vegan soup, it was plates of fried fish and then a finale of ambiguous, brown meat muck. I stare at my empty plate, unsure what to do other than quietly apologise for my own existence while the B.U.G. dominates the room, yelling stories I scarcely understand about truck journeys and food and Arabs.

He turns to me, face slackening with apathy and translates, 'Zee Arab make me coffee and ee poot pork fat in it. I take it. Because ee was nice. It was disgusting...AH!' All of a sudden his face changes, as though struck with genius. He dashes into the kitchen, and returns with a severed limb, hairy and hoofed. Horse, perhaps? His laugh rips through the room like an earthquake. 'IZ A FRESH ONE. I KILL YEZTERDAY!'

'Sacrebleu!' I say.

I hit the literal hay belittled and famished. Like The Very Hungry Caterpillar, I eat four oranges, twenty-five dates, and an entire tin of chestnut purée under a duvet, then fall asleep with sticky fingers and a guilty conscience. Morning can't come quick enough.

Another yogurt-advert day for cycling! Honey-sweet for a warm breeze that carries the scent of the last blooming flowers of spring.

'Right legs, no factor thirty for you today,' I slap my pearly-white thighs, as I often do, hard enough to leave a red handprint (call me crazy, but thigh slaps keep them slim). Thighs like gammon joints, I've often thought. Especially when I wear fishnet tights.

Seeing as the bike path is so smooth and flat, and admittedly still thinking about that skinny Dutchman from yesterday, I take the opportunity to complete a body check: coiling my thumb and forefinger around my wrist, clamping my waist with my hand, feeling over my collar bones. Still there, phew. Then I check out my tits: bigger! Suppose last night's chestnuts were a self-fulfilling prophecy. Stopping for a tea break, I Google 'does hot weather make your breasts swell?' (Google doesn't know), give them a grope and continue. Tits are a nice thing and I have the efforts of Big Portion Karen at the unit to thank for my own, which were at one point no more visible or impressive than peaks of whipped cream. It has been four years since I earned them back and still I can't help but find them just a little more fascinating than the silver river and endless cocky chateaus.

Predictably, I am burnt. My face looks and feels like Parma ham and as for the gentle breeze of earlier, it has swollen to such a hot, thick force, I might as well be cycling through custard. Knees rusting (especially my injured left one), I heave the remaining eight miles through the urban sprawl of Angers (um, actually, it's pronounced *un-jays*) lamenting loudly. 70 miles: not bad girl. Angers is your typical city. It has many McDonalds and groups of youths, playing music too loudly, revving their engines and bobbing their heads. But our English youths are much more impressive than these pansies: they're not even drinking beer or shouting.

Clarence opens the door. 'Bonjour, Aleece–' A screaming noise starts and with an exhale that deepens his hunch, Clarence says, 'Un moment, zat is my child.'

He tends to his littlun begrudgingly, holding himself as limply as the last deflated balloon of a long-finished party. His very small flat is thick with the sickly, mucky, sour smell of nappies and I can't help but breathe a little shallower.

'Aleece, can you come in zee room? He zink zat Mumma is ome. I tell im iz nut Mumma but he nut believe me.'

I peer into the room and whisper, 'Salut!'

The boy looks at me, painfully cute and glossy eyed from crying. He smiles a fascinated smile, giggles, then dumps his wee head of ruffled chestnut hair back on his pillow.

'Bonne nuit,' says Clarence, backing out of the room, closing the door. 'Zorry about zat Aleece. Pur-aps you wunt a showugh?'

Gosh, that little boy is so cute, so new and precious.

The doctor has chocolate skin and a chocolate voice. He shuffles his papers then circles things with a biro, muttering under his breath.

'It's been two years now, when will my periods come back?' I ask. 'I'm out of hospital and way bigger now, but they still haven't come back. I don't want to fry my ovaries, and... and, oh God! I'm just so tired ALL the time.'

I pinch the back of my neck excessively, trying to read my BMI stats from beneath his fingers. Ah yes, exactly as I'd suspected, down to the decimal point.

'Any day now.' He looks up from his papers. 'Your hormones have improved greatly, Miss Lushington, you've done so well. Keep going and be patient because your periods will come. They are controlled by your hypothalamus, in the centre of your brain, and so when your body is no longer under stress, everything will work again. And your energy and your periods will come back.'

I sigh sadly as my wet hair drips on the table. Clarence places a steamy bowl of pasta and tomato sauce ahead of me. My favourite. Dad used to make it for me every Saturday when I was wee. I'd drench it in cheese, wait for the shavings to melt flat, and then add more cheese. I always, always had seconds, sometimes thirds. Nowadays of course, I never eat it.

'I ope zat iz okeh,' Clarence rubs his sunken eyes, 'I zink I will go to bed now.'

The clock reads 9pm. Poor fella.

Clarence is busying in the kitchen looking even more depleted than yesterday. Perhaps because the daylight is illuminating his droopy eyes, crumpled shirt and Quasimodo posture. Or maybe this is how it goes: every day a little more wilted, until one day he'll be nothing more than a melted pink puddle on the floor. A broken mess, but at least finally able to recline. He hands me a baguette and goes about infant chores, leaving me to slice the bread a little too cheerfully and scar his table. Clarence returns and blames it on his child. I pedal away with a heavy heart, imagining my ovaries as two sad fried eggs.

It was a blur, a frenzy, a trance; I just couldn't stop. A moment or so ago I was peeling the lid off a tin of butter beans, cheerfully humming that tune from the 1-1-8 advert, then my brain snapped into some kind of primal state: focus sharpening, arms grabbing, nerves hot with yearning. Thing is, the more I thrust, stuffed and swallowed, the greater the hole of my belly yawned and to the stupor of everything around I felt nothing but unquenchable need until it was all gone. All of it. Not again, not again, not again. Humiliating. Disgusting. I run into the toilet, push my fingers to the back of my throat and relieve myself of my problem. Only that never works, does it? Because now my throat feels like a flesh wound, and I'm dizzy, shaking, hungry all over again.

'Fuck.' I hunch over the toilet and shudder, 'Jesus Alice. Not here, not now.'

These days, people throw about the word 'binge' as though it had to do with Netflix or finishing a *whole* packet of Oreos. Well, it doesn't. Anyone can finish a packet of Oreos, the manufacturers put yum-dust in them to ensure of it. If only it was just one packet of Oreos, oh what I wouldn't give for it to be *just one packet of Oreos*. Thing is, if someone catches you conquering a packet of biscuits they laugh, sympathise even, but get caught stealing, lying, riffling through the bin, scarfing raw pastry, and they'll out you in front of everyone: '*God, it's so obvious what you're doing*'. Or maybe they're the kind sort, and catching your swollen cheeks and watery eyes on the way out of the bathroom will ask, '*Are you alright?*'. Today's disaster was beans mixed with banana chips, followed by everything else. I can't even fucking remember.

After that disaster, cycling does not feel nice. Everything is spinning: the scenery, the wheels of The Insect, my stomach, my head. But never mind: I've left it behind, flushed it away. Only...God, maybe my 'recovery' is based on a lie.

'Hey! Aleece!' Remy (my host) bounds out the door, smiling wildly, 'Welcum to my ome!'

Oh well that's just typical. Charismatically dishevelled hair, a cheeky smile, artistic, the bright side of young, yet with that sexy weathering of a man in his thirties: Remy had to be a dish, didn't he? I'm really, really not in the mood for a dish of any kind.

'WOW! Did you paint that?' I ask, pointing to a massive psychedelic painting in Remy's living room.

'Yez! Ere. You wunt to see my sketch book? I take it on my travelz.' Remy pats the sofa and I sit beside him, 'Zo...Zis was when I taught some children to draw in Turkey...'

'Oh my gosh. You're– oh wow, I love that one.'

Remy's shoulders jolt madly, adorably, as he laughs the sort of laugh mistakable for crying. He does this at each of my squealing compliments until the last of the pages are thumbed and Remy suggests we hit the town. Time to loosen the goose.

With the goose loosened thanks to strawberry beer, we chit-chat the hours away, oscillating between his funky version of English and my awful attempts at French. My legs turn to liquid and everything is suddenly, from all angles, hilarious. One beer and I'm pissed, oh how typical. The expression 'light-weight' comes to mind and I smile, pressing the empty bottle into my eye socket, glaring at the dregs of red gloss.

'You muz be hungry Aleece?'

'Huh?' I unplug my eye from the iridescent world of bubbles. 'Um, well...'

'Lez go back. I make you dinni.'

11pm. Remy is cooking lentils. Lentils: a nice settling food.

'I az an allutment ere. But zee snails! Zey take over like crazy. GOD! So I keel zem wiz alcohol,' says Remy.

'Not a bad way to go really,' I say.

We laugh and laugh and laugh and then go silent. A lashing pain drives up my throat and I cringe at the memory of lunch.

'Je suis fatigue.' I excuse myself, and me and Remy go to our separate beds.

Sleep, please euthanize the day for me.

Slept and hopeful, off I go to Nantes, feeling as though yesterday didn't happen at all.

It happened again. And I don't even have the energy to hate myself for it. It started with banana bread (idiot, you never eat banana bread), then the urge overtook me. An urge, stronger than thirst, even stronger than the need to breathe. Dates, nuts, apricots – don't stop – bread, prunes – you'll pay for that later – more dates, more nuts. Chew, crunch, stuff, gulp, keeping the mouth always occupied. Only an avocado remains. Less savage than fingering it? Probably. I snatch my toothbrush and complete the frenzy. The wet green gunk clogging the bristles winks back at me. Me, the ogre.

'Ugh,' I moan, as a merciless midday sun beats me over and over as though my bowling-ball stomach, thickened to sludge blood, sticky fingers and even stickier conscience weren't punishment enough. I scan for a toilet: my retribution, my porcelain redemption. Then a shadow falls on my face.

'Excusez moi?' says a man, reaching out a handful of coins.

'Huh? Je ne comprends pas,' I say.

'Oh! Goodnez!' He backs away, 'I zo sorry!' and scampers off.

What the? He thought I was a hobo! I look down at my lap full of crumbs, packets, and that avocadoed toothbrush. Ah, well, fair enough. And then I laugh a little. A laugh which made the idea of a gruesome session in the toilets too jarringly sinister to go through with.

'No Alice, we're not doing that anymore.' I pat my bulging stomach. 'Time to let it go.'

I walk away from the public toilets, resolving instead to buy a probiotic. Come on Lactobacillus, I'll be rooting for you! Only, shoot, I've lost my purse. Ten minutes of prowling and scowling between the footfall of pedestrians and I spot it on the streets of Nantes. Phew. Only, not phew because in those minutes of purse-hunting, my phone has now gone AWOL. A few frantic minutes later I find it in a similar state and just as I go to fist pump the air in celebration, my water bottle spills inside my panniers, drenching all.

'MERDE!' I hiss, secretly enjoying the opportunity to curse in French.

'Ello!' says a man, smirking above me.

'Oh, hi! Désolé.' I lift my sodden clothes out of my pannier and say, 'Quelle dommage!'

The man giggles dangerously. 'Ey, I'm George. Ey, waz your name?'

My Spidey-senses tingle urgently: do not make friends with this man.

Fast forward ten minutes: me and George are *'going for a wulk'*. He'd insisted and compromised by a swollen belly I hadn't the energy to disagree.

'Iz nice, no?' says George as we wander further and further into the remotest parts of a very un-remote city. 'Ey, your legz are cycling legz. Très belle, très fort,' he goads, stroking my thigh.

I laugh nervously and walk faster. If he tries anything, I'm going to scrunch my face up as weird as it can go and spasm (I've been practicing in the mirror for occasions such as this). That'll freak him out, extinguish his interest. Also, note to self, add 'quiet walks' to my list of things to watch out for underneath: texts from the school caretaker, expensive hats, freebies, white transit vans, letters written on gold paper, phone calls under a full moon, marriage proposals, and invitations to nudist beaches.

'Oh, your air, iz so curly,' George reaches out and tugs gently on my ringlets. 'You muz be tired after all zat cycling. Ere let me giz you a massage.' He lets go of my curls and starts kneading my shoulders.

'NO!' I whack his hands away.

'Imagine you are in a special place. Tell me, where is your special place Alice?' asks Caroline, running her oily hands over my spine, shoulder blades, ribcage. Crunchy, crunchy, crunchy.

'Um,' I say, face down, wincing.

'Take your time.'

'The bus.'

It was the first thing that came to mind. I loved taking the bus in my pre-captivity days. My legs appreciated the rest from endless squats, and it was a relief to be away from diet plans, cupboards, worried faces. I miss it. I miss staring out the window, daydreaming, I miss watching the teenage boys scoff their subways, bragging 'A six inch could never fill me up, I always go for footlong'. I miss being a stranger. Now I am a patient, a file, an ever-increasing number, a problem.

'Oh?' says Caroline, surprised. 'That's nice Alice.'

Caroline's dainty hands weigh heavy on the jutting planes of my shoulder blades. Why do I even go to these stupid sessions? I dread them. More than the 6am weigh-ins, more than visiting time, even more than the days macaroni cheese and Big Portion Karen align. I stare at the locked door. Nearly over. This time I'll tell her, I'll tell her I hate her crunchy massages.

'Okay, there we are.' Caroline lays a warm towel over my back, 'Would you like me to book you in for next week?' she asks.

Book me in? Pft! Let me just check my very busy schedule of eating, angry diary entries, eating, staring out of the locked windows, eating, getting told off, more eating and crying in the 'panic room'. And no, Caroline, I would not.

'Yes please.' I say.

'Bye Aleece, It waz nice to mee–' George opens his arms for a hug, and I sprint off.

4

Suicide and a hot date

The French are curious creatures. Take breakfast for example: jam, bread and tea. Sounds normal enough, but there's a twist. Firstly, the jams come in all sorts of funky flavours like melon, fig, grape or even dandelion, which you then apply with a spoon rather than a knife (I guess because you can get more on a spoon) to bread so fresh, it's often still slightly warm. Then there's the tea: herbal and served in bowls rather than mugs. And as for plates? There are none! One is just expected to *not get crumbs everywhere*. This is impossible, but every day I'm rising to the challenge and every day I allow myself just a bit more jam.

Today's breakfast will be different though, as I'm currently face-down in banana chips and far too sticky for jam. The night before is hazy but – I peel a banana chip from my cheek and eat it – definitely featured drunken cycling, bars, a football game and some very loud frogs. So beans it is. Nice, cold, wholesome beans. I eat them straight out of the tin surrounded by unconscious students, laid about me like seals. The whole thing makes me feel like such a creep, I leave without even saying goodbye. Which is, in hindsight, perhaps even creepier.

La Rochelle is true to the delicious sound of its name though I keep calling it *'La Ferrero Rochelle'*. I glide along its harbourside, raising myself above the saddle, a warm wind whistling in my ears, pouring over my face, washing away my hangover. Between the crenelations of a tower, I catch a glimpse of a barman twisting a cloth inside a tumbler, gazing whimsically out to sea. All credit to the 21st century, in turning something designed for war, into a place to clink cocktail glasses.

Sharp right: I follow my indicating arm into a narrow maze of cobbled streets. Teaspoons chink inside cups, knives and forks rattle on plates, pastries crunch, orange juice is sipped: locals and tourists alike, breakfasting. Inspired, I decide to buy lunch. Yes, it is indeed only 11am. But like these many sunburnt baboons, I am British too.

Lunch was supposed to be my new usual: a sprout baguette. Cheap, cruciferous, low-fat, delicious but not *too* delicious: my way of accessing French culture. Only my legs, blatantly ignoring my frugal motives, seem to be carrying me straight towards a very expensive assortment of dried fruits. It was the smell that drew me in, that witchy concoction of pencil shavings, sage and that 'je ne sais quoi' I can never quite put my finger on. Of course, there's no way this health food shop sells tinned sprouts, so maybe I'll just have to blow my budget on— FUCK! Suddenly, my heart falls clean out of my arse. A boy with all the glow of a million full moons is tending to baskets of vegetables. I stare at him for infinity (two seconds) then bolt towards the exit but just as the automatic doors whoosh open, a slightly hurried voice says, 'Escuze me, ah you looking for somezing?'

It's him, the million-moon boy and gosh, his face is so startling, his hair so brilliantly blonde and fluffy, he looks like a freshly struck match. Oh bollocks. I'm in love.

'Ah, oui!' I meet his huge green eyes for a fleeting second. 'Um, I'm looking for *pâtes de champignons*?'

'Ah yez. I zink I know what you wunt. Come.'

The boy walks down the aisles and I follow him, willing my legs to gain back their strength, willing my face to fall into a normal shape. It's not fair: I can feel it contorting, giving away everything. And pinking because I'm painfully aware of my woefully inadequate outfit: the line of my cleavage, the unshaven hairs on my thighs, the scrunch of my exposed belly button all blaring out at this real-life man-angel who gestures to the mushroom paste gracefully and says, 'Zere.'

'Ah! Merci! Oui! Parfait!' I pipe. 'That's exactly what I'm looking for!'

'Yugh welcum. Oú habites tu?'

'Ah, well...' – Now's your chance GCSE French. – 'Je suis un anglaise fille. J'habite à la campagne dans le sud-est. C'est presque Brighton.'

'Ah! Oui! Yugh french iz very good! You learn well. An today, where you goh?'

'Ah, well I'm going over that great big bridge,' I point like an idiot, to what I think is West. 'I might sleep on the Island, maybe?'

'Ah, zis Island you go to today, I zink you mean ze Île de Ré, non? Ah! You will love it zere. And aftugh zat?'

'After that, I don't really know where I'm going. Maybe Spain, maybe Italy?'

The boy smiles at me, a special kind of smile: brilliant and trembling.

'What's yugh name?' he asks.

'Alice. Yours?'

'Loic.'

'Well *Enchaté*, and by the way, your English is amazing.'

Loic responds with a little wobbly grunt. Was that...a nervous thing? The thought fizzes in currents of electric thrill.

'Okay, Aleece, I'll leave you to choose.' Loic twists on his feet, then hesitates. 'Ur, do you ave Instagram? zo I can follow your journee?'

'Oui! Of course! Yeah!'

Loic walks off, leaving me with my 'Oui! Of course! Yeah!' to jolt in my head like a broken CD. It puts me in such a state, I actually forget to say 'merci' to the cashier. Loic returns with a fluffy-edged tuft of paper, but whips back from it and jumps behind the till as if suddenly busy as I kneel on the floor and try to spell my own name correctly. But just as I emboss the paper with the final 'n' of Lushington, a great thunder of a voice yells, 'GIVE 'IM YOUR NUMBERE!'

The heat of many staring eyes and blaring silence raise alarm in my scorched cheeks. Though I (like Loic) pretend not to notice and continue scrawling, adding a winking face next to my digits. I fold the paper, pass it to Loic and sprint out of the shop.

Air! I'd forgotten about you. Ah, solid ground! My old friend! Blood fizzing, heart galloping, cells jittering, mouth making all sorts of involuntary noises, I skip into the fluorescent depths of Carrefour as a broken instrument. Lunch will have to wait; I am simply too busy living the best day of my life.

The Île de Ré bridge twists into the oblivion of sea mist, too big to see in an eyeful, its foot congested with a clot of cars that have yet to pay their toll. This fills me with such self-righteous glee, I actually have to scoff some of it out because (like any true cyclist) I *detest* drivers. Especially when they knock you down as you're on your way to work (I was fine, a bit of tooth loss, bit of blood loss, bit of memory loss, all of which redeemed). Across I go, curving above the sea on a 4km concrete ribbon, high on the thrill of superiority.

The island too is full of cyclists, proper, down to earth ones with baskets, bells, and a sense of patience (not like those carbon fibre twigs with mean faces, fresh from the Strava factory). Naked children kick up golden sand, squealing joyfully, making sandcastles, splashing in the shallows, crying because their sandwiches are gritty. I laugh gently and make a highly appropriate sand angel. Mum rings and I tell her my news.

'And then this guy says "GEEVE 'IM YOUR NUMBERE!" so I did,' I say.

'Wow, just like a movie!' She giggles. 'That's amazing!'

'I know! I'm so happy I feel sick. I've opened my tinned spinach but, GOSH, I dunno if I can eat it. I can't stop jumping!'

Mum laughs. 'That's great Alice.'

'And you, how are you?'

'Well, I've just taken a B-vitamin and I'm on a cleaning rampage. I feel wired! I can't stop!'

I laugh. 'That's great Mum.'

Huh, maybe me and Mum are more alike than I thought. As I hang up, I notice a text:

'Hey Alice. Nice to see you today. Hope you pass a good moment on the Île de Ré. You can stay here if you like. I have Tofu in the fridge. I like to cook him with courgette. Maybe we can swim. Loic.'

I yell, bang my feet into the sand, check the text again, then reply, shaky with haste:

'Hey Loic. That would be great! That's so sweet! I'll meet you later to swim. About 5?'

I convulse, do a backwards roly-poly then gallop into the sea, one arm flailing, the other holding my bikini bottoms in place (the elastic has long gone, such as I discovered seven years ago as they slipped off and overtook me on a water slide. I still haven't gotten around to replacing them because I am afraid of shopping and sizes and numbers).

After a couple of swims, a tin of spinach, and third-wheeling a couple's picnic – I don't think they really minded – I decide it is probably about time to see Loic and his tofu.

Back along the bridge I laugh, sing, and squeal like mad, hoping to expend some nervous energy before my date. Is it a date? Must not get ahead of myself, it's just a boy and a girl sharing tofu. I squeal again at the thought, then fall completely silent, grinding to a halt halfway across the bridge. Something is very wrong.

On the opposite side of the road a man perches on the railings, his feet bare and dangling over the infinity of air between the bridge and the sea. There are three objects on the pavement below him: his trainers, a brown bundle of something, and a can of beer. He reaches down for the can, takes a swig, puts it back.

'EXCUSEZ MOI! EXCUSEZ MOI!' I scream. The bridge beneath my feet and the sky above my head drop away as I scream again with horrible, ear-cracking loudness, 'EXCUSEZ MOI! EXCUSEZ MOI!'

He turns his head, slightly and slowly, just enough for me to catch his young, empty face which flutters as though he's about to say something. But deciding better of it, he turns back to face the oblivion of blue sky, blue sea. My stomach churns with dread. A whisper of wind disturbs his beer can: it sways a little, and then falls silently over the edge. Suddenly, the air is too brittle to breathe.

'HEY!' I shout, jumping in the path of an oncoming cyclist, 'HELP! IS HE? I– HE'S– oh my God.'

'Geev me your fon,' she says.

I hand it to her, a shaking, panting, crying mess, eyes still fixed on the man who is now reaching for the brown bundle by his feet. With cruel calmness, he drapes the noose over his neck and sits a little more upright. And now I can't see him at all because a few different hands are lowering me to the ground as I cry with rib-cracking force, imagining over and over the man leaning forwards, his young neck striking as the rope yanks. The tilt of his body, the creak of the rope, the screaming of the witnesses recurs in my head.

I try to stand but my head fills with hot black fizz.

'No. Dun't move. Try to breathe, we az coll you a doctere,' says someone.

Sirens.

The sirens stop. I crunch my eyes shut and shriek. Because I can't bear to see what I might see or hear what I might hear. And if he dies, I have decided that I will die too. There is no other way. My God, he's going to die. I'm going to watch him die, then I'm going to die.

'Iz okay, hez okay.'

'Huh?' I look up at the woman.

'He's okay!' she repeats.

She and a couple of other people help me to my feet so that I can see for myself. There he is, completely indifferent as the policemen gently push him into the back seat of their car. I explode in a seizure of laugh-crying, cry-laughing. Then a doctor walks towards me opening his mouth to speak but I yell above him, 'HE'S OKAY!' and pedal away fast, slightly afraid of the white coats: been there done that got the paperwork to prove it, thank you very much. Besides, I, have a hot date to attend.

'Meet you at the beach,' I read the text again then look up at the cloying scatter of neon trunks and bikinis. This is like Where's Wally, only with no clues and no stripy jumper. Then I spot his beaming lit-match face, smiling wildly at me.

'Aleece!' Loic gives me a hug and kiss on the cheek.

'Hey! So, so sorry I'm late, I saw something TRÈS DIFFICILE! Il y a un homme dans le pont avec un...*rope.*'

Loic glares at me, totally confused, a laugh simmering beneath his face. 'Ere, come. I put my towelle juz zere. Yugh bike, Iz okay?' he says, ignoring my story.

'Oui.' I dump my stuff on the sand, 'I locked it by the *très cher* toilets.'

Loic erupts with laughter, his face flying backwards in a pinch. Having finally gathered himself he says, 'Shall we swim? I'LL RACE YOU!'

'Wait!' I shout as his trunks lunge ahead. 'Ur, I just need to get changed...'

If only I'd anticipated Loic's organisational grace, if only I'd kept my bikini on underneath my clothes, maybe I wouldn't have to wriggle on my back like an upturned beetle, one napkin-sized towel away from complete exposure. Loic pretends not to notice or feel sorry for me. A small win: I shaved.

'ALLEZ ALLEZ!' I shout and we dash into the sea, smiles ablaze, kicking the water either side of us into shimmering confetti.

'So, Aleece,' Loic says as we venture out to sea, away from the people, the noise, the expensive toilets, and the ice creams. *Breaststroke.* 'I zee you today on yugh bike wiz iz yellow bagz and I zink, "who is zis girl, where is she from?" Tu es étudiante? Oui? '

'Oui. *Le dessin.*'

'Ah! I like Art too! I show you in my ome. I like to draw maps. Very littul maps.'

For a while we chat in both French and English, about studies, Warmshowers, Couchsurfing, cycling and camping, Loic's face falling every so often into a humoured question mark as he tries to decode my galloping voice of improvised French. Eventually, we swim back to shore and drip our way over to our towels.

'Iz so smoll!' he says, laughing at my pathetic micro-fibre napkin, 'Ere, come on mine' he pats his towel, shimmies to its edge, 'AH! But please, don't get any sand on it.'

'Oui but we are on a beach! The sand is all around!'

'I know, I know but I JUZ ATE ZE SAND!'

I try my best to lay myself delicately on his towel like a Topshop girl but alas, my side of the towel quickly gathers a sugary coat. Look, I can't help it, it's in my DNA. Just ask my fortune teller who would tell you, as she had me, 'Ah, so that's it: you're a mermaid!'. I'd inwardly scoffed at the notion, slightly pissed that I'd let go of twenty quid. However, a week or so later while writing an essay in Caffè Nero, a live hermit crab fell from my head and landed on the keyboard. So there, can't help it: mermaid. I flick away the flecks while Loic rummages in his rucksack.

'Do you like zeese?' Loic asks.

'Figs! Mon préféré!'

'Oh my gud! Yez! Zey are my favorot as well! Ere. Take loads.'

'My God! I'm so happy to meet someone that loves figs as much as me, nobody likes figs these days, or prunes. Well,' I take one fig – honey-sweet, soft, chewy – and flip over onto my front, 'time to burn the other side!'

Loic explodes, one of those long laughs that dwindles and then starts all over again. It's such a delightful laugh I have to turn my face to one side, to hide the sheer victory pasted across it.

'Yez,' he says finally. 'You ah quite bughrned. Do you wunt some suncreame?'

'Nah...Je suis brûlé déjà. Anyway, I want a tan. What do you call this?' I point to my arm.

'Peau.'

'Ah, je naime pas mon anglaise *peau*. Trop blanche,' I say.

An enormous laugh ripples through Loic, flavoured with the sound of hysterical disbelief. This is actually the best day of my life.

'You wunt to go? To my ome?' he asks, still laughing.

'Sure.'

'Ah, zen Aleeece, come, we can go to the shadow of my ome'

I laugh, touched. Then say, 'um, you see that?'

'Yez?'

'That is a shadow. I think you mean shade.'

After one more session of squealing laughter, we pack up and mount our bikes. Loic cycles ahead and thank God because my adult baby-grow (a slinky, flowery thing, heavy on the cleavage that I decided to change into), its crotch buttons have popped out. A prophecy? Well, prophecy or not, these shorts are see-through and as always, I've gone commando. Loic stops. Fuck, he's noticed.

'Sorry. I muz show you zis. Look at zis.' Loic picks a leaf from a tree, 'Remember zis leaf, if you eza see zis leaf, iz a fig tree. Smell zis.'

'Mmm, that's so good, comme un rrrrêve, AHEM, cccckkkr-rev. Rêve.'

'Ah, you Engleesh! Cannut roll your R's. Iz so funny'

'CKKKRRRR. RL! CR-UGH! Oh! How do you do it?'

'Like ziz,' – a beautiful purring noise vibrates on Loic's tongue –'Zon't worry, Aleece, keep practice an you will learn. Ere, lez go, to ze *shadow of my ome*.'

For the rest of the journey, we talk about figs and the Hobbit (Loic loves the Hobbit) all the while my adult baby-grow slams its unbuttoned flap again and again against my you-know-what.

'Ere,' Loic opens the door, gestures me in ahead, 'welcum to my ome.'

Warmed by evening light, the wooden floors of Loic's studio apartment glow peachy, sweetening the air. In the centre of the tall room wooden ladder steps lead to Loic's mezzanine bed.

'Sacrebleu, your house is like a dream house.'

'Ah, merci Aleece. You wunt a showugh? You wunt to...how do you zay, laver?'

'Oui. Je suis dégoûtant,' I say gesturing to the cyclist tattoos of my shins. I close the bathroom door behind Loic's laugh and take a shower.

'I'm clean!' I sing.

Loic drives me back into the steamy room by my shoulders and spins me around to face him.

'Your back is very burned. See?' he points into the mirror behind me.

I look over my shoulder and flinch at the burgundy plane of my back.

Loic rubs his hands together and says, 'Turn aroun.'

I turn and watch the mirror in complete awe as Loic gently follows the contours of my back with cool cream.

'Voila,' he says.

'Merci,' I squeak.

'Also I have zis ozer cream, an it will completely fix your red skin but you ave to wash it uff because if you dun't it can give you brun spots.'

'Forever?'

'I zink maybeeee, yez.'

'Brown spots...forever? Comme un giraffe? J'ai peur.'

Loic's head flies backwards in a shock-fit of laughter.

'Um...Je ne veux pas être un giraffe. Non, merci,' I say.

Loic laughs even harder and returns to his sizzling tofu murmuring 'tuk-tuk-tuk' as he stirs things, adds things, chops things. The 'tuk-tuk-tuk' is a French thing, I have no idea why they do it but it's horrifically adorable.

'Do you wunt to try?' He asks tweezing a slice of pepper with his thumb and forefinger. I bite it straight from his hand. 'Uh, Aleece, I'm nut sure you really tasted zat... Have anuzer... Iz nice?'

I nod.

'I like zem togezer' he says eating a piece of pepper and a brazil nut in one mouthful. 'MM! You try?' He points the combination at me on the end of a sharp knife. 'NOT LIKE ZAT! IZ DANGERUZ!'

'Oh yeah, sorry' I say, flinching back from the blade.

'Hey Aleece, one day I wunt to do what you do an cycol. But in England and Erland.'

'Oh! My Mum's Irish!' – Mum's face scowls in my head – 'Northern Irish.'

'Really?'

'Yeah! And my Granny. Only,' I pause, squint and say, 'Elle est mort.'

'Oh!'

'Yeah, and Granny Lush is dead too. Now I have no Grannies.'

Loic erupts, belly-laughter spilling all over the place.

'Ah! Uh, gush!' he pants, holding his stomach 'Ah! "now I az no Graneeze" Zee English humugh!'

Loic presses his hand against his heart, takes a shaky breath then piles up two plates with rice, tofu and courgette.

'Here Aleece Zis one for you, we sit on zee sofa.'

'Cor! Merci!'

'J'adore riz. Look, iz like a cake of rice.' Loic picks up a fist-sized clump of rice with his fork, 'Bon appétit!'

We eat slowly, chat effortlessly. About bikes, life, diet ('I no eat much meat an I never eat gluten' he says), university.

'I zink Iz so cool you study art. Ey, let me show you my littul maps.'

Loic shows me his drawings: tiny trees, delicately inked, wiggly lines and land contours. We're sitting very close.

'Gosh, they're beautiful! So dainty...'

'Ah, zank you, Aleece...'

Perfectly ruining the provocative silence, a mosquito saunters in squeaking its way around our heads.

'No! Don't kill him!' I say as Loic picks up an electric tennis racket.

Loic pauses, 'Really? You be upset if I keel im?'

'Yes. He doesn't –ah!– mean it, not really. Ah! Ah! Aaaaah!'

'You sure dun't want me kill im?' Loic smirks.

'No. Ah! Ah! No. Let him –ah!– live. OH, piss off.'

Eventually, I let Loic kill him and without that shrill squeal, we are left in silence with empty plates and a heavy tension. Loic turns to face me 'Do you wunt to go to bed?'

'Um, urrr, um,' – I don't know what Loic means by bed. I'm way too excited to go to bed, but what if he's speaking in euphemisms? – 'Je ne sais pas!'

'You dun't know if you wunt to go to bed!' Loic laughs. 'You so funny. Ey, I know! Do you wunt to see ze stars?'

'Oui! Pourquoi non?'

'Aleece, in French we zay *"Pourquoi pas",*' he says, opening his front door.

'What do you call stars in French?' I ask, pointing at them.

'Étoilles.'

And so, we gawp up the many *étoiles* over our heads. In my periphery, I sense him looking at me. I turn to meet his gaze, but only catch the slight swing of his head. The silence is enormous.

'I ave an idea,' says Loic.

'Oui?'

'Lez go onto ze roof.'

Loic climbs the wall and reaches out his arm to me. I grab it and in one effortless sweep, he pulls me up beside him. We clamber onto his roof and lie side by side on the tiles, close. Silence again. Loic's fingers gently bump mine; he clasps them, his breath deepening ever so slightly. I really, really, need the toilet.

'Can I do mur?' says Loic.

I tense my bladder.

'Wee,' I whisper.

He leans towards me and plants a kiss so slow, so soft: the feeling shoots through me like an electric shock. A few more agonising minutes go by, a double-yearning from two neighbouring holes, causing me to squirm like a lubricated worm. Our kissing is silent but my head is screaming in rather annoying woo-hoos.

Loic pulls away, 'Lez brush our teeth. And zen... do you wunt to come into my bed?'

'Oui, S'il vous plait.'

'Hup!' He carries me to the ground princess-style.

I rush off, ungracefully desperate, release my bladder, flush, wash my hands, just in time for Loic to peer around the door with a small pot of toothpaste.

'C'est vert!' I cry, as he screws open the lid of green clay.

'Yez. I make it myself,' he says.

'Mine's black,' I hold my charcoal toothpaste in the air.

'UGH!' he says.

'BUT LOIC YOURS IS GREEN!'

We laugh, watching our mouths in the mirror as they gather green and black foam.

'Okay. Now we race.' he says.

Loic bolts off and I chase him, grab the back of his t-shirt, pull him back, and propel myself ahead.

'NO SHOES!' he yells.

I throw them behind me, my left trainer hitting him with a *duff*.

'EY!' he laughs.

I giggle my way up the stairs and dive into his bed. Loic follows quickly behind, crawls on top of me, draws closer. Our giggles quieten, our lips meet.

'Oh gush, you smell so good.' he says.

I let out a small moan.

'I love your body,' he says.

We melt together.

'Zis iz differunt to French bras,' he unhooks me. 'I wunt mur.'

I touch his hair, like I've wanted to all day.

'Oh... Aleece,' he says.

5

Light my fig on fire

Loic's eyes flick open: electric, green.

'I will be so sad to leave you today,' I whisper.

'No, Aleece,' he says in a gravelly early-morning voice, squeezing me tight. 'Dun't say zat.'

God, he's so warm, he smells so delicious, *Uh*, it's like being in bed with a hot doughnut, only with a six pack and a sexy accent. If I wasn't so damn hungry I'd have suggested round two. But I am, hungry.

'I recommend you eat within thirty minutes of waking, to reduce the likelihood of bingeing later in the day. Here is your food diary, write the time you wake here and the time you eat here.'

'It's quite late...' I say.

'Aleece, iz only eight. But would you like breakfaz wiz me?'

'Oh my God, *oui.*'

'Okay.' Loic kisses me. 'HUP!' then gets out of bed and steps into his pants. 'My breakfast zat I eat, iz...Ne pas normal.'

I stare at his panted crotch, 'Parfait,' I say.

We eat our *'ne pas normal'* breakfast (bran flakes, sliced peach and hazelnut butter) amidst the many blossoms of Loic's garden, the clink of our spoons, our crunching and appreciative *'mmm's*, muffled by the blankety softness of early morning sun.

'Best breakfast ever,' I say.

Loic laughs, not realising I was being serious. 'Iz gud, no? Mmm! Ey!' he throws me his jumper, 'try zis un.'

I pull it over my head, emerging pink, static and squealing as Loic snaps photos of me.

'Ere, look! Aw, Aleece...Oh, zat is very you,' he says, scrolling through pictures of a euphoric, tanned thing, looking thinner than I'd imagined, giggling into the baggy sleeve of his jumper.

'Ha! It's me!'

'Aw, you look zo appy, Aleece.'

I pull off the jumper and throw it back at him.

'Aleece.' Loic stares at my arm, horrified, 'What iz zis?' he points to a collection of raised scars, just below my shoulder. Damn heat has made them swell and shine.

'Oh,' – white hot panic – 'Uh, I'm just clumsy. I can't actually remember. See look, je suis maladroite.' I point at my thigh.

'Oh okay, tu es maladroite. An what you coll ziz?'

'A bruise.'

'Ey, Aleece! I av an idea!' Loic dashes into the kitchen, returns with a pen. 'Dun't move.'

For the next few minutes, I sit silently, trying not to squirm as Loic scritch-scratches my upper thigh with a biro. His head pops up, 'voil– No, wait! Stay zere.' he bends his head back down, scratches me once more, 'Voila!'

'C'est belle, merci!' I look down at my bruise, now a precisely symmetrical heart with an arrow through it. 'You're a bit, *OCD*, aren't you?'

'What does zis mean oh, zee, dee?'

'Hm, It's like, I– am ve-ry ti-dy,' I say in a robot voice. 'Liiike... Oh, Look!' I point to a stack of towels folded neatly, arranged in colour order, a straw hat balanced neatly on top. 'OCD.'

'Oh yez, I see what you mean. Per-aps a littul.' Loic wanders over to the towels and picks up the straw hat. 'Zere!' he settles it on my head, 'Oh, Aleece, It suits you. You keep it.'

'Can I brush your teeth?' I ask, because Loic is looking at me so adoringly and apparently I am allergic to romance.

'Okay,' he laughs. He's always laughing. God.

We spend the next five minutes bending over backwards, collapsing forwards, foam erupting through our giggling teeth. I really, really want to touch his chest but instead I find new, weirder ways of brushing his teeth. Loic laughs up a storm and green toothpaste goes everywhere.

With no more excuses to stay, Loic, me and The Insect loiter outside, a 'goodbye' hanging in the air like a bad smell.

'Ey, Aleece.' Loic turns around and squats. 'Get un.'

I leap on and Loic gives me a piggyback, running me back and forth, around in circles, spinning all different sorts of dizziness into my head. I barely notice the ground as he hands me back to gravity, squealing and gloriously broken.

'Bye Aleece.' he gives me one last kiss. 'I hup zat we meet again.'

'Et moi aussi. Maybe one day we'll cycle together.'

Loic stares at me, stunned. 'I wud love zat.'

I pedal away, not once looking back at my perfect rendezvous.

For the first mile, I keep my cool. Though this does not last and I am soon in a frenzy, zigzagging manically along the promenade, bursting into laughter at random intervals, frightening the pedestrians out of my way. Tara rings.

'Hey buuuu-ddy, how's it going?' she says.

'Ahem, well yeah, pretty good. I mean...Great! I have news.'

'Oh yeah?'

'The dry spell is officially over.'

Tara screams and whoops down the phone then catches her breath and says, 'Right, you need to tell me everything. Who was he? Where did you meet him? What did he look like? Was it *big*?'

Typical Tara.

After our chat, I find something while rummaging for a snack: a brown paper bag, folded precisely, weighted with medjool dates, brazil nuts, and of course, figs. I send Loic a text: 'J'ai mange les figs et je pense a toi.'

He replies in seconds: 'Oh Alice, you are the sweetest most cuddliest English girl I ever met.'

I sigh my way to Royan, a town that is, as my own kind would delicately put it, 'an absolute shit hole'. Like Butlins, but with an even smaller budget. Ray (my Warmshowers host) isn't much better either. He's an artist, about 50, a too-pissed-off-to-eat kind of skinny, ragged hair, slouchy jeans. There is just something about him I can't trust. Maybe it's the way he's harbouring Lu, a semi-Yorkshirian, semi-Filipino girl who's flouncing about his living room like an excitable puppy. Her hands are stuck naively to her hips and her face is beaming with the urgency of a child's. Lu and I hit it off instantly, spending the next hour crossed-legged, chatting about England, boys, France, uni, while Ray leans against the doorframe, a smirking vulture.

'Ray is teaching me how to paint, look!' Lu points to a painting of a cheese. Ray wanders over and puts his hand on Lu's shoulder. Was that a flinch? Hard to tell.

'Ah, wow! You're a natural!' I say.

'Thanks! I'm pretty pleased with it. I wasn't supposed to stay here this long, but Ray's training has been so good. So, hey. Tell me where you were this morning?'

'Oh, I was in La Rochelle with a boy called Loic. We... had a rendezvous...'

'Oh my god! ' she squeals. 'Was he cute?'

'Oh, God yeah.'

'Zen why did you leave?' Ray butts in.

'Uh–' Suddenly, the penny drops: he's gone. I'm never going to see that lovely boy again. And why the hell *did* I leave? 'Well, I want to keep cycling. It's...Important. And if I'd have stayed, maybe I never would've left,' I say.

Ray shrugs, drags himself into the kitchen and starts singing arrogantly to a sizzling pan of onions.

We eat rice and I think of Loic, *'Iz like a cake'*, wondering if I'll always be doomed to miss him.

'Living in Paris was shit, the peepol, zey live like rats. I fucking ate Paris.' Ray leans back in his chair, knife and fork left at jaunty angles on his plate. 'Do you want to do some shit painting?'

Here's another clue to Ray's character: he drives a four-by-four. Too late to back out now, I think to myself as I slosh about in the back seat, feeling increasingly queasy for a whole variety of reasons. Finally, we arrive at the isolated cliffs of nowhere. Ray hops out, slings a rattling rucksack on his back and storms up the cliffs with me and Lu following behind. Every ten paces or so Ray turns around to flash his DSLR at us, Lu posing cutely for each shot, me standing stupidly like a confused lemon.

At the top of the cliff, Ray decants his spray paints beside a small concrete hut which to my amazement does not smell even faintly of piss (the French, I am beginning to realise, are not as dirty as the English). So we do our 'shit painting': Ray spraying the worst of my mother tongue on an inside wall, Lu spraying love hearts on top of a wall already full of cocks and swears, and me, spraying one blue daisy, then retiring to the cliff edge.

The drop is vast and I think of the man on the Île de Ré bridge, his dangling bare feet. A thought that makes my chest so heavy with dread, I shuffle back from the cliff edge, in case the feeling should pull me over. It's funny because at the time the young fella was being rescued by the police, I laughed. I was over it right there and then. So where has all this sadness come from?

I dig into my pocket and take out the dried fruit I bought in Nantes: two kumquats, one slice of melon and two rings of pineapple left. Lu comes to sit beside me and I give her a ring of pineapple. We chat a little, then go quiet.

'You're tough,' I say.

'So are you,' she says.

I open my mouth to ask her if she's okay, if Ray is treating her okay, but the devil emerges from the chemical clouds with that bloody DSLR.

How I'm going to sleep tonight, God only knows. I check my phone: no new messages. Sigh. All this churning anguish, what am I to do with it? I can't stop thinking about that man on the bridge, the emptiness of his face, his tumbling beer can, the noose around his neck. Young people aren't supposed to die. It's sick, and I hate that he would do that to himself.

'Just those please.' I put a packet of bourbons and two packets of Paracetamol on the counter: the perfect finale. I pay. 'Want one?' I ask, opening the biscuits.

'No...' says the cashier boy, looking very grateful for the till between us. 'Thanks.'

I shrug and walk out the shop (what a perfect sunny day), back along the street, into my uni halls, bip the key-card in the lobby, up the stairs, into flat five, mouth filling with delicious biscuit cement. By the time I close my bedroom door and switch on Gordon Ramsey's kitchen nightmare, all of my packets are empty.

'FUCKING LIMP DICK IN THE KITCHEN YOU KNOW THAT?'
Gordon is ruthless.

Then black.

A hot, sour flash of poison in my blood urges me awake. I run to the bathroom and shiver and vomit and shiver and vomit and shiver and dry heave.

'Fucking hell Alice!' says Ollie, hovering in the corridor, 'What did you eat?'

'Oh God,' my voice echoes in the toilet bowl, 'something bad, I reckon... Ugh. I think I'm gunna... Go to bed.'

'Here, you might need this.'

'Thanks,' I slur, taking the bucket. 'I'm...Going to bed.'

Crawling on all fours, I make it back to my room. For the next 20 hours I fill Ollie's bin with bile until there is nothing left of me but loneliness.

Guilt drags me into a deep sleep.

Last night I dreamt of Loic. I dreamt he busted into Ray's flat declaring 'I missed you too much', that we escaped Ray's flat without saying goodbye and found a field to camp in. Then we cooked figs on a fire, laughing and laughing as they melted into glowing purple and amber drops. But morning rips me away, back to reality, back to Royan. How cruel the imagination can be: he felt so real and solid. Though I am glad I didn't dream about the man on the bridge, whose dangling bare feet are still haunting me.

I send Loic a text: 'I had a dream last night you came to see me and we cooked figs on the fire together.'

He replies: 'Oh Alice, I want to make your dreams come true.'

With robotic steadiness, I pedal through the hustle and bustle of Royan, quietly thanking the sky for being considerate to my state. No brilliant blue or shrill sunshine: it's overcast, cold enough to warrant a jumper, raining ever so slightly. I start to cry. And cry. And cry. Then I meet a Yorkshireman who insists me into a cafe.

'I've bin livin' ere eleven years and I still can't get me 'ed around French. But I can say this – it's a good wun so you remember this –

ahem, "Gee swee fatigue".' He hands me a steaming cup, 'Ere, get that down yer. Ey! It's joost a coppa tea lass!' he says, as my tears plop into the tea.

After the salty tea, Dad rings and I cry at him. I cry into my yogurt, I cry through the bike-paved forest, I cry eating tofu, I cry all the way to Hourtin where I retire by the lake with tear ducts like sun dried tomatoes.

A swim and a nap later, my hosts Alexa and Hugo come to meet me. From a distance, their blurred silhouette looks kind of like a tractor. Then I realise this is because Alexa and Hugo are body-builders and there is a very tall man walking between them.

'Ee is Diego, from Spain,' says Alexa, panting as she lifts weights. 'Ee's retired an ee stay with us tonight.'

Alexa, Hugo and I stare at the Spaniard, now splashing about in a lake too shallow for his long body. 'I think he's funny.' I say.

Alexa laughs. 'Exactly,' she says.

Hugo says nothing but steals the odd cautious glance at me, holding his mouth down as if a smile would burn him.

'Ee's shy.' Alexa whispers.

'Oh! Me too, sometimes,' I whisper back, blushing at the thought.

Alexa smiles at me, as if to say she already knew that.

The sun sinks and we amble back to Alexa and Hugo's flat for dinner.

'No, merthi.' Diego screws his face up at the lentils, 'J'amie azúcar' he says in part-French, part-Spanish, lifting a beaten up selection of pastries out of his pannier. He tells us, while sipping his sugary coffee mischievously, that the word retirement in Spanish, 'jubilación', comes from the word 'júbilo' meaning 'joy', and that as soon as his pension landed he was off, navigating only with the sun. And when it's cloudy? He scratches silver beard, 'Es difícil,' he says.

Diego might be the most delightful thing I've ever witnessed. The way he hangs over the table swirling his big hands as he tells us with extraordinary excitement that he nearly drowned yesterday, the cartoon sea lion on his T-shirt, his adversion to legumes: he's like a big kid who's run away from home. After his sugary dinner, he packets his long body in a sleeping bag on Alexa and Hugo's balcony, because he only sleeps under the stars. Without even really meaning to, Diego has completely cheered me up.

I shimmy under the covers, about to text a friend of a friend who lives in Bordeaux, then I notice an MMS from Loic. Heart lunging and belly contracting, I wait for the image to download. Laid in a neat grid are the following items: a water bottle, sun cream, a sleeping bag, a stack of socks and a neatly folded towel. I text back demanding an explanation, holding my breath, holding my thoughts. He replies with another picture: a train ticket, La Rochelle to Pau, arriving Thursday, 19:00. Captioned: 'To go to cook fig together.'

I text back, 'Really?'

'Look like truth. Quit my job tomorrow. We go together on the west. What do you think in this moment?'

'I'm so excited I feel a bit sick.'

'That's all I want to know. Good night Alice, see you soon.'

What a turn of events. One minute it's nightmares and suicide, the next it's all dream-come-true, fairy-tale romance. In all my life, I don't think I've ever been this happy and I have no idea how I'm going to hold my cells together, how I'll stop them exploding into luminous glitter, how I'll ever sleep again.

Woo-hoo! New day, new journey.

The next morning I pedal off so fast, my legs almost whizz off like helicopters. It is as though the close buzzing of trauma and excitement in my brain have sent currents of shivery electricity through me. Which is rather treacherous because it has left me with no patience for red lights or to wait out the scuffle happening on the bike path in front of me. I try to get around the three thicky-thumpies, but their tussle seems to worsen as I get close, so I wait. Finally, after a bit more shouting and a touch of theft, they all chase each other into the sunset.

Bordeaux is as posh as it sounds, excessively so. It has historic toothpick-whittled buildings rubbing shoulders with shiny shopping centres, carved into graceful shapes. The cobbles and tourists are shiny too. In fact, the only thing neither posh nor shiny in this city is me. Aware of this, I actually ruffle my hair a bit, like

I've seen other girls do, but this just makes me look more frazzled.

'HEY!' Flora waves me down, 'Come in, great to meet you. Oh, these are my boys, they can speak English *and* French. Here come in, come in. Can you eat peanut butter? My husband is going to make a curry with peanut butter. Here, here, take a seat. Oh, and how do you know Shamus?'

'Oh um–'

Flora's brother Shamus manages my local Holland and Barrett. Back at uni, every morning at 9am I'd shiver into his shop dripping and salty from my swim, to scan the three main numbers on the back of packets (fat, sugar, calories) and Shamus would follow me around the shop chatting about this and that, his days as a vegan butcher, his new suit, my purple fingers. Then one day, while I was buying my usual 88-calorie packet of dry roasted chickpeas, he asked me out for cider, an event that ended in him reading me porn, while I drank a cup of tea made using a teabag he'd already twice used. 'I find it very loosening,' he'd said.

'We're friends...' I say.

'Oh, that's great yeah, nice. You know, he's never come here to see us. Here, you must be hungry, eat some nuts.'

The next morning, rain wakes me up. Not as a cosy 'pit-pat' or even a heavier 'TAP-TAP' but a deafening 'SHHHHH', relentless, severe, dark.

'You can stay anuzer day if you like, iz so wet out zere, you'll be froze!' says Flora's husband.

I almost jump out of my skin. He hadn't said a word to me up until now. But I guess that's because Flora talks so much.

'Merci mais,' – I flex my pathetic bicep – '*Je suis fort.*'

'But... iz so wet.'

I stare out at the swelling and merging puddles. '*Je suis fort.*' I repeat.

Loic. I have to make it to Loic.

After a couple of dark, watery hours, my cold bones have started to creak. Yet I rattle on, face stuck in a champing grimace, fingers clawed and frozen, my once-pink now deep red trainers heavier than moon boots. Even the appreciative toots from lorry drivers (I decided to cycle in my bikini) have lost their sense of novelty. Ah well, only fifty miles to go.

'ESCUSE MOI!' I yell to a woman as she dashes through the rain, 'AIDE-MOI?'

'Uh-,' she hesitates by her front door, looking from me to the cosy yellow light of her living room.

'Je suis tellement froid et mes vêtments est NE PAS SEC!' I plead.

'Viens,' she says.

The nervous woman hands me a second cup of tea, a banana and a bundle of clothes as my wet ass prints a motif on her sofa. She sits next to me but quickly jumps up again and starts pacing again. Wincing with each quiet word, she says that her husband will be home soon. The sky shrivels at this comment, and I take my cue to leave.

Though my belly is warm with tea and snacks, I leave feeling even worse than before. That woman's frightened eyes seem to be still flittering in my head, her nervous feet replacing the 'tip-tap' of the absent rain. But I've got to say, my new outfit is brilliant: pyjama bottoms that flare just below the knee (perfect length for getting caught in my chain), *fresh* pink socks, a slightly see-through floral top stamped with the words 'never stop love' on the back (how apt!) and finally, a multi-coloured raincoat that would've given Joseph's technicoloured dream coat a run for its money.

77 miles spent and dry everywhere apart from my squelching shoes, I arrive in Lacquy, at Henri and Sigrid's house.

'Ere, welcome. An watch out, zere is a snake by your feet' Says Henri, opening the front door.

I look, but only catch the rustle of long grass by my feet.

'Aw, I missed it!'

Henri smiles. 'Come in, meet my wife,' he says.

Henri's wife Sigrid stands in the kitchen with a face so true and warm, it makes me ache with the weary relief of coming home. She pushes me into the shower with the benign insistence of a mother and when I hop out again, I notice a pair of slippers waiting outside the door. I slip them on and shuffle into the kitchen.

'I have a trick,' says Sigrid, handing me a wad of newspaper. 'Put zese in your shoes und you vill find zem dry. Zen you can help me make dinner.'

'Thank you,' I say stuffing the newspaper in my trainers, 'hey Sigrid, how come you speak French *and* English so well, even though you're German?'

'It's my job. I can speak Arabic too. I teach English to Islamic cult schools und I am not allowed to teach zem anyzing except for zings to do with Allah. But,' she leans towards me and winks, 'I teach zem other zings, in secret.'

'But that's so dangerous! And you never got in trouble?'

'Never. I trust zee children und zey trust me.'

For dinner I polish off three bowls of pasta and a baked apple, much to the delight of Henri and Sigrid, who gleam at me proudly, willing me to eat more and more while we chat away in my wonky version of French.

'I sorry, we ave to go to bed so early.' says Henri, cleaning the plates. 'Tomorroh, we both leave very early to go on separate holidays.'

'Oh!' I say.

'Yez' says Sigrid, 'Henri likes to go on long, painful adventures und I like to remain horizontal. Zo Henri go to Zcotland und I go to Zpain.'

In bed, it suddenly dawns upon me that this will be the last time I sleep alone, apparently, though I haven't actually heard from Loic. But whether he does or doesn't come, I know I needed Henri and Sigrid today. I needed their homely warmth to fill my bones, their parental comfort to supply me with the strength for tomorrow and I really needed them to feed me in the vast quantities they did because...well, I don't know.

That night, fragmented by a very vocal and flirtatious mosquito, I have another dream about Loic, a different sort of dream. I dreamt that we were travelling together and he began to change. Not only his character, which soured with arrogance, but his appearance changed too, gradually metamorphosing into that familiar face: Matt, my first boyfriend. The last time I saw *him*, I gave him (and his bitch) my middle finger and I feel a little horrified at his uninvited dream appearance. I shake the dream out of my head and pedal off, a trembling mess of excitement and apprehension.

Today's journey is dry, hilly and long, ideal for pouring all this nervous energy into. Hopefully I'll arrive tanned and dry, rather than looking like a used toilet brush. This seems feasible because there are no clouds above head, only strange jagged ones, sitting on the horizon.

'It can't be...It's just a cloud, just a cloud, just a– BUT ALICE! CLOUDS AREN'T SHAPED LIKE MOUNTAINS!' I scream.

I jump off my bike, sprint into a supermarket, ask the lady if those pointy clouds are mountains.

'Oui,' she replies. 'Les Pyrénées.'

I burst out of the shop in a fit of howling tears.

Just two weeks ago I passed a blasé comment about 'maybe cycling to the Pyrenees' and now here they are, straight ahead, paper-thin, but definitely, definitely there.

I stare at the mountains all day, watching them solidify and take up more of the horizon as I close the 70-mile gap between myself and Pau. Mountains that, even from this distance, seem to be pulling at the fibres holding me together. Perhaps this makes no sense. But how could anything as beautiful as a mountain make sense! And just to add to the heart-skips, I have a text from Loic:

'Train is delayed expect at 21:00.'

My heart, full of weighty mountain awe, seems to lunge in my throat. Because maybe this was all a cruel trick, maybe Loic isn't coming.

It's 19:00 and I arrive in Pau. The mountains are thick in front of me and the next hour spent staring at them seems to slip by like water.

With time to murder, I make use of France's very curious 'self-cleaning toilets' (basically, they just blast the mess about with water between each visit). First a nervous wee, then I wipe a circle in the condensation of the mirror, fluff up my hair, pat it back down, settle Loic's straw hat on my head, suck my stomach in and then finally enter the station.

What can one possibly do with 42 whole minutes? Pace? Yep. Learn a few cheeky words from my pocket French dictionary? Yep

(LA PUTE!). Survey the vending machine options? Yep, and what idiot is going to pay more than a whole two euros for a packet of crisps? Oh, that one.

Ten minutes to go. Giggle a bit, pace a bit, sit, swing legs, stand up again, sit down again.

Nine minutes. Try to make friends with the guy next to me, fail, watch him walk to the other end of the station.

Five minutes. Drink water, squirm, fiddle with straw hat.

Four minutes. Watch the ticking clock: three minutes...two minutes...one minute.

An enormous hissing noise blasts through the atrium, then a series of beeps and hustling footsteps. This is it. Beneath the clutter of noise, the slow spin of a bicycle wheel ticks in my head and I know he's here.

A bicycle, a boy, a fluff of blonde hair, blazes right in the dead-centre of the atrium. The whole world tumbles away as I hurtle towards Loic and leap at him. With one effortless sweep he whips me off my feet and I kick and we spin and we laugh, gripping each other with the intensity of wartime lovers. He puts me down and I stare at his face, flaring with wild euphoria, for all of two seconds then I yelp again and squeeze him desperately. His laugh beats through my chest, warm and strong.

'ALEECE!' He beams.

'I– I can't believe it's YOU!' I tip-toe on the spot, as though the ground was scalding my feet, 'Oh my God, oh my God, I can't believe you're here.'

'You zought I wouldn't come?'

'Oui! Non! Je ne sais pas! Oh my goodness. I'm– I'm just so happy.'

'Et moi aussi,' he says.

'Oh gosh,' I look around, at our smiling audience, 'Sorry, for the reaction.'

Loic laughs, 'It was pughfect"

After a quick stumble, fumble and tumble, in perfect synchronisation we push on our pedals and begin our journey together.

It was only five miles to Anne's house (our warm shower host I'd pulled out the bag last minute). Even so, it's taking us ages: too busy giggling, going the wrong way, chatting, giggling more. I look at his glowing face, for the hundredth time: yep, he's definitely real.

'Aleece, let's stup! Look,' Loic points down to the river.

We park up, giggle our way down the ledge, crouch beside the river and swash our hands in it. Twilight falls, yet Loic's face seems brighter than ever, looking at me like— we kiss.

By the time we make it to Anne's, it's completely dark.

'Bonjour, enchanté,' She says in a fragile voice, holding her frail hands together in a gentle clasp on her chest.

'Ah! Enchanté mademoiselle! Bleugh bleugh bleugh bleugh bleugh,' says Loic.

Bloody hell, I didn't know he was *that* French. I hadn't even considered the fact he was French and I was English and how this might demote me to the foreign, plus-one, goofball tag-along. A minuscule twitch of regret makes a fleeting visit in my mind. Then I remember it doesn't matter, nothing matters! I am nothing but a fiery throb of love and all that matters is being able to touch Loic's arm.

'Elle est très jolie,' says Anne's husband, looking at Loic but nodding at me.

Loic strokes my chin with his thumb. 'Oui,' he agrees.

I feel so shy.

6

Love, mountains and hanging resentment

We wake up in a naked tangle. I tense my limbs in a good morning gesture and Loic responds with a giggle then a long, savouring kiss. Look at his eyes. Look at them, looking at me! My toes are flickering like a distressed flame and it is thanks to one single thread of self-control that I don't scream in his beautiful face.

At the breakfast table, tidal waves of rolling R's and gag noises gush between Loic and Anne, little of which I understand. It's all 'seurgh' this, 'bleurgh' that. I could try to join in but God knows at the hurdle of my poor English lips, those melding sounds would be chopped into ugly, awkward chunks. So instead, I inconspicuously stir my fruit compote with a teaspoon, stealing glances of Loic when I know it's safe. But I misjudge and trip into his eyes; my appetite shrivels immediately. I feel about as powerless as a turkey at Christmas. Dad rings.

'How's it going sport?' he asks.

'Amazing. Wonderful. Dad, Dad, Dad! I'm so happy! GOSH! See, I'm no longer solo.'

'No way! What's his name?'

'Loic.'

'They're always called Loic!' – One time Dad, it was *one* other time – 'Well, I am glad there are four eyes rather than two to see things with. Is there *romance?*'

I can see Loic through the window, folding his pants carefully.

'Maybe a little bit,' I say.

Gosh I'm so excited. Does happiness breed more happiness, or am I burning through a lifetime of dopamine reserves? My soul is volcanic, hence the scream trembling beneath the threshold of my lips. But I keep my composure, siphoning little giggling squeaks out in the shower. Gillette ProGlide? Anne's husband, you beauty! I do a few happy shower jumps – '*You'll fall and break your neck,*' says Mum's voice in my head – then waggle away the expression of wild ecstasy, in the steam-free circle of the mirror. Deep breath. I step out of the bathroom steamy and completely unable to conceal my teeth.

'Okay?' asks Loic, panniers in hand.

'Oui. Let's go,' I reply, cooler than a cucumber sorbet.

It's 12am, and all me and lover-boy have managed is a trip to Decathlon (basically Sports Direct, only with happier staff that are allowed to go to the toilet) and now what? An aimless wander around Carrefour, deciding how much sweetcorn to buy. In the end, Loic insists on the biggest tin.

'We eat ere? Iz okay?' Loic says, pointing to an island of anaemic grass surrounded by concrete and dodgy looking men.

'PARFAIT. My Dad used to work in an industrial estate and so they're very nostalgic to me.'

'Yez, I like too. I zink zey are beautifol, nut even because nostalgia. We eat zen we go to zee mountains?'

'Oui.'

Lunch is hummus, tofu and sweetcorn. Lots of different stressful packets and no sprouts and no fresh bread (Loic is *'nut to eat gluten since I waz eleven'*).

'I eat like yogurt,' says Loic, spooning hummus into his mouth.

I laugh, nibbling raw tofu in small bites.

'Gosh, pffft,' Loic pats his belly 'I zo full. We eat zo much.'

'Yeah...' I say.

'Full' is a lonely word, to me. The last time I was *'full'* was in 2015, May the 16th , 8.30am. Rice Krispies: the final bowl. And I remember it vividly: the malty, sugary smell, the initial crunch of the first bite and the melted mush of the last; the scratchy netting of the tutu I'd pinched from dance therapy; the packed suitcase waiting at my side; the way HCA Debbie had put a hand on my shoulder and said *'Well done. Let's get you home now'*. The reeling stopped right there. My stomach, my bones, my very soul, collectively agreed on a feeling of fullness as I stepped outside to all the beckoning things of the real world, two stone more alive. But that was the last time. On that very same day I started a diet; the hunger came back twice as strong and I haven't been able to shake it off since.

Loic finishes the hummus, then we do roly polys – God, I love him – and finally, we head for the mountains.

'Aleece! You ride very dangeruz like zat!' he says.

I brake, just as we emerge out of the bushes and attempt to cross a dual carriageway.

'But I always cycle like this.' I say.

'I zink you nut to go in front.'

'Oh.'

'I zink you follow me, come, we go zis way.'

Loic places his phone, alight with the demands of Mrs Google Maps, in his pocket, pedals on.

'Uh–' I open my mouth to protest but Loic carries on ahead, steering us wherever the hell that shrill and bossy robot woman has decided to take us. Fucking Google Maps. If you are a cyclist then heed my warning: Google Maps wants to kill you. But it's fine. Really, it's fine. For the next hour we climb beside a whoosh of relentless traffic – you know, I'd never noticed before that some lorries have more than four wheels – for the next hour, I gawp mindlessly at his back. Two thoughts relay in my head: 'go away Loic' and 'I'm hungry', though I can't tell how related they might be.

'J'ai faim!' I yell.

'Olready?' says Loic.

A feeling of hatred flashes in my belly. Filling me up, undermining my hunger. He thinks I'm greedy, he thinks I'm fat! Fuck him. If he thinks I'm so fat and useless he can fuck off on his own. I was fine without him anyway.

'Oui,' I say.

We stop for figs (eight for Loic, five for me) munching through them without 'mm'ing nearly as much as we ought to.

'Shall we goh?' asks Loic, crunching the empty packet in his hands.

'Just...' I lie back on the grass, 'give me a minute...'

'Oh, okay.'

Loic wanders off, slack with sadness, and sits by the riverside, hands clasped over his bent knees, staring into the babbling brown water as if wishing it would swallow him up. I sit beside him and kiss his shoulder, which drops just slightly.

'Allez?' I ask.

'Oui.' He smiles, weakly.

We continue, pedalling through a day that brings me little interest. Look at his lovely back. Look at his stupid fucking back. Oh my goodness he's looking at me and well, isn't he beautiful?

Suddenly, the meander of the road swings us around and our uphill efforts show us their yield. I grind to a halt and gasp at the great roar of mountains, too big to fit underneath the clouds, the pine trees that soak them looking no bigger or more impressive than tufts of moss, the ribboning silver roads appearing thin as threads. The Pyrenees.

Loic whizzes on ahead, clearly not as awed as me, and for a split second I think to let him go on while I bolt off in another direction, somewhere he won't find me, somewhere I can hang out without him third wheeling my mountain. But this thought, though initially sweet, quickly rots down to guilt and I catch up with Loic fast, hoping he hadn't noticed my hesitation.

We stop in the first village, Castet, for no reason that I know of. Maybe Loic is getting tired. *Pussy.* No, not pussy, a very nice boy, Alice. Besides, with its wonky stone cottages, glass lake, and heaped emerald mountains, Castet is a bit of a fairy-tale. There's an icy chill in the air sweet with the anticipation of snow and the swirly-horned sheep have a medieval quality to their countenance.

'Aleece. Your...' Loic points at my bike, 'what you call zis? Gearz? Zey are not good.'

For the last hour, my chain had been crunching desperately and finding the worst possible moments to slide neatly off the cogs, but I had secretly been enjoying the inconvenience.

'Oh, it's fiiiine! ' I say. 'C'est ne pas grave.'

'Ah, no Aleece, Iz grave, nut good.' Loic inspects my back wheel and points at what I've heard other cyclists call a 'Jockey '.

'See zis? Zis is not suppoze to be broke like zis. Iz broke like a giraffe trying to sit on an aeroplane, wiz iz neck all bent like zis,' Loic crooks his neck theatrically.

We keel over, laughter beating away all the doubts of five minutes ago.

'Get un my shoulders' says Loic, squatting in front of me.

'But I'll crush you!'

'You wun't! Come!'

'WAH! Nous sommes un giraffe!' I scream up in the thin air above Loic's head.

With my thighs either side of his warm face, I can't help but hope we have sex tonight.

'Shall we camp here?' I ask, determined to protect our joy. If here we are happy, here we must stay.

'Aleece. It iz very culd for zat. Ere, lez tulk wiz zeese people,' Loic talks to a young family stood outside the stony walls of their home while I, after pretending to understand for about five minutes, hold a telepathic conversation with one of the swirly-horned sheep. Loic turns to me, looking so damn pleased with himself for speaking his own language and leaving me out.

'Come,' he says walking off, 'we stay wiz zees peepol but fughst we go for a wulk, up zere to zee church. RACE YOU!' Loic sprints up the hill.

I let him, and in those few seconds on my own I retrieve enough energy to persuade myself to not be such a bitch.

'Beacoup des personnes mort!' I announce theatrically.

'Ah, zee Engleesh!' Loic laughs, 'You av such dark humeurgh. Ey, Aleece! Regarde!' Loic collapses on top of a grave.

We flap with laughter, great belly-aching thumps of it. Watching him flailing about beside that tombstone, I notice the softness of his blonde hair, the safety of his arms, the beam of his face and my own awful luck. Loic must've noticed my noticing because he comes to sit on the wall beside me and we stare ahead at the mountains, shoulder to shoulder, a quiet smile growing in our hearts. I'd have felt light as a feather, easy as the cold, thin breeze, if I weren't so riddled with guilt.

'Aleece?' he says.

'Oui?'

'We must remembugh zere names; of zee peepol we stay wiz. It is zee most important zing. Zumtimes iz zee only connection we az wiz peepol. Yez?' He says, all wise and sexy and Frenchy.

Pasta without gluten: what a sad, sad world we live in. Look at it, pasta should not be that yellow. Never mind, Loic is obviously pleased and jabbering away with Daddy and Mummy Pyrenees (I know, I know, *'zee only connection we az wiz peepol'*) leaving me to the terrifying company of their tiny offspring who attack me with a screeching of French words. I try to entertain the two girls by reading them a story: the hungry caterpillar or, as it read 'La chenille qui fait des trous'.

'Mais elle avait encore faim!' I say.

What a relatable book. Loic smirks at me wickedly. Does he love me, or does he hate me? Do I love him, or do I hate him?

'C'est pret!' says Daddy Pyrenees.

Pasta, my childhood favourite. Loic has seconds.

'Aleece?' says Loic as we undress and huddle.

'Huh? Yeah?'

'Do you know my name?'

'What? Yeah, of course. Why?'

'Oh, I zought you didn't know my name,' he chuckles. 'You never say my name...'

Generally speaking, we don't say each other's names in England, unless it's a nickname, or the person in question is a stranger, or in serious trouble. I should've told Loic this, maybe we'd have laughed at the culture clash, but instead, choked by a broken heart I say, 'Oh.'

And that was the last word of the day. No sex tonight. I'm so lonely.

Morning: I gaze out the window. A bird of prey – I'm sure it was an eagle – flies across the window and for a split second, I convince myself he is I and I am free, flying away. Away from Loic, away from guilt, away from the twisted knot in my stomach. Then I brush my teeth, pausing to stare into the mirror as my mouth fills with foam. Look at those dead eyes.

Spain was my idea. Mine. If I let the thought be loud enough, maybe I'll stop noticing how lost I feel, how much I miss myself. And maybe if Loic doesn't speak Spanish he'll feel lost and lonely too and, and –then what?

'Regarde!' says Loic, braking beside a gush of water falling down the mountainside.

'Une douche!' I shout, ducking under it.

The cold shrinks my brain and knocks the air out of me but it's worth it: all of my doubts collapse at the sound of his laughter and the touch of his hand on my arm. I feel good, for about ten minutes but then the loneliness returns. A special, horrible type of loneliness somehow catalysed by the 24/7 promise of Loic's company, spreading through me like rot. Even our wee-stops don't find us far enough apart. I just want him to piss off. Yet at the same time I want *all* of him. Now. Desperately.

A couple of hours of pedalling go by and the mountains part, making way for a river so blue, it looks like a dribble of spilled sky.

'Oh, I just love the mountains!' I say to Loic, as we skip down the valley and crouch beside the river.

'Yeah... But zee mountains are bigger in zee 'obbit. ALEECE! No! Zon't drink zat!' Loic's face fills with panic as I draw a handful of river water towards my lips. 'Sumzing might have dies in zee water and you might get sick!'

Something comes over me and holding his gaze I lap the river water from my hand like a mischievous dog. It seizes the walls of my throat in a cold strangle, and shocks my belly rigid.

'Mmm, best water ever,' I say.

1500 metres climbed, 300 to go: the air bites hard. Our breath puffs out in tight clouds and there's snow on the mountain tops either side of us. Us! Oh yes! I turn over my shoulder but Loic is nowhere to be seen. I'm free! Put it down to madness, a crazy hallucination.

A tuft of blonde hair emerges from down the hill and I wonder, heart pulling away from my chest, arteries taut from the tension, I wonder whether there has ever been a person as bad as me.

'We are near SPAIN!' I yell.

'Yez! ALEECE! I zink we will camp in Spain tonight!'

'And eat RICE!'

'Yez! Water, rice, sleep!'

'WATER, RICE, SLEEP!' I yell.

'WATER, RICE, SLEEP! WATER RICE SLEEP!' we chant our new catchphrase over and over until a wind flattens our pathetic little voices to nothingness.

At 6000ft, the pass looks like hell, or perhaps the surface of Mars. Nothing grows up here, not a single blade of grass. It's just mean silver rock, a bruised sky, a bitterly cold wind, thin and fast like a whip, and one spooky hotel. The hotel sits rigidly at the tip-top, no frills or tables or anything to be ripped away by the wind. Like everything else, it's cruel-looking. Who knew Europe could look so foreign? We enter the hotel and the silence and warmth after all that cold wind lays over us like a warm blanket. Loic chats to the hotel manager, who fills up our bottles. Loic nods at me and we head back outside.

'ZE MAN SAY ZERE ARE WOLVES IN SPAIN ZO WHEN WE CAMP, WE HAZ TO PUT OUR FOOD AWAY!' shouts Loic over the wind.

'OKAY!' I return.

He kisses me, a proper one, an adoring one.

'READY?' he yells, eyes watery.

'YES!'

'LEZ GO!'

Loic shoots off ahead. Meanwhile I fall behind, trying to get my head around a sign that casually presents 'ESPAÑA'. In three weeks my pale English legs have taken me all the way to here, how wonderfully ridiculous! The screaming wind scrapes away my tears and squashes my delirious yelps as I watch Spain rise in front of me and Loic fall further out of sight. Try as I may, I can't help but feel a bit furious with him for rushing away, for acting as though the only important thing was the next thing. It's like something very uncomfortable has gotten under his skin. Is it me?

I join him at the bottom of the hill. What's the damn rush? Why haste away a sweep down the mountains? Loic you are fucking annoying sometimes. Loic I fucking love you but I also fucking hate you. All of it lurches behind my throat, threatening to spew in an upset, heartbroken torrent.

Instead I say, 'Sorry.'

'Zat okay,' he says with a tinge of passive aggression.

Jesus, this whole 'couple' thing is an absolute fucking nightmare (if you can even call us that).

We approach our first Spanish civilians, two forgettable faces next to the river.

'Hola!' I smile.

'Hola señorita! ' says Loic. 'Dónde está uh- uuuh. Oh Gud-dónde, ur–'

The Spaniards hasten off.

'I can't believe I forgotten Spaneesh...' Loic says to the abyss. He turns to face me, 'I need to get a phrase book. I need to eat words!'

'Okay! Tomorrow we can go and buy Spanish books. It's gunna be great. We're in Spain! Water, rice, sleep!'

'Yeah! Water, rice, sleep...' He says, half-heartedly. 'Aleece, you nut to camp in Spain. And zee police might find us. So we az to hide an camp where nobody find us.'

I, imagining the Spanish police have better things to do than to shout, 'PUT THE TENT PEGS DOWN YOU'RE UNDER ARREST!', think Loic is being a drama queen but I follow him anyway, to camp next to the shallow and depressing lake.

I can feel Loic's morale depleting fast. What's worse, I can feel it top up my own a little bit. So the purple sky punishes me, cracking open with hard pellets of rain. Not rain, hail. Glorious, glorious hail. But alas, they stop as soon as they start.

We set up camp at the lakeside. We? Loic sets up camp, meanwhile I read my French dictionary, calling out random words to him while he fumbles with poles. I actually did offer to help. But anyway.

'Hey! I'm going for a pee. Don't look!' I say.

'Mhm,' he says.

As I squat in the grass, sharp pinches prickle up my legs, towards my-

'AH! FUCK!' I scream.

Ants! In my literal pants! I close my bladder, scream like a banshee, flick my legs either side of me, run in circles, trying to pull my leggings over my bare ass. Loic ignores me, preferring instead to stir a pot of rice, a look of contemplation brooding on his face. Maybe he's just hungry.

Nope, that wasn't it. Rice is clumping in our bellies and still, the atmosphere is so thick, you couldn't even cut it with a meat cleaver. Loic laughs to himself, staring into the screen of his phone. A new kind of laugh, cruel.

'Quoi? What is it?' I ask.

'Oh. Iz zis girl zat I like at work. I was zuppose to go to her show today where she is dancing and she dun't know I'm not zere. She texts me, she say "where are you!"'

'Oh, poor girl...Won't she be looking for you?'

'I dun't care.'

The anxious knot in my stomach coils up tighter. What did he want me to say? What did I want him to say? Is he trying to make me jealous, or reassure me, or make me feel like an idiot? We shimmy into our sleeping bags, side by side in Loic's one-man tent, emotions of all flavours condensing in my chest like my soul was eating lemons, gherkins, sponge cakes and onions all at once. For hours upon painful hours, neither of us sleeps and neither of us say a single thing.

7

Light at the end of the tunnel

'The world was young, the mountains green. No stain yet on the Moon was seen. No words were laid on stream or stone. When Durin woke and walked alone.'

Did we really need an alarm?

'Qu'est-ce que c'est? That song playing on your phone, what is it?' I ask the fluffy, blonde mass a couple of inches from my nose.

'Iz zee Hobbit.' Loic turns over to face me. 'You like?'

The lyrics lilt soulfully in the tent, lifting the atmosphere.

'Very much.'

But alas, as the music abandons us the atmosphere drops with such cruel steepness, our tent suddenly feels like a shared coffin. So I excuse myself, and crawl out of the blaring silence into the company of twinkling dew. On goes the bra, crop-top, shorter-than-short shorts, limp socks, scuffed pink trainers.

'Zzp.'

Funny, that used to be one of my favourite things about camping, that cosy ripping noise of a tent zip. Not this time though. Loic's face, soft, sleepy, soured by something, pops out. Yet he's just too beautiful to be cross at. I look away.

Things happen, tarmac passes beneath our wheels, then we stop in Biescas because I said to Loic I, 'would like a coffee'. Really, I just want to talk to someone else.

'Un café por favor?'

'Sí.' The bar lady exchanges the euro from my hand for a coffee.

'Gracias,' I say.

'De nada,' she returns.

A small interaction, but still, it blunts the internal sear of loneliness. Loic meanwhile loiters behind me. Ugh, doesn't he know? If I wanted to see a sad, lifeless face, I could've just looked in the mirror? Spooked, I whip my head about, searching. The bar lady has swiftly occupied herself with another customer, so I grab the attention of another random Spanish woman, hunched over the bar.

'Hola, hey,' I say, like some kind of arrogant piece of garbage. 'Can you teach us some Spanish? He's French, and I'm English'

'Sí.' The woman snatches Loic's notebook from his hands with an aggressive, flamenco flourish. 'I teach you.'

She scrawls, 'BAÑOS, DONDÉ, SI, NO, GRASIAS' in obese handwriting that busts through the neat grid lines of Loic's notebook, and Loic is horrified. This delights me so now I am horrified. Poisonous bitch. Nasty, evil cow. Unworthy of love.

'Did it make you enervé?' I ask Loic, as we pedal further south, 'When she scribbled a mess in your very tidy book? Oui?'

'Oui!' he says, 'She write zo big und I olways write zo littul und keep in ze squares, UGH! An zese words she write, I know zem anyway!'

I laugh, he laughs, our morale bubbles back afloat.

A few hours later we stop in Sabiñánigo, our morale completely, do-not-resuscitate, time-of-death-14:00, drowned. Me, Loic and the tree: three fed up, hunched over, dehydrated figures in the middle of a sleeping town. Cowering under the woefully deficient shade of the tree, we crunch through a bag of cashew nuts. One for me: four for Loic. Half for me: three for Loic. Two for me: five for Loic. A secret game.

'Do you want to tulk?' says Loic, cocking his head to one side.

'Huh?' I lose count. Oh, okay.'

'Ow you find travelle wiz me?'

'Uh– I don't know. It's...different. Why?'

'I dun't zink you want me here. I zink you prefugh to travelle alon.'

'Um...' I stare straight ahead, unable to look at his face, suddenly gorgeous, suddenly so loveable.

'Oh Aleece!' Loic puts a hand on my shoulder, 'No, Aleece! Zon't cry, Iz okay. If you want me to go, Iz okay. Zis is your travelle, nut mine an I feel zat you are not appy. You zon't have to feel– what iz zis word, oh I forget zis word...' Loic quickly taps something into Google then looks at me and says, 'guilty. You nut to be guilty, I know I quit my jub but iz okay, I can still go back ome. Aleece!'

'Oh God,' I sniff, 'I'm just, so sorry.'

'Iz okay.'

'It's not that I want you to go, it's just... Oh God, I'd be so sad if you left me. But travelling with you it's... I guess,' I pause, take a breath, 'I worry about making you happy. And on my own, I go further and longer.'

'Aleece! You wunt to take care of me?'

'Yeah.'

'But you dun't have to do zat. I can do zat. I dun't want you to travelle like zis if you'd be happier alon.'

The desperate need to know a million things boils in my head: why he's blowing so hot and cold, what the hell was with 'zis girl' he spoke of yesterday, what the hell he expected from this, from me. I want to tell him I feel trapped and panicked but that I also think the world of him. I know it doesn't work, I've known this from day one of staring at his back. But all this boiling despair fills my head with hot fog and all I can really say is, 'I don't want you to go.'

'Okay. Iz okay Aleece, I stay.'

'But how do you find it, travelling with me? What's it like?'

'Hm,' Loic pretends to hesitate. 'I dun't like Camping and I dun't like Spain. My Spanish iz nut so good and I wunt to go back to travelle in my own country'.

'Then let's make it better! Tonight we can stay in a hostel, no camping, and we can buy books to learn Spanish! And we can head back to France, if you like. And swim and write postcards and eat rice. We can make it GREAT.'

'Yez. Zat would be nice. And, Aleece? You say you goh furzer wizout me? How far you goh, normalement?'

'Normalement, cent kilomètres.'

Loic goes pale but says, 'Zen tomorrow we go one undred kilomètres.'

'Really?'

'Yez.'

Our room is sterile and soulless but Loic is obviously relieved by its order. €30 for emptiness: that's the equivalent of 30 baguettes or 60 tins of beans. I go into the bathroom and begin yanking at the hard blonde nests baked into the back of my head, staring straight through my reflection. Apparently that foreign, bewildered face, is mine. Loic walks in behind me and I watch in the mirror as his clothes drop to the floor, as he steps into the shower, as he reaches out a wet, steamy hand.

An hour goes by. Nothing is said. Our kisses are wet and slippery. I know what is going to happen but it's been so many, many minutes of it not happening, that my fingertips have become the texture of raisins and I can barely contain myself. Loic turns the shower off and while he faffs, I sit naked on the end of the bed, waiting. Loic stares at me, ruffling his hair with a towel, then storms towards me and pins me down. I feel like a porn star.

Loic is lying on his front and I wake him by biting his left bum cheek. He shrieks, then whips out his phone and snaps a picture of me.

'I will zend zis to my muzer,' he teases.

'No! *Mwa*. No! *Mwa*. You're so cheeky!' I squeal, pecking kisses around his face, 'Coquin. *Mwa*. Coquin!'

We squirm, giggle, kiss and tumble like puppies (I even give him a quick blow job). Today sparkles with hope. Today, I will give him everything, I won't piss him off, I'll be a good dog, a nice person: call it a fresh start. Loic fusses with his gorgeous flames of hair in the bathroom while I, star-struck, stumble half-dressed into my pannier. It knocks over and a pool of fizzy black liquid pours out.

'Allez! Let's go!' I insist, pulling my shorts up. Big day today!'

'Un moment...' says Loic.

'Allez, allez!' I insist again, staring at the dissolving puddle of ants next to my pannier.

Ten miles in we approach a blue sign, as big as a cinema screen. It reads, 'AUTOPISTA'. This is not good, I've failed already. But maybe Loic won't notice.

'Aleece, we can't go zis way. It's le auto route.'

'Oh! Um, are you sure?'

'Yez. We are nut allowed. Iz interdit.'

'Oh, ummm...I mean...' I look left, then right. 'We can cycle on that!'

'Aleece. Zat is a drain.'

'Oh, oh bollocks. Well, maybe it's only a *tiny* bit of motorway?'

Loic ignores me, conniving with the evil likes of Google maps. 'Yez.' He looks up from his phone. 'Zis is the only way to Huesca, tout droit.'

'Well, what do you think? We could go back, then go the longer way around but it'd be an extra thirty kilometres. It's your choice.'

An hour later and we are still on the motorway, chugging up a 12% incline that just seems to go on and on and on. I'd much rather be between a rock and hard place, than an ever-deepening precipice and a stream of angry drivers. One of them honks at us and I near enough eject my own skin.

'OH FUCK OFF!' I scream, making good use of my wobbling middle finger, 'WE CAN'T TURN AROUND, CAN WE?'

Just as things could not possibly look more perilous we approach a sign: 'TÚNEL NO ILUMINADO 2KM.' Loic and I stop beside it, stare into the noisy black hole, then at each other.

'DO YOU AVE LIGHTS?' shouts Loic above the mechanical howling.

'UR, NO!'

'OKAY. FOLLOW ME, WE AZ TO BE QUICK!'

'NOUS SOMMES DES BÊTES!' I shout.

'WOO! NOUS SOMMES DES BÊTES!' he returns. 'LEZ GO!'

The tunnel, lit only by the luminous 'SOS' telephones haunting its walls, is hellishly dark. A darkness made thick as soup by heat, pollution and noise. Breathing becomes a nightmare. I focus on Loic's hazy silhouette as the rhythmic bu-bumps of tyres on cat's eyes ripple through me like a heartbeat.

A deafening groan swells behind us, followed closely by thumping lights and screeching tyres. The car swerves around me, then Loic and I scream, but the sound is hollowed out and lost to the howling soup of anguished car engines. This happens a few times, and I resolve to shout and scream as loud as I can to warn the impending traffic not to crush us. Then finally, it happens: a circle of yellow light dilates around Loic's silhouette and the air begins to thin. Daylight throws itself onto us and we escape, squinting.

'NE PAS MORT! NOUS NE PAS MORT' I yell.

Loic laughs, I laugh. Then we stop laughing. A sign reads, 'TÚNEL NO ILUMINADO 4KM'.

Twice as long means twice as dark, hot, noisy and polluted. I misjudge a cat's eye which clips my bike and sends it wobbling all over the place. My attention sharpens, cutting the seconds into fractions, as things blur to gut-dropping, left-right swerving. But I steady myself. Not dead. Ahead, Loic's blonde hair flaps dark grey in the tunnel. God, he's so brave and so thoroughly handsome. I think...I love him. A speck of gold pierces through the blackness: light at the end of the tunnel, indeed.

Oh Jesus, when will it end? We enter our third, then fourth, 'TÚNEL NO ILUMINADO', with nerves like tobacco onions. Our optimism, will, humour, personalities are shattered: for now, we are stripped down to raw, non-whooping focus. We survive our fourth motorway artery and face another sign, a glorious sign, a sign that, after three hours of motorway, came with the same erotic relief of a cool glug of water.

'IS THAT WHAT I THINK IT IS?' I shout.

'YEZ!' Loic shouts back.

'WE MADE IT! IT'S OVER! NE PAS MORT! Jesus, I'm so sorry for the danger. *Stupid* Google Maps, I knew we should never have trusted Google Maps. Anyway, I'm just so glad you're okay.'

'Aleece, iz okay! We did it togezer an I nut to tell my muzer.'

For a while, we snog underneath the motorway-end sign, until our PDA is interrupted by a police officer who lisps furiously at us from the open window of his police car.

'Ah! Engleesh? You cannot cycle without a helmet. Iz a crime. We will fine you two hundred euros if we catch you again!'

Me and Loic nod, agree, apologise.

The policeman goes 'HMP,' stabs a button and waits for his window to close. It does so in slow motion, then he revs off.

'Aleece, I nut wunt a helmet. I want my hair to go blonde in ze sun.'

'It's alright,' I laugh. 'Let's get lunch instead.'

Leaning forward on the supermarket trolley, I fly down the aisles like I used to do as a kid, whizzing past a euphoric Loic who throws yet more treats in the trolley – 2kg of dates, tofu, rice cakes, nuts, figs – laughing, shining. This would usually have bothered me (be it healthy or not, food is ammunition, and I don't particularly want to shoot myself) but today is different, I don't even check the nutritional information. Nope, I tuck straight in unabashed, shoulder to shoulder with my favourite person.

'Zees lentuls are zo good. What Iz in zem?' asks Loic.

'Oh, let me check,' I grab the tin, scan the ingredients, 'Lentils, Onion, Bac–... bacon fat, lard...Fuck! Oh God, I feel sick.'

'Aw, Aleece!'

'I haven't eaten meat in...nine years. Oh dear, oh God, oh dear.'

'I zo zorry for you Aleece, but iz only a littul bit. An iz good to get your B vitamins up!'

Touched by the earnest in his face, I lean a thankful head on his shoulder and shrug away the guilt more easily than I would've imagined. But I guess as we've just survived three hours of motorway, 0.2 grams of pork isn't going to end my world, surely. And look at Loic, just look at him. How could *0.2 grams of pork* mean anything when he looks at me with such vividness, when he laughs that belly laugh, when he... He leans towards me and kisses me.

More happy pedalling. I stare at Loic's back again. What a lovely back! We whiz through dusty nowhere until finally, we find a bookshop. This is great, another move in the 'make Loic happy' mission. Fantasies of me and Loic bloom in my stupid, naïve head, of us lying side-by-side on our bellies, kicking our feet like girls at a sleepover, learning Spanish together.

'No,' I grab Loic's T-shirt, 'I'll pay.' I pull him aside.

'No Aleece, *I pay.*', he drives my shoulders backwards.

'No!' I tackle him out the way and slam a €20 note on the counter.

The book seller takes my cash, smiling.

'zank you,' says Loic, touching the small of my back.

Shivers prickle up my spine then fizz in my head like popping candy. This boy.

Our next stop (I have noticed that Loic likes to stop), is beside a well because Loic (I have also noticed) really likes water. Stopping was worth it this time though because there's a lizard in the well, about as big as a year-old baby, his turquoise skin glimmering with glints of pink.

'WOW! He's *beaut*-iful!' I say.

'Yez. But ee will die.' Says Loic.

'Huh? Oh. Well... How about we make him a ladder so he can get out?'

Loic replies with a wholesome smile then lies on his back, letting out a long but happy sounding sigh. Can I? Shall I? I crawl up to him and draw close. He laughs at the tickle of my curls on his cheeks as I give him an upside down spidey-kiss.

'Today I get a text from my Dad.' He says, out of the blue, 'I meet 'im for the furs time laz month.'

'Woah, that's huge! But, gosh, going all this time without knowing your Dad? I feel sad for you. My Dad, he's kind of my best friend.'

'Well, I never ad a Dad before so iz great... Iz like I gain a Dad!'

'That's *beautiful*, I *love* that you said that.'

'UH!' he gasps. 'You said you loved me!'

'No...'

Hot face, hot face, hot face. Stop blushing Alice, he's going to think you love him. You don't, do you?

8

Onions have layers

The highlight of today was the motorway, second only to the meaty lentils, then the lizard. It was all downhill from there. Although we did find an almond tree (Loic loves trees). We climbed, gathered, munched and giggled but as soon as the taste of nuts had let go of our taste buds, it was unhappy radio silence again. Didn't we wake up naked and happy? Didn't we laugh on the motorway? Seems like a lifetime ago, if it ever did happen.

'Aleece, can we stup? J'ai faim.'

'Bien sûr.'

So we take un petit pause and I watch with euphoric glee as Loic tosses back handfuls of nuts, chews on dates, inhales rice cakes.

'Gush, I dun't know why but I'm zo ungry, you wunt?' he says.

I take one rice cake and watch with twisted satisfaction as Loic completes the rest of the packet, then eats yet more nuts, more dates.

'There. Will that do?' Matt asks, his face grimaced with nausea.

'Nope. You have to eat it all. That was the deal.' I reply.

Matt makes a small 'ugh' noise then continues, shovelling the last fistfuls of cake in until all that remains is smeared on the cellophane box and buried in the brown corners of his mouth.

'There.' He looks around – nope, no tissues– then cringes as he licks butter cream from his fingers.

I smile at him. He thinks it is a loving smile: it isn't. Then he kisses me and I panic because it tastes like chocolate, fat, calories.

'Now can I have a picture of you?' Matt asks.

'Fine,' I say.

Matt picks me a daffodil, 'Hold this,' then steps backwards, aiming his phone at me. 'Oh my gosh, you look so pretty! Now look at the camera... Alice? Please! You promised!'

I cry into my hands, suddenly aware of myself. Matt never gets his photo.

'I eat oll,' says Loic, patting his belly.

I smile, wickedly.

After an hour of pedalling, yet another tree finds us at a halt. A strange tree, its branches slouching with small fruits that look like bleached apricots. Loic tears one open: its flesh is a translucent milky-orange colour; its pip is black, thin and slippery.

'Let's eat it!' I say.

'No. I zink it cud be poizun.'

I glare at the very serious face of Loic.

'No! Aleece! Don't eat zat!'

'Mmm! Delicious!' I say, slurping up the wet sinew.

I polish off the rest of the disgusting fruit (to prove a point) and then we continue in deeper silence. Why do I do it? Why do I spend so much time and energy trying to keep him happy only to leap at the chance to piss him off? Because I'm toxic, a twisted nutcase, unworthy of love. A big, fat, horrible monster.

Almu opens her front door, lazy-eyed and casually beautiful. 'Hey guys!' she says.

'Hola!' I beam, beating Loic.

'Hola!' Loic repeats.

God, I hate myself.

'Here, welcome. Yes, leeb your bikes dere. I was jus about to walk de dog, but Oscar will take care of you.' Almu points to a man sitting on the sofa.

He looks up from his laptop and waves in quick, shy flaps.

'I hope you okay with dogs,' says Almu, patting her thighs. 'Here girl, here girl.'

A ginormous dog comes bounding, two pendulums of drool hanging from each side of her massive panting mouth. I pat the dog's meaty head, trying to forget the transfer of dog-smell onto my hand.

'Can I come?' I ask.

'Of course! We can leave de boys to it.' Almu snips a lead on the beasts. 'Good girl, *good* girl.'

Sigh, if only Loic treated me like that. Yes, I get hair everywhere yes, I'm scrappy, grubby, badly behaved, messy but at least I'm not constantly drooling.

A little time away from one another, I naively thought, would have settled the seething misery between Loic and me. But seeing the distress on his face now that me, Almu and the enormous beast she calls a dog are back from our walk, I realise it has somehow made things worse. He doesn't even talk to me. Then again, I guess I don't even talk to him either.

Almu quickly fusses about in the kitchen whispering with Oscar about the gluten-free options for Loic and vegan options for me. She sits us both at opposite heads of the table like a king and queen, filling the chairs between us with her friends as they arrive. Neither me nor Loic look at one another.

'Hey. Iz nice to meet you, I'm Silvia,' says my immediate neighbour, helping herself to all the best bits of the salad. Silvia is a short, choppy sort of lady and she speaks in punches. 'So cool. You travel by bike. All here? So cool,' she says.

'Ah well, you know it's just a bike ride, only quite a long one,' I say. 'But hey, can you teach me some Spanish?'

'I'm Portuguese.' says Silvia. She swallows a mouthful of feta, 'But sure. What you wanna know?'

'Oh! Jeez. Sorry! Ur– How about... "I am happy"?'

'Yo. Estoy. Feliz.'

'YO ESTOY MUY FELIZ!' I shout.

Everybody laughs, except for Loic who is reaching for a white bap.

'Ah! Loic!' Almu stops Loic. 'Dey are not gluten free. Sorry. But here, you can eat de salad and dese burgers!'

'Oh, Iz okay. I can eat,' says Loic, grabbing the damn thing anyway.

'I nut to eat gluten since I was eleven,' he'd said. Liar! Absolute liar! He's made me look like such an idiot. If there is one thing I can't stand, it's liars. God!

Tonight there is a third presence between the two single beds of me and Loic. A full bodied clot of things to say that won't be said. The thing is, I don't even know what they are but I know they are extreme and hurtful, on both sides. Despite the thunderstorm, I'd sooner be out in the rain, than in here with this churning sorrow.

Another day, just like yesterday only more barren and thanks to heavy cloud, pretty much no colour. Between the odd quiet town, there are no trees or shops or people or *anything* to distract from the broken tethers of me and Loic.

'What is your dream?' I ask, as we pedal east.

'I want to grow lots of crops and feed people. I dun't know how or where. But I want to feed peepol who do nut have much. And I want to live in a tower zat I build myzelf. I like towers alut.'

'That's *beautiful*,' I say, a massive surge of love flourishing in the pit of my stomach.

'What is your dream Aleece?'

'Well, I mean... I want to travel, LOTS, by bicycle and–.'

'En Français?' Loic interrupts.

'Oh, okay. Urrr, Je voudrais voyage avec vélo et... Dessiner pedant pour l'argent?'

'Zat is a good dream,' he says.

Loic has forgotten to mock my awkward French. No laughter, no, '*You sound like a witch*', no corrections or humiliation. This is not a good thing. Something has died, but we are still dragging it around. Maybe this explains the dark chill glazing the air, the electricity keeping me and Loic at a distance, the bruising clouds hung heavy over our heads. They finally erupt, throwing a great relief of cold rain over my sad, sad self. Poor Loic, I'm probably the worst thing to ever happen to him .

An hour of rain has broken me, my shivering brain dispelling any clear thought like dandruff. This is a blessed relief, although my hands no longer work and my stomach is sick with chills. So we take respite in a bar, empty but for one fat man watching the football and one bored-looking barmaid. I wander up to ask her a question using the Spanish I'd been secretly practising in my head but Loic steps in front of me, stealing the chat I really, *really*, needed. I bite my tongue. Hard. Something I used to do as kid when I thought I was talking too much, being too loud, too annoying, just 'too' anything.

But it's not all bad because Loic's passive aggressive misery is evaporating with the steam of our lunch, kindly microwaved by the bar lady. He seems content, my peas taste nice, my wet hair is drying, the football commentator on the TV is rattling nice sounds into the empty bar: these are all good things. The rest of the day is a blur of wet dust.

Caesar's house, like the man himself and like the essence of mine and Loic's day, is cold. For a country that switches off at 1pm everyday because of the heat, Spain has proven impressively chilly today. As for our host, Caesar stands the very epitome of coarse: wire-wool hair, mean eyes behind narrow glasses, thin, unpleasant.

'Come. Dis is your room,' he says, throwing open a door. 'Dere are rats. You can have a shower. But only a cold one. I'm going to do some dings.'

After a cold shower, me and Loic join Caesar in the kitchen.

'Here. You can cook dis if you want,' Caesar dumps a couple of dusty tins on the table. 'They're three years out of date. Someone cut me some cheese,' he snaps. 'Do you want beer?'

I look at Loic, who says, 'no zank you.'

'No thank you,' I confirm, nervously cutting cheese to the best of my ability.

'What? Neither of you drink? What kind of people are you?' says Caesar.

Beer is disgusting. To this day I have no idea why people like this gassy, pissy, gut-crunch of a drink. And yes, I want one. To be a girl drinking *cerveza* in *España*. For the dizzy hit of blurry courage. Still I side with Loic, because tensions aside, I really care about that boy.

'Whatever,' Caesar takes a swig, 'You know you're in Catalan, right? You know about Catalan?'

Me and Loic exchange a confused look.

'Oh my God, do you guys know *anything*? Well, dere are dese people who want to leave Spain. Most people don't want to leave Spain but dese liars say *"we all want to leave Spain."* All winning and shit. They are destroying things and they're stupid, violent, awful people. Don't believe a word dey say. NO! Don't wash that up, you won't do it properly.'

Loic drops the spoon back in the sink.

We sit down to rice and beans: Loic eating thrice my portion while Caesar laments about the ills of the world.

'Dese pesticides are shit. When they spray de crops next to my house I can't leave because it's not possible to breathe. De children can't go outside. Dey are not safe.'

'Zis iz why we need permaculture!' agrees Loic, proceeding with a gallant speech which I zone out of. Not because it wasn't interesting but because I am consumed by the mysterious magic causing this plate of rice and beans to swell as I eat it. I'd originally estimated 600kcal, now I'm thinking 800. Not that it matters.

'Loic you know a lot about permaculture and Alice, you just sit dere agreeing with eberything de world has to offer.'

I nod and Caesar's face twists up all sour.

'Ey,' he says, 'Someone needs to take de keys, I'm going to bed and I won't be here in de morning.'

I point at Loic.

'You're going to leave the one who speaks bad English the key?' says Caesar.

'Yes. He's much less stupid than me.' I say, suddenly protective of Loic.

'Whatever.'

'And grasias, Caesar,' I continue. 'What an amazing dinner.'

'Yez. Zank you,' Loic agrees.

Caesar scoffs, 'Thank you for a couple of tins of out of date legumes that I didn't want? Thank you for cooking your own rice?'

'Sí,' I reply confidently. 'I thought it was completely delicious.'

Caesar accidentally smiles.

Bedtime. Loic unzips our sleeping bags so we can touch, and I take the gesture as a massive compliment. He even kisses me. A weak kiss, but a sweet one.

'I like Caesar,' he whispers.

'Yeah, he's a bit strange but quite hilarious.'

'He cares about zee important zings.'

'Yeah...'

I think, Loic, you'll actually find that Caesar is a racist.

Kisses and deep inhales: I want to drink him in. I definitely love him in the morning, not sure about the rest of the day. Breakfast (cashews) eaten, note to Caesar scrawled on a piece of toilet roll ('we hope the Catalans don't come knocking. From Loic and Alice'), we hit the road. For some reason, the more we pedal the less I like him. Which inspires such a struggle in my soul: I love him and want to touch him, but I also want him to fuck off to Timbuktu and leave me alone. Can I pocket him for late-night thrills? Is that shallow? I guess I just want to be wanted.

A while later, exhausted by the relentless thump of a midday sun, we take a drink of shade beneath a tree. Trees are impressively rare in these dead ochre parts. As much for a wee as for my own sanity, I leave Loic's unhappy radius and walk behind a derelict building and squat: my new technique. Being the only girl of four I'd always assumed that al fresco weeing had to be done standing. That is, until one day while I dashed off for an eco-wee in the woods, a friend asked me 'Alice, why does your wee make such a loud noise? FUCK! WHAT ARE YOU DOING?!'. It was that day I bade farewell to my usual A-shaped stance and pressure thrust and learned how to pee like a lady.

After my flawless squat-wee, I hesitate. There's a raw ache in my chest, eating me up. I can't go back. Oh my God, I can't do it. I stare into nothing for a while, then I pace a while. Back and forth, back and forth: weirdly comforting. I feel stuck and stifled and lonely and panicked and– then I notice, a little purple flower growing at the base of the concrete warehouse. An idea.

'Pour moi?' says Loic.

I nod.

'Oh, Aleece. Zank you,' he takes the tiny bunch of flowers. 'I zink you want a kiss?'

Loic's lips, tense with heart ache, but smiling slightly, meet mine.

'Ça va? What's wrong?' I ask.

'I dun't know. Sometimes it is juz like zis. I cannut be appy oll zee time.'

'I know. But how can I make it better? Would you like to do less cycling?'

'Well, my legz urt a bit. But I can stretch. Maybe we go find zum water to swim and ave a rest zo I can write postcards?'

'Of *course*. I just want you to be happy, more than anything. Tomorrow we'll go to the sea and write postcards and swim and do nothing and rest and it'll all be fine.'

'Yez, okay,' he says, with the cautious enthusiasm of a nun at a disco.

Off we go again, heaving our heavy hearts someplace else.

'Hey, Aleece, you zink one day our children will ask me, "So Dad, ow you meet our muzer"? OH! STUP! OH MY GOODNEZ. LOOK!' Loic shouts.

'Quoi?' I ask, confused by both the mother comment and the happy shouting.

'STUP. I muz take a picture.' Loic jams on his brakes and dismounts.

'QUOI?' I repeat. 'What is it?'

'ONIONS!'

For ten whole minutes I hang about the field of onions waiting for Loic to finish taking pictures: up close, crouching, from above, panoramic. Don't they have onions in France? All I can think of is Shrek, *'Onions have layers'.*

We stop again with only three miles between us and our host, Joan. Why? Loic wants to take videos of himself doing handstands. I can't figure out if I find it aggravating or arousing. Both, probably.

'Aleece! Can you do zis? HUP!' Loic takes an impressive leap and clicks his heels.

'Um...I don't know' I run, jump, '...HUP!' fail, then run again, jump again, '...AH....HUP!' ... *Merde*...HUP! I can't do it! It's too difficult!' I pant.

'Okay. We run and we jump like zis: HUP! Okay?' Loic props up his camera to film us. 'Zree, two, one...GO!'

We hurtle towards the camera, do our jumps then check out the footage. Loic looks like a film star, while I look like a daddy long legs with wet legs. After four failed attempts, a slightly frustrated Loic suggests we move on. *Sigh*, I just can't do anything right.

Mum rings. I can't even remember what we spoke about but I do remember her saying, as I wandered off somewhere Loic couldn't hear me, 'this is *your* journey Alice, don't forget that'.

Joan is a gentle man with gentle features and three bright daughters (five, nine and fifteen years old). I'd found him on

Warmshowers especially, because he speaks French and I thought this might cheer Loic up.

Warm under our feet, soft and comforting Joan's house is all timber. Joan is saying things and showing us around but I'm not listening.

'Ey, Aleece,' Loic picks up a book from Joan's shelf, 'Iz French! Ere, read to me.'

I do so, quietly, cautiously.

'Oh Aleece, you're so funny. Iz like watching a child learn to read.'

I'd have been offended, if he hadn't smiled so lovingly and planted such a sweet kiss on my cheek. Maybe things will be all right.

By the time I've come out the shower the loving look on Loic's face has entirely eroded to an upset wince. He *hates* me. Why does he hate me?

'Can I help?' I ask.

'Ur...' Loic chops slower but does not look up, 'You can cut zat.' he says, more to the chopping board than me.

While cutting 'zat' tomato, feeling rejected, a sheet of paper flaps under my nose.

'Oh! My... Gracias' I take it.

'I made dis for you,' says the youngest girl, swinging her shoulders in front of her while I admire the sausage fingers and alopecia of her figure drawing.

'It's... beautiful,' I say.

She dashes off, dives onto the sofa and writhes in giggling fits. *That* was what was missing from today, I realise: a laugh.

We eat. Loic piles rice high onto his plate, I take a small portion.

Dinner over, belly and soul still empty: bedtime. Joan and I blow up two camping mattresses while Loic brushes his teeth. I'm left dizzy, but cautiously hopeful for a late-night hug. It'll be dark, thus finally I can let my face express its heartbroken worry.

'Oh. I zought Joan was joking when he said we haz to sleep on zee floor' Loic says, exhaling a condescending laugh.

'Well, it was very kind of them to have us. There was nowhere else we could've stayed, unless you wanted to camp? It's very isolated round these parts. I tried all the Warmshower hosts.'

'You dun't olways az to find us a ost. I could az done zat.'

'Okay. You do it next time then.'

'Okay,' he says.

Brushing my teeth, I turn away from the mirror, away from a face wracked with a starkly familiar emotion I don't want to believe. By the time I've made it downstairs, Loic has moved the mattresses to opposite sides of the room. This isn't good.

Something drops. Something that had been hanging a very long while. And the feeling of falling, that same old horrible feeling I'd left in England, whooshes through me as I crawl into my sleeping bag and crunch my eyes tightly shut. Oh God, oh God, oh God.

I hold my breath, hoping the effort might calm my arrhythmic heart while Loic storms over to the light switch. The flick of the switch shoots through me like a knife and I plummet into panic. I can hear myself panting. Not again, please not again. I thought I'd left this behind. It can't happen, it'll freak Loic out and he'll leave me. They *always* leave me.

'Aleece? Aleece!' Loic is at my side, he places his palm on my left shoulder blade, just like a good HCA, 'Aleece? What's wrong?'

I press my palms into my face, I pull my hair, I rock back and forth but it's useless, the awful sounds keep heaving in my throat. Sounds that should come from a torture victim. But I guess it is, torture.

Some of the patients from 'the other unit' are singing Christmas carols in the dining room and we, the bony audience, watch.

Suddenly, the singing faces become garish, jarring, and my heart dips, trying to duck away from the fear, the noise. God the noise... I push my hands over my ears, hard so the flaps of cartilage overlap and I can hear only muffles and my own terrible heartbeat. Simone pokes me.

'Hey Al, do you want to go outside?' she asks.

I nod.

She takes me by the arm outside, onto the stairs but the noise is worse out here because someone is screaming. Jesus. It's me.

What I didn't know back then in the unit (and thank God for my ignorance) was that I had released a demon. A demon that five years on, would still terrorise my days.

My thoughts go as follows: 'Oh God, oh God, oh God, not again, Oh God,' and pray to the highest heavens no-one can hear them.

I cower behind the 'Architecture' bookshelf (the quietest part of the University's library in the far corner), willing it to stop. A futile effort, I know this. Then my vision goes strange, the books recurring, gaining on me, filling my eyes. And my hearing sharpens horribly: every 'DUFF' of laptops closing, every 'SH' of pages being turned, blaring in my head. I have to get out. Now. Fast.

Keeping my eyes fixed on the spinning floor, I walk out of the library, tapping my chest with my right hand (a weird ritual that keeps me contained just a few seconds longer) then down the stairs – don't look up – and into the disabled toilet. I fall against the cubicle door. Wet cheeks, racing breath, and then the screams. Ripping through my throat, splintering my brain, making the air ugly. There's a banging noise: that's my fault too.

But eventually the screaming subsides, because I am now just too dizzy. I like this bit, the wooziness that blunts the humiliation, the humming quiet. And there is always a nice lady ready on the other side of the door with a cup of water.

'Phew! That was a big one.'

Today it was Sam.

'Oh dear, sorry about that,' I laugh, moving snotty clots of hair away from my face.

'You know, seeing as you spend so much time in here, don't you think we should jazz it up?' Sam hands me a tissue. 'Put in a fun poster on the wall, maybe buy some pot plants?'

Good old Sam, she always has something fun to say. Not like that other woman from living support, who sometimes turns up, utterly petrified, waits for me to stop screaming and awkwardly asks if I'm 'stressed'. Unlike Sam, she never laughs at my dark jokes.

Me and Sam chat a while longer, about where she might go surfing this weekend (Godrevy, always Godrevy). It's my way of putting off the outside world; it's her way of skiving library admin.

'I wish I could help you,' she says fiddling with her lanyard. 'I googled it last night.'

Sam's kindness breaks my heart, and so I laugh.

'Ah well,' I put my sunglasses on, like I always do, 'I think I'd better call it a day.'

Loic sighs, a deep, disappointed, fed-up sigh, takes his palm off my juddering back and goes back to bed.

The next morning we pack up, brush our teeth, eat breakfast, say goodbye to Joan, then loiter outside, saying nothing to each other. Not a word. My mouth is clamped shut by frustrated shame, Loic's by... I can only imagine hatred.

'Shall we tulk?' he asks, finally.

I shrug. Ten more minutes of silence. Then I take a deep breath and finally ask, 'What did I do wrong?'

'Hm. I zought to myself last night, I can't believe she'd leave ze light un, why would she do zat? And you, *ugh*, juz like my last girlfriend: over-dramatique like zat.'

'I'm sorry, it's just, well, I have problems, at home...It's um...I was in hospital for a while and... Sometimes I panic. I don't know why.'

'I understand,' he says.

Liar.

'Okay. Well, I guess, let's go.'

There we have it: a completely unresolved disaster. If anything, the talking made it worse. Maybe screaming fits are not all right. Maybe six years on, I should've made a visit to the GP. You think I hadn't considered this? They'll just pill me up, just like they did in the unit until I'm crushed down to something acceptable. Because apparently drugged-up zombies are acceptable and screaming banshees are not.

After a short while cycling in strict silence I break the silence again and ask, 'What else annoys you?'

'I feel like you are my child and I ave to look aftugh you all zee time and do everyzing. And your mess, I ate it.'

'Oh.'

Bleak and dead, dry and soulless, one fed-up boy and one

bewildered girl: the road ends at a T-junction. To the left: dust, dirt, cacti. To the right: cacti, dirt, dust. The atmosphere between us is as heavy as the heat. We stop.

'I wunt to travelle alon,' says Loic.

'Huh? Oh, okay.'

'So you go zat way and find a place to charge your phone and I go zis way,' he gestures. I nod. 'Will you be okay?'

I look down at my dead phone and empty water bottles.

'Yep,' I say.

He leans over his bike to kiss my cheek, then shuffles backwards.

'Bye, Aleece.'

I turn towards my dictated fate (cacti, dirt, dust) and pedal away.

9

No date, no dates

Is this the desert? Maybe. It has all the stereotypes: dryness, dust, cactus plants, profound sense of desolation. And just like in the movies my phone is dead, my water bottle empty. I pedal on steady and silent.

A village appears on the horizon and I dismount as I near it, walking The Insect beneath ghosts of laundry strung between villas, into its un-beating heart. There is no sound, no chatter, footstep or sizzle of chorizo sausage. Even this strange bunting of t-shirts and dresses lacks the courage to flap. It is, I think to myself as I begin panting, the best place in the world to die of sadness.

I let go of The Insect's handlebars. He clatters on the ground, disturbing a dust that rises in mustard clouds, and I fall to my knees beside him. Seizure-like waves of sobs thump out of me. How could he do this to me? Then again I should have learned that they always leave me, they always leave me when I go wrong.

> '*Stop. Stop screaming. You're upsetting everybody.*'
> '*I just want one day without you in it.*'
> '*Look at you! It's like fucking a skeleton.*'
> '*You have no idea the misery you're causing everybody.*'
> '*God... It's like you've taken to your skin with a cheese grater.*'
> '*You're dead to me.*'
> '*Stop it, be quiet, stop screaming. Everyone is going to look at you.*'
> '*I think I want to move on now. Just leave me alone.*'
> '*I zink I want to travel alon.*'

My stomach is reeling, eyes sore and flooding. Just me and The Insect curled up together: the end of the world.

Then a soft, elderly voice trickles into my ear. I peer over my fingers at the man standing above me, his chequered shirt tucked neatly into his jeans like an old cowboy. He has dark pebbly eyes, kind eyes, a golden collection of wrinkles rippling around them.

'Perdón. I'm English,' I sniff.

The old man rambles on, lisping through a toothless mouth.

'So sorry, I'm English,' I repeat.

The old man's brow squeezes into a dense crumple, then he changes tactics and starts speaking in French: why am I crying, have I had an accident? No accident, I've just been abandoned by a beautiful French boy, I explain. He points, horrified, at my knee – oh, it's bleeding – then scuttles off, his small steps kicking up dust.

Oh how I'd wished Loic away on that first day in the Pyrenees, how that wish had flavoured every day since. Dare I the right to be sad? But I loved that boy. But I guess love isn't made for broken monsters like me, but for pretty girls who cry quietly, delicately, in controlled drip-drops.

Before the dust has had its chance to settle, the toothless old man returns with a couple of policemen, thumbs poking out of the breast pockets of their unnecessary bulletproof jackets.

'Passeporte?' asks the taller one.

The other policeman cowers behind, looking very grateful for his jacket.

I hand over my passport and after a teenage-girl whisper session, the two men turn back around and nod at me.

'Sí,' says the taller one, handing it back to me.

Not sure what else to do with themselves, they trundle off, at once disappointed and relieved to be left without an excuse to arrest, chase or tussle.

Still lisping, the old man props up my bike, then me, and escorts us both into a bar. Inside, a woman is dragging a cloth over the bar, her other hand propping up her bored head of badly cut hair. She looks up, immediately alarmed by my leaking state (blood and tears) then quickly relieved at the sight of the old man stood beside me. Spanish conversation rattles in the room; I understand only 'señorita'.

'PUE-DES QUE-DARTE EN MI CA-SA ES-TA NO-CHE,' says the lady, loud and slow.

No luck. She repeats herself, louder and slower with the

additional theatre of charades until I realise she's inviting me to stay. Touched, I nod and start to cry again. The old man responds to this by loading my arms with food and giving me the most aggressive kiss of my life. He scuttles off, satisfied.

I spend the rest of the day in the bar, growing fonder of the barmaid's charming wonky teeth and chaotic hair (I used to have hair like that, when I was seven and I borrowed Mum's scissors). At times I remember Loic and the sting of it finds me hysterical. But sadness eventually gets boring; I blow my nose on my t-shirt and start to eat. And eat. And... eat. I chomp through five bananas, seven apricots and a tomato baguette, realising that my arms look different, less...soft. In fact, all of me is slightly less soft: my knobbly shoulders jutting like two tennis balls, my collarbones like twigs and my spine, as starkly bumped as an old cat's. My clothes seem to hang. My skin, even, seems to hang a bit. How has this happened? At this point I also realise Loic has pedalled off with all the food, including the two-kilogram box of Medjools I'd bought us yesterday. I chuckle at the cruel humour of it: no date and no dates. I never want to see that boy again.

Deciding that I'm over it all – Loic who, sorry? – I begin humming cheerfully, swinging my legs as I thumb the pages of my Spanish phrase book. I try out a few phrases on the Spanish lady and we manage an almost conversation.

'Los chicos son malos. mejor solo.' I say, banging my fist on the table.

'Sí. Mejor solo,' she says.

I cry, drink coffee, speak more bad Spanish, cry, take a wee, cry again. Perhaps this is where my life ends: as a legend of this ghost town, the strange girl who turned up reeling until her crying eyes shrivelled up and her aching heart refused any more languished beats. Or maybe I'm just too sad to die.

It is 5pm and not a single customer has been in the bar. So we call it a day and head to the Spanish lady's home.

The Spanish lady's home is as gleefully chaotic as her hairdo. Imagine a tornado of Tasmanian devils on cocaine had hit a charity shop, and square it. Huge mounds of toys, clothes, papers dumped on every level: the floor, the sofa, in corners, on counters. It's actually worse than my bedroom at home, which is extraordinary. Her children come home from school aggressively manic, though less so after a snack, and even less so in my company. They follow me and sit close next to me yet pretend not to notice me at all. We watch Peppa Pig. Daddy Pig has lost his glasses, typical. Daddy Pig finds his glasses and this makes my tear ducts explode.

We share a skillet of rice and courgette for dinner, great mounds of it, impressively both under and over cooked. I crunch on the mushy lumps, thanking the woman again and again.

'De nada' she says.

I even have seconds.

Comatose by indigestible rice, I stumble towards bed. But a tiny bronze girl (about four years old) jumps ahead of me and gives me a little pink pot about the size of a two-pound coin. She puts her finger on her bottom lip and I mirror her, my finger landing on a sharp red slice (sun-burn had bust my lip open). I wince, she winces.

'For me?' I ask.

She nods and scrambles off before I have the chance to cry all over her.

I smush the pearly lip balm over my busted lip and wait for the sting. A sharp throb of pain slices my bottom lip, sweet and metallic with the taste of blood.

I collapse into bed, feeling dark and rotten, wondering how to sleep with a heavy heart, wondering whether I should sleep at all. Tomorrow I am on my own. Perhaps I will die in the night, as the last of my heartstrings are snipped. I cuddle my ribs (an old habit) and wait for the oblivion of sleep to put the worst day of my life in the past.

wow, I'm amazed by how ~~QUICKLY~~ QUICKLY,
loss of my ~~travelling~~ pal. I don't u
- after I'd stopped crying of course, I
I felt .. Better. Travelling solo I fe
again. I feel I can be more strang
to embarrass *can't spell*. NO EXPECTATIONS
and more confident. I regret ha
I don't regret that we have l
amazing and bizarre that yo
without someone. And someone y
too. Because I did REALLY
am more happy without hir
I thought I hated my ou
trip but now... It cannot
I'm not sure I've ever
of the earth.

FAR OUT MAN.

10

A good old clear out

Is it true? I look around: no fluffy blonde hair to run my fingers through, no warm arm to touch, no early morning whisper-chat to land on my ears. My world and my world only.

'I'M FREE!' I hiss. Then, 'Uh-oh...'

An avalanche ruptures my belly. I throw the covers back, run to the toilet, and so it happens: a whole week of intestinal stage-fright finally gives way in a knee-buckling, earth-shaking, shiver-inducing torrent. 'A good ol' clear out' as my Dad would have delicately put it. Quite refreshing, quite appropriate: I can now *'leave all this shit behind'* and start over. Only thing is, the toilet won't flush.

'Adiós Aleeth!' the Spanish lady waves wistfully from the front door, not yet aware of my parting gift. Whoops.

Solitude is a dream. Ironically, without Loic my 'joie de vivre' restores fast, as does my concave belly which fills and thickens throughout the day as I eat gluten-heavy feasts with fervour, talking to the ants. I whip up and down the barren roads, singing *'that's what friends are for'*, dust sticking to my sweat. Ten, twenty, thirty, forty miles? Easy. I even pedal up a couple of mountains in my bikini (much to the amusement of truck drivers), the sun scorching my nose to a scab and my lip to a bloody crust. I couldn't give two hoots. I couldn't even give one hoot! I'm having a hoot! Even as my chain crunches itself to death, my glee is true and unwavering.

Twenty euros later my bike is fixed, oiled, cleaned. The bike shop man even pumped up my tyres and let me eat my lunch in his office. Didn't he know? I'm English! And would've therefore paid way over the odds. Anyway, I wave him goodbye, grateful that I have enough change to buy gazpacho.

The final ten miles to Manresa were strange because they were overwhelmed by the presence of yellow ribbons tied to cars, graffitied onto bridges, walls, abandoned buildings, shops, chalked on pavements. Forget the fact they are ribbons and they are yellow, there is something distinctly eerie about their frayed edges, capital-lettered captions and uniformed rows. Manresa has these ribbons too, but amidst the hordes of people and cars and tall buildings, spotting them is a bit of a 'Where's Wally' mission. Though make no mistake to search out peace and quiet here: these parts, I quickly realise as a hooded creature nearly vaporizes me with a single stare, are quiet for a reason.

So I wait for Etoire (tonight I'm trying 'couchsurfing.com') in the heart of the city, a heart that's manically pumping civilians in different directions, all of them in a pissed-off rush. All except me, who sits bum-to-kerb outside number 197, talking to a packet of dry spaghetti.

'Hey!' a man calls from across the road, running towards me, 'I saw you outside from my office an had to come chat, where are you from?' he pants, crouching down to my level.

'Englaaand!'

The man has wild hair refusing to conform to a ponytail, and wears a shirt refusing to stay tucked-in. And me? I'm just my usual pile of bloody, oily disaster, a stray dog. We shake hands, like two chimney sweeps.

'Wait...' he studies my bike, 'So how did you get here? You didn't... cycle all the way here, from England?'

'Hell yeah!'

'Woooaaaah! Dude, that's amazing! Hey if you need anything, I'm just across de road. You can stay at mine if you can't find anywhere, but I guess you're waiting for someone.' He smiles at me. 'You have the right idea about life, girl.'

The hippie fella gives me a high-five and runs back to the grey block, slotting himself among a line of spiny chairs (not that they'll do much spinning). I can see him from the window, the life draining out of his face lit by the saccharine glow of his computer screen. Poor dude.

It then occurs to me as I resume my conversation with my spaghetti, sat on the curb of a strange city, that I am one of those 'mad' people. You'd have thought, having done my time and earned my paperwork, I might've already clocked this. Of course, I always knew I was mad, but not 'a mad person', that's different. A mad person is not so passive. A 'mad person' sleeps in strange places, babbles to herself, makes friends with objects, laughs too loudly in supermarkets. And she's emotionally volatile: never far from crying or laughing or falling in love. Huh, no wonder I scream and scratch and panic, I've had all this belated madness bubbling beneath.

'Hi. Sorry. I was working.' Etoire interrupts my epiphany. I instantly dislike him.

'Hola!' I return.

'Cummon, let's go. You can lock your bike just here in the atrium.' Etoire scowls at my bike. 'No one will steal it. By the way, we're not taking the lift.'

I pant clumsily behind him, trying to lug my panniers up six flights of stairs.

Etoire hates me. And I don't know why. It makes no sense, because in Couchsurfing profile he's claimed to 'love life and every moment' and his photo looked so cheesy. But standing here, his face looks not like cheese, but curdled milk, which I suppose isn't far off. His apartment is hardly more inviting. It has marble floor the brown-red colour of stale blood, lanky mahogany cabinets lurking in the hallway and creepy wooden masks swimming in the walls. Then, out of the dark appears the most beautiful woman I have ever seen in my life. She stands, long and sculpted, the epitome of grace, her ebony skin glowing slightly lilac. I've never been much a religious woman myself (though I did go to Sunday school as a kid for the free biscuits and we did go to church once, just once, because Dad 'wanted to try it') but I think this woman might actually be God.

'Helloh, welcum to ah hum,' she says.

She tells me her name, but I am too busy wondering why she has a massive purple scar across her head to remember it.

Etoire allows me to cook for myself, begrudgingly. Then we sit around the table, all eating our different things.

'That's all carbs,' says Etoire, pointing at my sloshy red mountain. 'There's no protein.' He shoves Parma ham in his mouth arrogantly.

'Well, I'm a cyclist. Carbs are good for cyclists,' I say. I then turn to God-woman. 'Hey, what's this stuff?'

I knew exactly what plantain was but wanted an excuse not to look at Etoire's mean face. He was putting me right off my spaghetti.

'It's plantain,' she says, slipping some onto my plate.

'English people can be so stupid.' Etoire interrupts, 'They come here and want to eat only English things. They hate it when they don't get what they want.'

I laugh, too loudly.

Etoire grunts, looking at me nastily. 'So you like adventure?' he snarls, 'Well the world is pretty dangerous. I nearly died in the desert once, had to eat scorpions. And see this?' he points to the angry six-inch scar slashed across God-woman's head, from her crown to her forehead. 'We were attacked. It was all a fucking setup.'

I can't help but notice Etoire doesn't have a scar of his own. I almost mention it too, but I'm too engrossed in squiggle-slurping.

'You know,'

Oh god, here he goes again.

'*Usually* when I have guests they clear up after themselves. Go and mop the floor,' he snaps.

So I drag a mop over the floor then sneak the rest of my dinner to bed and eat it in the dark, in peace.

The following morning, I hasten towards the front door without breakfast.

'Good luck,' says Etoire, not meaning it at all.

'Thanks.' I say, just as genuinely.

God-woman meanwhile stands radiant in the hallway. She opens out her long arms and folds me into a hug. She smells like meadows.

'Um...Can I just say...?' I begin, and God-woman's smile urges me to continue. 'That you are the most beautiful person I have ever met in my whole life.'

She giggles into her folded arms while Etoire intimidates me out of the marble dungeon and closes the door.

On the prowl for somewhere vegetable-ish to eat breakfast, I spot a sign: 'EL TASTET VEGANA'. From zero to hero! In I waltz, never more grateful to be on my own. Confusingly, the menu seemed to have been written in wrong Spanish (even Google Translate had no idea), so I crouch down to cake and pastry level and decide on which devilish thing to point at. I eventually decide on an artery-busting mountain of whipped soya cream, with a side of cake. Have I finally let go? The waitress, seeming to know all of my everything, beams proudly at me as I lick the plate clean. High on sugar I speed off, deciding not to ever worry about calories again.

The cake keeps me going a long while. In fact, it takes two mountain climbs (twenty miles, three hours) to regain that hollowness which I was starting to miss in the same way a child misses her mum when lost in the supermarket. But mum came back. Phew. I keep the fill of emptiness another hour until I start shaking, just a little, then stop for lunch: peas, my efforts at re-balancing my cake-greed. Only, my hand won't fit in the damn jar. Now frantic and swearing, I try to pour them out, but the watery peas go everywhere but my hand. Like a confused monkey I try to scoop them out with a stick (too thin), a leaf (almost successful), receipt (it dissolved), tissues (same issue, but worse), and then a stroke of genius: I gnaw my cucumber into a spoon shape and polish off the jar. Did I mention this was up a tree?

I'm lost. Up another mountain whose promising bike path has dissolved to nothing. It's just all rocks. Way down below I can see a silver strip of motor way snaking in the valley carrying red, blue, white, silver dots that glide smoothly along it. Sort of beautiful. I tumble my way down like a mountain-biker, screaming like a girl.

The remaining ten miles, though increasingly isolated, featured more of those yellow loops, graffitied in uniform rows like army troops. Note to self: ask Mark (my Warmshowers host) what the hell is with these ribbons.

I nourish my sixty-mile-spent body with a skinny-dip in a lake. Skirted by mountains and as still as glass, I slide into the soul-soup. The cold rush is sublime; I don't even mind the passing boats.

'Alice!' says Mark, opening his arms out in welcome, 'You swim in de lake? Sí? Iz beautiful, no?'

'I think you must live in heaven...' I reply, staring whimsically at the mountains above Mark's head.

Mark laughs, 'I know. I am so lucky. Oh by the way. Queralt and

I are began.'

'NO WAY! I'm vegan too!'

'Oh dat is so cool Alice! And dis is my uncle,' says Mark as a man emerges onto the courtyard, 'and my aunt,' he says as a woman appears from behind him, 'and my cousin, my other cousin, my niece, my nephew, my Farther, Grandpa...' Mark goes on as more people emerge, like the end of a panto. 'Dis is my family. We all libe here.' He says, as fourteen different pairs of eyes glare at me. 'Oh! And dis is my wife, Queralt, and our baby.'

A blonde woman appears from behind Mark, balancing on her hip a fleshy little thing with a chaos of black hair. The fleshy thing squirms – please don't cry, please don't cry – then shows me her lack of teeth, giggling.

I spend the evening playing with the fleshy thing, sort of how I'd play with a cat: shaking soft toys by her cheek then tapping them along the floor, hoping she'd chase them. It worked a bloody treat, although her company (as I find the company of all babies) makes me sad.

'God, *gracias*, these chickpeas are de-liscious! Oh and by the way, what are all these yellow ribbons I see everywhere?' I ask.

The clanging of knives and forks stops and Mark and Queralt's faces shadow with grief. They look at each other, then at me, like two parents whose child had just asked about death or babies.

'Do you not know that this is Catalan?' Queralt asks.

'OH!' I say, too excitedly, 'so *that's* why that menu in Mandresa was written in bad-, wrong- ur in something I couldn't understand...'

'That's right. You are in Catalan, that menu you read was in our Catalan language,' says a watery-eyed Queralt. She looks at Mark, who nods at her to go on. Queralt then tells me the opposite variation of what Caesar had said, telling me that, 'we just want our country back, to speak Catalan, our own language. But those who speak out for Catalan are beaten and put in prison. Some have died.'

'We don't want to be part of Spain,' Mark adds, 'Spanish culture is bery biolent. Like the bullfighting, *ugh*.'

A sad silence falls on the room and I realise how blatantly insensitive my conversation gambit had been.

'Can you teach me some Catalan?' I ask.

The mood lifts at my request. In-between mouthfuls of chickpeas, Queralt teaches me a few words in Catalan which I instantly forget, then I hit the hay. Having said that, *hay* is not the right word, *marshmallow* would've been more apt. A mass of soft, white, sweetly fragranced duvet whipped onto a bed the size of a trampoline. I sink in, tired bones melting into the mattress, the delicious ache of a long day coming in one final surge.

I wake up pressed deep within the whipped linen and let out a long, 'ahhh.'

For breakfast: croissants and an oat milk latte. Life is sweeter than a sugar sandwich.

It's been two hours of 'cycling' and I am only seven miles ahead of Mark and Queralt's house. But it's impossible to chug on, when the fruitful green mountains and glassy lakes surround me so severely: the perfect antidote for all the dust and desert and dumping of two days ago. Besides, to someone who has spent the last six years worrying about being too big, the enormity of the mountains makes me feel perfectly small.

Twenty miles on, busting through the threshold of mountain, I realise I have left my technicolour dream coat and my M&S bra behind. Suddenly hot and inspired, I'd taken them both off halfway up a mountain and then forgotten about them. It's a shame because the bra had nice frilly bits on it and cradled my wobbling lumps perfectly. Any girl will know the near-impossible challenge of finding such an unknown specimen as a 'fitting bra'. As for the coat, well it was the most beautiful coat I'd ever seen. But I'm not here to be beautiful.

3pm, I roll into Girona on the lookout for a man called Cyril. Along the river, sunset-coloured houses jut out irregularly, a jimble-jumble of them in mustard yellows, wotsit oranges, strawberry reds (I think I might be hungry). I turn into the neat cobbles of the highstreets and try to weave between a tsunami of shopping bags and obnoxious hats. Bloody Tourists.

'HEY! Aleece!' shouts a very attractive man wheeling his bicycle towards me.

'Cyril! Bonjour!' I reply.

Mike (my Warmshowers host) had suggested I cycle with a Frenchman called Cyril who was also coming to stay with him. And here Cyril stands, the rugged end of thirty, looking like he didn't need the height he didn't have, or the hair he lacked. Buzz cuts have never really done it for me, but Cyril's cheeky grin more than makes up for it. Before I'd even got round to properly admiring his arms (I like arms), a shiny sort of girl bursts up to us.

'Excuse me! Do you know where the Cathedral is? You know, the one from the game of thrones?' she pants, definitely more at Cyril.

Cyril does his best to point at Cathedral-like building then the shiny girl dashes off, 'Don't worry!' she says too sweetly, her white doily top flapping, her long legs trotting away in new sandals.

'Cummon,' says Cyril turning to look at me, 'let's go get a drink, yeah?'

I shake the envy out of my head, 'Sure! And hey, what's with the jazzy tyres? Do you not get punctures?' I ask gawping at the fat black cushions of Cyril's wheel.

'No, zese are great! zey're worth hundreds but I got zem for free because of my sponsor. Zey never puncture.' he says, leaning his bike against the wall. 'After you,' he says, opening the bar door.

I scurry through, hoping my tan is disguising my blushing.

We nestle ourselves into a groovy Latino bar, adorned with dark wood and embellished cushions too small for an ass bigger than a pin prick. I decide on the left cheek. Latin music twinkles in the background.

Two plates of bruschetta arrive looking like someone had tried to grate a tomato with them and we tuck in eagerly, our teeth first crunching, then squelching through the bread, generously lubricated with olive oil, tanged by tomato and polluted by the devilish warmth of garlic. Tiny crystals of salt make delicious jabs at my taste buds. Cyril, I notice as I unpeeled my eyes, is looking at me, confused and amused. Then I realise, in a strike of self-aware horror, the orgasm noises I was making.

'Ahem, Ur, so how come you're out here?' I ask.

'Ah, I had a few days uff work and decided to cycle here. But what about you? Yugh so young to be out ere alon.'

'Oh! Yeah, dunno, just got on my bike and cycled here...'

'From England?!'

'Mhm. *Jesus* this is *so* good.'

Cyril laughs, orders another drink, downs it in thirty seconds, pays for us both (despite my very English protesting) then off. Oh but wait.

'Quelle dommage!' I say as Cyril inspects his puncture. Fortunately, unlike me, Cyril knows exactly what to do. I admire his grunting effort a little too much, and then we pedal east (towards the coast) as the sun goes soft and amber.

'You have a guitar?' I ask, pointing at a sky-blue ukulele strapped to his bike.

'Yez! I can play if you like, but on one condition: you ave to zing for me.'

'I can't sing!'

'I dun't believe that. Cummon, we'll zing togezer....ahem....'

Cyril wobbles frantically, arms flailing either side, one holding the ukulele. He eventually steadies himself and begins to play. We first sing 'in the jungle' but my 'Wimbe-weh' is so out of sync Cyril decides instead to play a much slower 'Major Tom' while Spanish children point and laugh with amazed delight.

'Can I take a picture of you? The light is pughfekt.'

Cyril is not the first man to ask for my photo, and after the whole 'naked bike ride' catastrophe, after the stalkers and threats, I had planned to always say no.

'Yes!' I say.

Cyril choreographs the scene: me in the grass, with the last of the golden light of a sinking sun. He then points what looks like a bazooka at me.

A few flashes later he says, 'wunt to see?'

'Nah.' I say.

On we go.

There she was, looking more magnificent than ever: a brilliant blue, edging the sand beneath our feet, expanding out to infinity.

'THE SEA!' I yell.

Cyril laughs then gets out his bazooka, 'will you do somezing for me?' He asks.

Of course, I acquiesce. Only, thing is, this 'somezing' was propping up my bike in front of the sea then running away from it so Cyril could capture it upright and isolated.

'Ah non, non,' Cyril scowls at his camera. 'Can we do it again?'

So again, I prop up my trusty steed then let go. The Insect clatters even louder and more upset.

Eventually, after five whole heart-crushing clatters, Cyril says 'Zat will do' and we chug to the top of the hill, to Mike's house...

'Hey!' beams Mike, 'Come on in guys! This is my friend, he's from Argentina,' he says, pointing to a man weathered by a life of travel and, judging by the look of his eyes, sadness. His hair falls down his back, silver and fizzy.

'Hey,' says the Argentinian, softly.

Asparagus hisses on the barbeque.

'Seriously Mike, you are an epic cook. This is INSANE!' I insist, knocking a little couscous off my fork.

Mike, Cyril and the Argentinian laugh.

'What!' I accuse.

'Well it's just, you're so English,' says Mike, 'Everything is *Amazing*'. I show you my pool and it's "the *best* pool" and I cook you asparagus and it's "the *best* asparagus". You're just so English.'

'Whoops, sorry!'

'Hey, no problem. Anyway, it's quite nice to have a young girl like you here rather than another sixty-year-old German man who goes to bed at six. They can be so damn boring. And I can say this because *I'm* from Germany. I'm going back there to live soon.'

'Why are you going back if the people are so boring?' I ask.

'Well yeah, that's why I'm leaving. It's *too* nice. So I'm going to live somewhere boring so that I actually get things done.'

I cup my full mouth and laugh.

'Do you find it hard travelling as a girl, alone?' Mike asks. I think it's so brave. If I were you I think I'd be too afraid.'

'Yeah well...' I collect another asparagus from the barbeque, limp and charred, 'I actually think it's kind of safer travelling as a girl.

People see you as vulnerable, and help you out. Also, I think I look *really* young, too young, which kinda helps.'

'Yeah, you do look really young, I'd ave zought you were maybe, like, sixteen!' Says Cyril

'Well hey, you know what they say...' Mike continues, glaring at Cyril, 'If it's hairy, it's legal!'

All of us but the sad Argentinean laugh up a storm.

'You know, I used to be Vegan, like you' he says, breaking his whimsical silence, 'I did it because I thought meat was bad Karma. But then when I was in Israel a lady offered me to eat a meat stew with her family, she'd been preparing it all day. I realised it is worse Karma to reject her. So after eight years, I ate the meat.'

Everyone goes quiet because it was a bit of an awkward interjection. Then Mike finally says, 'You know, usually, I ask my guests to cook. To taste their culture.'

'Well, I'm glad you didn't ask me,' I say, 'I can't cook to save my life.'

'I wouldn't dare ask you to cook Alice,' says Mike sternly, 'you're English.'

With the asparagus, couscous, courgette and inappropriate banter down to their last remainders, I bid the lads goodnight

It was a treat to catch Mike on his own at breakfast. His company is soft, easy and generous. 'Here take these.' He hands me fruit. 'Oh and these' He hands me flapjacks 'I'm pretty sure they're vegan. Oh...And these are great. You'll need electrolytes for when you sweat. I thought they were bullshit, but I swear after taking them I cycled faster.' He hands me some tablets. 'Take this too.' He hands me a bike light. 'Oh, and remember, try to get a tent, and not a girly one. That way you won't look like like bait.'

'GRACIAS!' I shout, waving behind me with such force, The Insect and I swing to the wrong side of the road and crash. But thankfully Mike has already closed the door and misses this.

I resist the sea for two miles before I strip off and slip in. The tide is high and so I lift off the ground in two steps, treading water clearer than air, a lattice pattern dancing over my toes. Deep breath, plunge. There is nothing like the thick silence of underwater, the way the water gives grace to normal movements, the slowing of time, the dimensional freedom. A blurry world, free from gravity, from my own weight (which is especially nice given how much oily asparagus I ate last night). I could stay down here, watching the glossy sun above, and wait to run out of air. It would be the perfect place to die.

Being too young to die, I bounce back to the surface and swim to shore, leaving behind me the best swim of my life. It was special because I hadn't seen the sea for weeks and because I was the only one swimming, like everybody knew I needed it to myself.

The rest of the day goes like my swim. I even weep with joy as I tumble into Platja Grifeu.

'HEY!' shouts a voice from a balcony. I look up. 'IT'S ANGEL!' shouts my host of the day.

Angel is stocky, a sea-urchin of black hair spiking from his head as though he was permanently surprised. His tan is extreme; surely his organs are brown too. He hugs me like a daughter and says, 'You cycled all the way from England? Alone? Cool. Here, look. I cycled to China and this is my book.'

'That's insane, you're a hero!'

Angel laughs, 'No, I'm just crazy. I think you are too,' He winks. 'Do you want a shower? Or maybe you want a swim?'

I nod and throw my micro fibre towel on my shoulder.

'You won't need this' he says, stopping me on my way out, tugging at my high-vis.

I blush.

'Don't worry, look, all the women wear bikinis here,' he points to the Malibu Barbie figures bellow to reassure me. I release the Velcro, and my shoes, give Angel a cheesy thumbs up and skip downstairs.

Angel's hair must've been an omen: I alight from the sea limping, with five black spindles burrowed deep into my big toe.

We spend the rest of the evening drinking gazpacho, each member of Angel's family taking their turns with the tweezers.

'ARGH!' I yell.

'Sorry,' says Angel's daughter, giving up.

We also watch a demented lady through binoculars swashing about. She dances, swirls into the sea fully clothed, cries a bit, lies awkwardly on the sand, face-first like a dead fish, then drives off. It is very strange, floating above someone else's madness and though Angel and his family are rightfully disturbed, I can't help but relate to this woman a little.

11

France encore

'I don't like to swim here. I like to go to a quiet beach and be naked and free,' says Angel, passing me a soya yogurt and a teaspoon. 'Fucking vegans,' he winks at me.

'Gracias.' I close my eyes and chew my yogurt. Gosh I love breakfast. Hey Angel, I think I'm going to swim naked today.'

Angel laughs, 'Great. If you go just around the corner, you will find a nice nuddie beach. I'll show you to it when you're ready to go. Ah! Wait there. I have an idea.'

Angel dashes off, leaving me to squint at the sea, shimmering madly like tinsel.

'I never used this when I went cycling.' Angel steps back out onto the balcony, carrying a large blue sausage-shaped thing, 'I was too lazy to camp and stay in hotels instead. Hotels have showers, see. Anyway, it's yours. If you wan it.'

I gasp, slapping my hands onto my cheeks a little too hard. 'Oh my God, YES! Only, how would I carry it?'

Angel tosses it in the air and catches it again 'Let's find out.' He wheels my bike onto the balcony, scratches his head, then slots the tent under the buckled straps of my panniers.

'Perfect, perfect, perfect! Look! Now I'm a proper cyclist, I've got my own house. Hey, maybe ...I'll *never* have to go home.'

Angel grins.

'Hey, Angel?' I ask. 'How far is France?'

'About twenty kilometres. Twenty hilly kilometres'

Can I skinny dip here? Angel said it's fine, that it would be quiet and nobody would mind. Well it's definitely *not* quiet but that lady over there has got her tits out, so maybe it's fine. Inspired by those two bare nipples eyeballing me, I drop my micro fibre towel and everybody watches, stunned (even tits-out lady's plucked eyebrows near enough eject) as I wobble and splash vigorously towards a blue horizon. It's low tide.

After all that I eat 600g of oats (that's right, that's over a pound of oats), seasoned with sea water. I tried to stop after bowl three, I really did, but something deep within me begged for more. As I try to iron then punch my belly flat (this never works), I think for a moment about relieving my problem (oats are easy to throw up). But I swiftly toss the idea in my inner landfill of bad ideas, deciding I don't nearly hate myself enough to do something so violent. Besides, I'm sure the beta-glucans will do me good. Besides, besides, there are no toilets here.

Hilly was right. It's so hilly in fact, people seem to think my earnest pedalling is some kind of miracle. Tooting coaches overtake, fully loaded with posh tourists that wave, take pictures, bash each other's shoulders –*have you seen that girl on a bicycle?'*– as I wind up the precipice, the sky and sea swelling, the buildings and people shrinking to mere speckles.

'WOO! YOU CAN DO IT!' shouts a BMW driver, swinging a blinged-up wrist out of his tinted window.

Then down: the sky and sea shrinking, the buildings and people swelling as a well-earned wind washes over my sweaty forehead.

The next few hours are spent like this: up an hour, ten minutes down. And I just keep chugging. God bless those beta-glucans indeed.

The final climb: four miles uphill. Spain shrinks away. I stop between two signs plonked on top of the hill.

'FRANCE'

I look over my shoulder.

'ESPANA'

I freeze in the no-man's land between the two signs, my eyes prickling with imminent tears.

'Alain!' shouts a woman, 'Arrête ça!'

'NON!' Alain retorts, 'Je pense que-'

'Alain!'

'JE PENSE QUE SI J'APPUIE SUR- '

'ALAIN!'

A small woman, in a bright red mini dress barks at a man, apparently called Alain. Alain barks back defensively, furiously bashing an iPhone with his enormous index finger.

'Excusez–moi?' I interrupt, 'Peut-être... Je peut prends un photo? Pour toi?'

They nod gratefully, handing me their phone and assuming their position next to the 'España' sign. The tiny woman leans playfully into Alain who leans forward, mouth ajar, forehead a maze of confused lines. A laugh bubbles up my throat, I squeeze my lips together to push it back down then say, 'Voila!' showing them the photo.

'Merci! Je m'appelle Nelly' says the lady. 'Et c'est Alain,' she says pointing at Alain, who is frowning at the vista, looking cross.

The exchange ends with a bag of cherries, two peaches, three oranges and a place to stay in Cap d'Agde tomorrow.

'AU REVOIR!' Alain screams.

I walk back towards Spain and sit on the ledge feeding fruit to the ants (and a little for me too), much to the annoyance of the Germans picnicking to my left.

'HI!' I yell.

They grunt, pack up their cheese, and huff off.

'Alright...' I say, unusually quietly, 'Bye Spain...'

So that's it: Spain over. And why should I be so surprised? After the desert-dumping, I'd made a beeline for France. If I was being honest with myself, maybe I secretly wanted to bump into Loic, knowing he'd head for the sea first *'to write pozcardz an rest'* then straight back to France *'I dun't like Spain'*. So this evening, as my host Xavier tells me a French boy, 'a cyclist, like you', will also be arriving sometime soon, my stomach back flips.

'What was his name?' I ask, the bang of my heart making my voice wobble.

'Hm.' Xavier stops chopping aubergine. 'Hold on...CILY?'

A cute, sunburnt thing strides into the kitchen, her blonde hair tied tightly in two plaits.

'Bonjour!' I say.

'UGH! Don't tell me jor going to shtart shpeaking French,' says Cily, 'I HATE French.'

'Oh je suis– Ahem, sorry.' I say.

'I'm Dutch,' she says, then turns to Xavier, 'Yes?'

'What was that boy's name again?' he says.

'Shomething beginning with "L"?'

'Fuck.' I blurt.

In a jolt of panic, I realise I'd rather eat my own toenails than bump into Loic.

'Whats up?' asks Xavier.

I tell them the story, Xavier nodding along, Cily more focused on fanning herself with different objects from around the kitchen. Eventually, she settles on an invoice.

'It was intense,' I sigh, 'even when I went for a wee, me and Loic were never more than two metres apart. A week felt like a very long time, more like months.'

Xavier leans towards me, his eyes following the back of Cily's pigtails as she storms out of the kitchen huffing about how 'fucking hot' it was. He lowers his voice and says, 'You should try three years.'

I chop onions, glad of the sting fizzing in my eyeballs which would've been watery anyway. What if that boy 'beginning with an "L"' is Loic? A flash of bicycle zooms by the window and the soothing aroma of cumin and onion suddenly becomes stifling. Please, God, I'll never pray for anything again, not even snow: please make the boy not Loic. *Not* Loic. The ring of the doorbell hits me like an electric shock.

In walks a boy, my new favourite boy of the world, a scrawny thing, a flop of brown hair obscuring his eyes.

'Hi, I'm Louis.' he says, scooping the hair-flop to one side.

Louis is seventeen, gracefully awkward in that way teenage boys are when not yet familiar with their newly elongated limbs. Xavier puts us both to work shelling nuts.

'You should visit my contry, iz beautifol,' says Louis, depositing a handful of shells into the bowl.

'Wait, you cycled here? From Switzerland?' I ask.

He nods.

'But,' I look over his shoulder, at his bike, 'where are your bags?'

'Oh, I don't az bags. Only zis,' he pulls out the contents of his pockets: one mobile phone and about twenty euros. 'When I get ungry I eat fruit off ze trees.'

'You little rock star!' I say.

Louis laughs.

'It's ready!' Xavier dumps a huge pot of curry on the table.

Louis out eats all of us three-fold, while Xavier and Cily tells us stories about their travels.

'This Arabian guy came into our tent and asked if he could rape Cily, and when I told him "no", he tried to set us on fire!' says Xavier.

'He was so fucking annoying. I just wanted to shleep,' says Cily. And that just about sums Cily up.

Bedtime.

'Do you az a charger I could borrow?' Louis whispers.

'Sure,' I whisper back. 'Oh hey, just so you know,' I toss it to him, then shimmy under the duvet of bed number two, 'I think you are so brave, really, the absolute coolest.'

Though it is dark, I know Louis is blushing.

From the window, we watch the silhouettes of Xavier and Cily crawl into a tent at the end of the garden. Nothing they do makes any sense.

The next morning Xavier sits me and Louis with a crate of dates.

'Eat as much as you like,' he says in his London accent, gesturing sleepily to the ten-kilogram mass, 'I got them from this dodgy shop. The guy always gives us freebies.'

Me and Louis, having already discussed our zeal for fruit, exchange a frenzied look then tuck in eagerly. Eight, nine, ten, fifteen... We lose count.

'When my friend left me in Spain, he took *all* the dates. *Je deteste.*' I say.

'No!' says Louis. 'But les dates are zo good!'

'Merde,' I hiss, raising my fist.

Louis laughs. I am so down with the kids.

Cap D'Agde is a full 85 miles away. But with my new friends Alain and Nelly waiting and a stomach full of dates, I'm pretty sure I'm invincible.

Too many dates and too many centigrade have rendered me as useless as a drunken slug wading through cold gravy. Thirty miles done, fifty-five to go, I slump under a tree, feeling... peculiar. A text arrives in my inbox, it's a boy from uni and all of a sudden my wriggling stomach doesn't seem so important. I ignore the message and glug gazpacho arrogantly. Then I reply, bragging about my gazpacho.

A while later I wake up to three empty cartons, and a stomach that feels like a tumble dryer full of raw meat. Despite the shivering surges of *'ugh'* rippling through me, I manage to put up my tent, nude myself, and crash.

Crunching intestines startle me awake. In a frenzy of sweaty, naked nausea, I snatch some napkins from my panniers, dart as far from the tent as I can manage, squat, and...a violent substance like hot egg-mayonnaise shoots out of my arse.

Deep into the hours of the night, the episodes continue. And to make a desperate situation worse, horror of all horrors, it's round five and I've run out of toilet roll. But alas! According to my creaking guts, the show must go on. There are no leaves on the trees, only spikes and pinecones so I riffle through my bags, to no avail other than a small bunch of old receipts. Not that I could use them, they're too small, too shiny, there's no grip! They won– too late. The deluge commences and I clutch the receipts miserably, wishing I'd bought more items in Carrefour.

Morning comes and I feel emptied, better. My first time solo wild camping had been a success! Well – I peer out of the tent, still naked, and stare at the aftermath – *mostly* a success. Who knew so much could come out of one 5ft 5" girl? Come to think of it, where the hell am I? It's all rocks, dust, pine trees and a bridleway. Though I'm not sure the white trail of her gown would be safe around here after my– let's not think about it. No phone battery, a woefully inadequate water supply and no food: well, shit. I pack up camp and go north. At least, I think this way is north, it seems upward enough. But how is a girl to know?

Ten minutes of (probably) northern cycling later, I wave down a man, thickly built and heavily bearded, walking a dog the size of a peanut. I yell at him to help, that I need a boulangerie, urgently.

'Uh– Je ne sais pas! Suivez ça?' he laughs, pointing at a disused railway.

I parallel the railway, groaning loudly into my elbows, staring at the rocky terrain zipping beneath my tyres. If I should look up, it's just more rocks, more railway. So I do not look up, not for an hour until, hallelujah praise the lord, it happens: civilisation. Just in time too, according to the apparently not yet spent gurgling of my guts. I sprint into a boulangerie and beg for a toilet and a baguette (in that order) but the terrified bakery lady only shakes her head.

Slumped outside, I clutch my stomach and moan into my knees, considering the possibility that I might be sweating it out. The thought makes me shiver.

'Ça va?' asks a passer-by.

'JE BESION UNE TOILETTE!' I yell.

A crowd gather around me, each taking it in turns to offer their solution. Water? A snack? One of them points me to a pharmacy and I try to tell him I cannot walk that far, but my desperate pleas are drowned out by the shrill (though pleasingly foreign sounding) call of an ambulance.

Three high-vis men fall out of it, hurrying to my side with kits and instruments.

'Ello zere. Az you ad an accident?' asks one of the men, opening his first aid kit.

'No. I just *really* need a toilet... Une toilette! UNE TOILETTE!'

The saga finally ends in a bank where I am allowed (just in the nick of time) to use the toilet. I complete my evacuation with neurotic glee, gripping fistfuls upon fistfuls of *real* toilet paper. Then I pay a *little visit* to the bakery bitch who wouldn't let me use the toilet.

'Du pain et un té, *s'il vous plait.*' I say confidently.

She brings me my bread and tea, delightfully pissed off. Two baguettes and two cups of tea later, I'm pretty much recovered.

Alain's mouth is still ajar when I arrive, as though he hadn't got round to closing it since I first met him and Nelly at the pass. Nelly's mouth, however, is much busier, explaining dinner (did I like falafels? She'd bought them 'spécialement'), showing me around the flat, and going on about '*tapis rouge*', which I think means red something. She hugs me then throws me into the shower.

I'd barely stepped out of the shower and she's started fussing again, pulling hangers out of her wardrobe, tucking the different outfits under my chin, tossing each option on the bed. We decide on a little black dress, a pair of strappy sandals and a denim jacket. Then we're off (God knows where), Nelly driving, Alain sitting in the passenger seat shouting excitably to no-one in particular, and me sitting in the back, admiring the liquid-soft viscose of my dress: three completely separate planets.

Stumbling in my skimpy sandals behind the quick, short steps of Nelly, and clumsy lope of Alain, I wonder to myself just what the hell is going on. Hordes of ladies and gentlemen nurse cocktails and laugh delicately, mingling in an orbit of booze. Suddenly we all stampede towards the new hotspot: a red carpet. A limousine appears. According to the clutter of flashing cameras, the sequinned specimen stepping out of it is famous.

More sequins, more heels, more underweight women and a few groomed men make their way down the carpet, Nelly pointing out each one excitably. This goes on a while until, noticing me staring at the sky, Nelly suggests we head home for dinner.

Leaving this morning is almost impossible. Nelly, with the same loving insistence of a grandmother trying to will you to eat 'just a little bit of cake', keeps trying to give me things meanwhile Alain keeos yelling at me about the 'common wealt' and 'brexite' to which I kept responding with 'quelle dommage!' and 'sacrebleu!' and 'JE N'AIME PAS LE BREXITE'.

Eventually I do leave, five kilograms heavier with: cable ties, three Tupperwares of food, cutlery, toiletries, bungee straps, a map, a bunch of flowers, and a collection of dangerously white clothes. These featured: a white dress with the words 'A-team' on it, white shorts, and a white top with the words 'something odd, yet beautiful' on it. I wear the 'odd yet beautiful' top and heave away, my poor bike swaying lazily alongside the sand dunes like an overworked donkey.

Throughout the day I find convenient places to accidentally leave Nelly's gifts behind: the food was eaten, the flowers left in Sète, three bottles of shower gel left in Frontignan. I was just looking for a convenient place in Montpellier to leave the wipes, when a Tour de France legend approaches me. I really wish I'd remembered his name, because there's something distinctly cool about cycling alongside a *real* cyclist. My Lycra compadre convoys me for a whole ten miles in fact, riding uncomfortably slowly while I ride uncomfortably quickly, so our paces match. He tells me I am beautiful and adventurous, two things I've wanted to be since I knew their meaning, then sprints off.

It is dark as I arrive outside the green spikes of Marie's enormous gate, my whole body jolting involuntarily. Marie is not impressed by this.

'Oh, zis is vewy bad.' she says, scowling, 'you are vegan, so you are too thin.'

Two impulses flash through me. Firstly, I wanted to tell Marie that I am thin because I keep myself hungry all the time, not because I'm vegan. Secondly, and more importantly, that I am not thin at all and she shouldn't be playing these mind games. Couldn't she see my dinosaur thighs? My plump cheeks?

I laugh, and say, 'Je suis fort.'

Marie does not laugh.

Dinner went about as well as our first encounter. The only difference being the presence of her microscopic husband, who stayed silent while his mean wife barked at me, correcting my French, dumping rice on my plate. I thank her and she grunts, her eyes squinting behind round spectacles.

'Et pourquoi! Pourquoi vous voyage comme ça?' She demands.

And then I say something that changed everything. I watch the mean pierce of Marie's eyes melt as I tell her I travel because *'comme être en enfant encore'*, because it's like being a child again. For some reason, this strikes a chord with Marie and she here on out decides to love me.

'You must stay anuzer day. Iz no pwablem. You stay. We're going to a party tomorrow, you come.' she says.

'Oui,' I reply.

The day, like any great day, begins with Jam. Then I visit Nimes, as suggested by Marie, for an oh-la-la day of culture. I run rings around the Roman temple, buy four postcards, then hit the Roman amphitheatre. Eight euros. *Eight* euros to get inside and the whole damn thing was webbed with scaffolding and disco lights because apparently Elton John was on his way. Wanting to get my money's worth, I do five laps of the top steps, nick a colossal amount of toilet paper from the toilets, then collapse into a café, starving hungry. Lunch is bought for me by three different women: one Irish, one English, and one French.

After burning myself to an unholy shade of burgundy I return to Marie and her husband, who sit in the garden, he reading, she sewing.

'Tank you fow what you wote,' she says. 'It was so bewtifaw.'

She must've been talking about the note I left this morning.

'Tonight, we are going to a pawty. We bought you a ticket. Iz okay?' she asks, handing me a leaflet.

The words 'paella' and '$30' both disturb me. Marie must have sensed this because she says, 'Oui. No pwablem. I pay alweddy. And we can do somezing for you to eat, for vegan.'

Man, I hope this 'somezing' isn't picking bits of fish out of the paella.

I glare at the Paella, lips curling inwards at the sight of the two squirmy mussels they'd forgotten to pick out. It stinks of a dodgy orgy. Loic wanders into my head *'Iz only a littul bit. It good to get your B vitamins up.'* I shake his memory away as I mummify the crustaceans with a napkin.

'I've been ill,' says Marie's husband, staring at the back of his wife who was jabbering away with a friend a few metres away. 'Iz ard for me to wulk.'

This is not the first time someone has confessed illness to me out of the blue. And just like the last time, I just gawp at Marie's husband, the threat of tears paralysing me. Bad news always seems to do that, as if the rug really had been pulled and so comes the whoosh of a fall, then the stun. But Marie's husband changes the subject, asking me in French if I like dancing, pumping his fists playfully whilst a woman in red leather trousers walks onto the stage. Everybody claps and I win because mine was the last. The leather woman has a voice like Robbie Williams which I was really appreciating until the worst thing in the world happens.

'Viens!' says Marie, offering her hand.

'Non, merci. Je suis *anglaise*,' I reply, shaking my head.

This does not satisfy Marie, who cruelly and insistently pulls me off my chair and hurls me onto the dance floor.

There are about ten other men and women in the dance-zone, swinging their hips and clicking their fingers with candid style. All but me, who stands among them in my white "A-team" dress with my legs apart and arms suspended like a computer game character waiting to be selected.

What is a poor English girl to do! I try swinging my arms but look like an orangutan. Then I phase out the swinging and deciding I'm maybe more of a lower body dancer, I start to kick my legs. This looks even worse so I jump on the spot, which at least blurs all the staring faces. But after about twenty stiff jumps, I get a headache and instead start swinging my hips, trying to copy the eighty-year-old to my left. Hip swinging does not work if you're as stiff as a corpse though. Oh dear. Horror of all horrors, my incompetency has climaxed: ignoring the points and titters, I start doing the robot. Damn you Peter Crouch.

Just as I was beginning to wonder whether a bit of actual suicide might be an option, *finally*, the middle-aged, leather-trousered beast puts down her microphone and leaves the stage. People applaud and I dash towards my seat. By this time, it is dark.

'Time for le feu. Allez, allez! Viens, viens!' says Marie.

We slip into the tsunami of crowd, which disperses around a fire in a circle. Marie and I join the circle of held-hands, the warmth of the fire glazing our faces in brassy light.

To my gasping astonishment a young boy sprints towards the fire and takes an enormous leap over it. What is even more amazing than that is that instead of being grounded, everybody claps.

Then another boy, then another. Throwing caution to the wind, I let out a little warning squeak and sprint towards the fire. As I take a screaming leap, a blast scorches my feet and crackles in my ears. I land, feet still hot from the lick of flames. The crowd goes wild.

'Why don't you stay anozer day. Iz no pwablem. It will be vewy, vewy hot. Iz dangewous. We can go watch Elton John play,' says Marie.

I reply, in the best French that I can manage that although it would be lovely to stay, if I always stayed when I loved someone, I'd never make any progress (this makes Marie well up). Besides, I tell her, my next host has invited me to watch her daughter play the guitar at a summer fête tonight so I didn't need to see Elton.

'You are weally such a lovely girl. Dun't eva change,' says Marie, gripping my arm. Her husband smiles in agreement behind her.

As soon as Marie and her husband are out of eyes reach, I bawl my eyes out, thinking of those words, 'lovely girl', 'dun't ever change.'

12

Better

Alice is late: how classic. Not even a cold slither of fried onion remains of the fête and I pedal off to Geraldine's house full of apology.

'Je suis *tellement* désolé!' I pant as Geraldine opens her front door, then her arms, 'I got lost in a quarry! Where are they, your daughters?'

'Oh,' Geraldine pulls away from our hug, 'Zey gone ome to zere Dad. Zey live zere now. Ee lets zem do everyzing zey wants,' she sighs.

Geraldine has that gorgeous bloom particular to only French women: her motherly curves, chesty accent and slightly ruffled black hair, seeming to unfurl in front of me. And her eyes are a very true dark, almost black, her face shadowed with a disturbingly familiar kind of sadness.

'Zere. You can watch her sing on zis, I filmed it,' she passes me her phone, 'and I will make uz some food.'

I dump my ass on the sofa and watch the bad quality footage of beautiful singing. Meanwhile, Geraldine opens and closes all there is to open and close, cupboards, drawers, the fridge, trying to solve the puzzle of cooking for a vegan. After a bit of blank staring into the glowing abyss of the fridge, she gets out two things: fennel and tomatoes. The fennel sizzles, sweetening the room, then comes a loud clattering noise. I look up from the video. Geraldine is dropping tomatoes into a blender.

'Okay, iz ready!' she sings, loading the table with a pan of fried fennel, and two bowls of tomato slush, before proudly announcing 'Zis iz tomato soup.'

I concentrate hard on the ground, locking the muscles in my face, trying to think of anything other than the 'soup'. But I can feel the laughter bubbling so dangerously in my chest so I grunt and say, 'Merci. This looks de-liscious!' I sip a spoon of tomato smoothie. 'Yum!'

'Iz good! My friend let me borroh er blender, iz a very clever machine.'

'Well, it's great. Oh and thanks for showing me the video, your daughter, she has a lovely voice, and she's...' I admire the paintings in the hall, 'very talented.'

'Oh gush. Yez. Zere iz nut nuzing she could nut do. She's a *genius*.'

Geraldine's face does something I'd seen before. So I ask her, 'Is she okay? Your daughter, I mean. Has she... had problems?'

'Yez.' she says.

'Mental problems?'

'Yez!'

'God, I'm so sorry,'

'Iz okay. She is better now. But she was really nut well. She ad to stay in a...how you say *opital psychiatrique*?'

'That must've been so stressful for her, these places... They can be so...difficult. And actually, sometimes they make things so much worse.'

'Yez! Zat is exactly what appen! I get calls from ze opital saying she az done somezing bad. Like she urt erself.'

'My gosh. I'm so sorry-'

I blush, because I was about to call Geraldine Mum.

It's been three days and still, no calls. I've been waiting all day for 7pm to come and near enough tackle my way to the front of the queue as the HCA hands us our Nokia bricks. I turn it on. Nothing. Not even a text. I wait, waking up the screen every few minutes just to check the signal is holding true. Then it happens, shrieking and vibrating on my lap and, though I had planned to let it ring a little, if he called, I pick it up after the first ring.

'Hello? Matt? It's been so many days! How are you?'

'Yeah, fine...' he says, sounding bored.

'It's nice to hear from you anyway, this week has been absolutely crazy.'

'Yeah,' he says.

We chat a while. Or rather, I chat at him, sounding insatiably perky, telling him about mine and Georgia's new Mary Berry poster we've stuck on our wall, but Matt's responses dwindle to nothing. Eventually, I let the silence speak. Was that...did he sigh? Or yawn?

'Um, Alice?' he says, 'I think I want to move on now.'

'What?'

'Yeah, sorry.'

'No, wait! But I'm getting better! I swear, I swear. And I'll be out soon. Please! I'll try harder, I really will. And I'll wear those clothes you like and be anything you want, please, Matt!'

'...Sorry.'

'NO WAIT! THAT'S NOT FAIR! YOU CAN'T LEAVE ME IN HERE!'

'Bye Alice.' He hangs up.

I have now lost everything. Two years of love and laughter, gone. 'There's no one like you.', 'I'll always love you.' Gone.

In a fit of tears, I rummage through my drawer and grab one of my long socks. My ears ring and I rasp, pulling it tighter around my neck, as tight as it will go. Light head; heavy heart. Static vision, brain throbbing. The doors burst open and Jivito shouts, panicked, yanking the ligature. Another HCA crashes in, shouting even louder than Jivito. The pain around my throat slips away.

Footsteps, the rustling of plastic, the crackle of walkie-talkies go on. They bag up and confiscate all my things (even my teddy), slip me a blue pill, put me on 24-hour watch and then do the worst thing they could have possibly done: they ring home.

'Iz okeh Aleece, she iz bettugh now,' says Geraldine.

'That's wonderful, she's lucky to have had you. It can be lonely in that kind of place, I'm sure. And hard to get out, once you're in. You must've been exhausted, you know, not knowing if she'd get better.'

Geraldine looks at me, startled, 'Yez, exactly!' she says. 'But I ad to forget about myzelf and be strong for 'er. Iz like I switch myzelf uff and only zink of her. I was exhausted. I could nut sleep.'

'I understand. And... I'm just so sorry.'

Geraldine is about to say something so I ask, 'Do you sing too?'

Geraldine smiles and sits herself in front of the piano. And so follows an ebb and flow of tinkling notes, Geraldine singing 'J'ai demandé à la lune' in a treacly voice.

'Bravo! Amazing!' I say, clapping.

'I zink we should zing togezer.'

I stand with my mouth open, blushing.

'Say yez! Iz good to try!'

And so we sing: Geraldine's treacle voice melting along, mine coagulating alongside in mumbling lumps.

'Louder!' She says.

'Et la lune c'est moquée de moi!' we sing, filling the room with smile.

The next morning Geraldine says to me, 'Goodbye Alice. An zank you. I knew before you came we would az a special connection. I ad a good feeling.'

'Et moi aussi,' I say.

We embrace and I leave thinking of Mum, I think of when I screamed at her to take me home, the exhausted worry in her face. I realise then the duty of being a daughter I have mostly failed at. Which is probably why I bought her that £400 coffee machine after my release, which still sits in our house, it's beady lights and unnecessary compartments bullying our small kitchen. Really, I should've just said sorry, and thank you.

My God it is hot. Sacrilegiously hot, pushing beyond the 40s, slapping every inch of bare skin, thickening my blood, cooking my organs.

Lidl offers respite, not only from the heat. But the no-frills, no-radio, functionality of it I've always found pleasingly meditative. An elderly woman in the queue holds my face in her palms and says that when she looks at my face, she can see a good and beautiful heart. She kisses my cheek. I almost cry.

Fifty-five lava miles later, Claire opens the door and I gasp. She'd warned me she had a baby, but I wasn't prepared for how frighteningly delicate, pink and tiny it would be. It is like she's holding a rose petal to her chest.

'Enchanté...' I whisper.

Claire smiles, glowing her motherly glow, and gestures me into her vigorously air-conditioned house. I soon get a headache, which might be from the menthol air conditioning or might also be the pained regret I always feel in the presence of babies.

Today is somehow even hotter. It is only 11am and already it's

45°, which is impressive because anything above 42 is cooking temperature. Even I, one who has spent a large portion of this year in a mild state of hypothermia, find that a little severe. Even my phone cannot stand it and so I sit cross-legged in the chilliest aisle of Carrefour with my head in my hands waiting for it, as much as myself, to cool down and work again. The checkout lady stops on me on my way out, soured by suspicion. She checks my bags and seems somehow disappointed with my innocence. Not a thief, not carrying drugs, just a little too hot, *actually*. Stepping outside is like opening the door to a steamy oven, or hell. Flinching is useless.

60 miles later, I arrive in the very coarse city of Marseille. Cars toot, men shout, and the continuum of traffic from a multi-tiered lattice of roads, moans. Poor foreign families sheltered under motorway bridges stare at me distrustfully, eyes as dusty and sunken as the mattress they sit on. What a sad, sad place. My phone rings.

'Hello?' I answer.

'Oh hi, is this Alice Lushington?' says a nicey-nicey voice.

'Yes?'

'Hi, it's the Truro mental health team. How are you?'

'Oh! Well actually, absolutely excellent! I'm on my bike, in France!'

'Oh! That's...amazing!' says the lady. 'So would you say that you're doing better now?'

'OI! FUCK OFF! Ahem, sorry, *Men*. Let me pull over...What was I saying?...Yes! I have actually never been this better in all my life!'

The lady laughs, the professional crispness to her voice waning.

'Yep, you can go ahead and discharge me!' I say.

'If you're sure Miss Lushington?'

'Never more sure of anything, Au revoir!'

I wonder who tipped her off? Maybe it was that nice psychologist I'd been forced to see after that awful day. Anyway, what a nice emotional checkpoint. I take a deep, satisfying breath of pollution and continue deeper into the thickening smog of Marseille.

Honk number five of the hour blares in my ear. What *do* these men want!

'HEY! BEAUTIFUL!' shouts a man with three and a half teeth,

'YOU AND ME DO SEX!'

'NO, MERCI!' I yell back.

'IT WILL ONLY TAKE SEVEN MINUTES!'

Charming!

Finally, I escape Marseille and its men and arrive at my host Lois's house. A magnificent tree, heavy with sunset orange apricots, shrugs amber fruits onto the ground. I pick one up, dazzled.

'Take as many as you like,' says a voice. It's Lois. He is my age, blonde, an artist. His name and his face remind me of...No. I won't think about it. The rest of the evening proceeds as a blur.

Life has many lessons. One of them is that tinned potatoes should not ever be allowed. Another is that Nice is wonderful.

'Hey Aleece!' says Roman, opening the door to his flat.

Roman stands, true to his name: golden, strong, worshipable, looking exactly like a better version of Johnny Depp, his top loose and gaping. So is my mouth. I shut it quickly. Then Roman leans towards me and kisses my cheek.

'Je suis dégoûtant!' I squeal.

'Nut at oll.' He says, cheekiness blooming in his face, 'come up, you can meet my girlfriend.'

Girlfriend. Phew, thank goodness.

Roman goes to kiss her but she shivers him off.

'She says I'm too sweaty and disgusting' he says, shrugging, 'So Aleece, what would you like to do?' he asks, handing me a dark chocolate sandwich.

You, I think. I want to do *you.*

'NAGER!' I shout, 'Oh merci pour le sandwich, c'est un bon combination!'

'Iz good, right?' Roman giggles. 'Come on, let's goh.'

We whiz through the city: Roman's girlfriend speeding ahead while Roman and I try to work out the tandem. I'm afraid this hasn't helped my perving. Roman's sweaty back is right in front of my nose and his muscles are undulating beneath his transparent t-shirt.

We pull in, and wait for Roman's friends to arrive (four in total). But I haven't been paying attention to their names, or their gender. Basically, I'm hypnotised by Roman, his manly giggle, his agonising sexiness. All seven of us clamber over rocks then wade through the sea, carrying our bags on our heads like tribal people, giggling as the waves swell under our chins. We make it to a little cove and cheer a collective 'Eyyy!' as we dump our bags on the technicolour shingle.

'But wait! What about when the tide comes in? Won't we get stuck?' I ask.

Everybody laughs.

'Ah Aleece, zee tide ere, it does nut move like in England. It stays right zere,' says Roman. 'Come, lets swim.'

With Roman's girlfriend flouncing about in the shallows, Roman, Roman's friend Ludic and I swim out to sea, then into a cave. Sea water flaps against the walls as we rise and fall with the waves.

'You trust me?' asks Roman.

'Oui.'

'I love your accent,' he laughs, 'Okay. Come.'

Roman takes a deep breath and disappears. I take a breath and follow him underwater. Our heads surface inside a tiny, dark cave and I stare into Roman's giggling face, lit by the luminous turquoise of the sea. Our elbows brush. Maybe it's the travelling or the romantic cave or maybe it's just me, but I think I have fallen in love again. But I am rescued by the gasping head of Roman's friend Ludic, who wants to know if me and Roman want to jump off some rocks.

Dripping on the shore in the peachy late evening, we all share pretzels. Roman's girlfriend has left early, leaving the rest of us to laugh away the darkening hours, lit only by the technicolour pebbles and glossy sea borrowing their light from the moon and streetlights.

By the time we make it back to the flat, it is past 12pm.

Roman wanders into the bathroom where I am brushing my teeth. I pause and swallow mouthfull of foam.

Roman laughs, that gorgeous, throaty laugh. Ugh, I could eat him, or kill him, or...No Alice! His girlfriend is right next door.

'Let me show you a magic trick. Give me zis.' He takes my toothbrush with a 'wup!', throws it in the bin and waves a brand new one in my face. 'Look, zere we are!'

Roman's cheeky face sparkles at me, wisps of hair escaping his ponytail; the climate of slight sweat renders me woozy. But I don't let on. At least, I'm pretty sure I don't.

I sit upright in my sleeping bag, jotting things down in my little red diary, checking the map. Italy is not far. Then he the almighty God walks in, bringing with him that agonising charm.

'Bon nuit Aleece,' he whispers, leaning across me.

A great dizziness washes over me. Then, FLICK. The light switch...Of course.

The flat is quiet this morning, and I know exactly what I must do. It's impossible to face them today, not after last night's dream. I tear off a piece of toilet roll and write, in *French*:

'Sorry to leave without saying goodbye, I've many miles to do today. But thank you for everything, it was FANTASTIC. I hope we meet again. Alice. PS I had a dream last night Roman turned into a goat.'

Why would having sex with a man turn him into a goat? I think to myself as I gently close the door behind me. And if I were to sex a man into goathood, surely then I would stop? Anyway, onward. To Monaco and beyond.

Monaco is as ridiculous a place as I ever saw. A great monopoly of over-dressed snobs, strutting, determining where next to spend their excessive income. The casino? The opera? Monte-Carlo? Or, if desperate, just toss it straight in the fountain! No wait, they don't do that here. That would be too earnest, too peasant-ish.

Everybody clip-clops in shoes as shiny and important as their uppity selves. And everything is trimmed, finessed, symmetrical, unblemished: the place, though soulless, is beautiful beyond belief. Ah but that isn't quite true because there is one blemish: in the shine of one of the limousines, I catch her bruised legs spinning, her clumsily stuffed panniers, and her freckled face contorted in bewilderment.

'EY! YOU CANNUT BE ERE!'

I pretend not to hear the suited man, despite the intimidating black coil dangling from his ear.

'If you muz be ere, you cannut cycle!' He says, charging at me like a sexy and annoying rhino. 'You might scratch ze cars. You muz wulk.'

My middle finger quivers with intention, but the man is too

damn sexy to insult.

The thing about Monaco is, because everything is private (even the bloody beach), it is very difficult to escape.

'FUCK!' I yell, watching a spiky black gate close behind me, 'I HATE MONACO!'

Imprisoned like a filthy dog, I dump my ass on the tarmac and rip open my fruit compote.

'EY!' shouts a woman, strutting furiously towards me.

'QUOI?!' I yell back.

'You cannut be ere!' she snaps.

'JE SUIS PERDU!' I roar, 'YOU LOCKED ME IN!'

Eventually, deciding I was too dirty and cumbersome to remain a feature of her enormous garden, she clicks the gate open.

'Merci,' I say.

Mercy, indeed.

After all that snobbery, meeting Pete and his family is just about the best thing that could've happened. His two nieces from Madagascar have come to stay and, their spirits are so tropical, their laughter so quick to surface and so genuine, I know they're breaking my heart. Nice children always do. They do a show for me then we play Uno cross-legged and then we brush our teeth in all the strangest ways yelling, 'BROSSER LES DENTS!' and 'LAVER THE DENTS!' over and over.

The next morning, the heat urges me awake at 5.30am. Wandering over to the balcony, I can see it has done the same to Pete.

'Hi, iz beautiful, non?' he says looking from me, to his coffee cup, to the sky.

'Jeez...' I agree, staring out at the sky brewing in deep reds, throwing rusty warmth on the jumbly undulations of houses.

Pete laughs softly and takes a sip of coffee.

'Combien de kilomètres à Italie?' I ask.

Pete smiles. 'Hm... Dix?'

'Wow. So today...I'll be in Italy?'

'Oui.'

13

Italy

'ITALIE'

Just like that. One flimsy, blue sign and a couple of bored security guards: pass these and it's au revoir croissant, ciao pizza. The guards (if you can even call them that) glare at me from beneath their sunglasses. But the very sight of my curly hair and bulging panniers exhausts them, leaving them with not quite enough energy to bother asking about my passport. I cross the threshold, holding my breath.

And what do I expect? Italian accents? Flags? Deeper tans? Black hair? Moped engines spluttering impatiently? Scent trails of pizza? Twenty minutes in and I have already completed stereotype bingo. Yet I can't help but look over my shoulder and wonder if I should go back to France because, and try as I will, I can't deny this air of hostility lurking beneath the weather of garlic.

Ventimiglia. I wander into my first shop, a fruit shop, stomach crunching with hunger. But inside there exists only three things: one scowling woman, one shelf of apples for apples, one for oranges.

'Alice, that's a warning. You know oranges are banned, please take an apple next time. You only have one more warning and then you'll be taken to the upstairs dining room.'

Spooked, I put the orange back and pick up an apple. But the cashier lady throws me such a look, like I'd walked into a synagogue with a bacon sandwich, so I put that back too and go hungry. What the hell is with this place?

'Ello!' two men shout, cowering in the shade thrown by a corner shop.

I smile, pleased to have somebody to talk to and skip up to the two ragged and wild-eyed men who talk in succession:

'Can you elp us?' the shorter guy begins.

'We want to get over dere. Croz de road,' the taller guy points.

'We can't walk in de sun,'

'Iz too ot.'

The chuckle brothers point at a zebra crossing struck by a thick ribbon of sun.

'Oh. Can't you just run across to the shade quickly?' I ask.

'No. We can't do dat,' says the taller guy.

'Iz too ot,' says the smaller guy.

'Sorry, I don't know! But hey, maybe could you teach me a couple of words in Italian? I've only been here twenty minutes and I can't speak a word!'

'But why you ere? You should torn aroun an go back. Yes, go back to France cause Italianos are no good. Dey is arrogant, terrible people. Yes. Go back. Now. Iz a good idea,' says the taller guy.

The shorter guy nods in agreement, looking petrified.

Fatigued by a vastly depleted morale, empty belly and the weight of the sun, I walk my bike across the shingle of a – can this be called a beach? Not really – a coastal place, littered with cigarette butts, rags, debris. A place for some unhappy non-Italian bodies to lie on dusty pebbles, surrendering to the pounding of the sun for the sake of... What? Respite? A tan? To socialise? Nobody wants to be here (myself included) and so even though the 'beach' is busy, no one says a word. Each miserable him to each miserable self.

Alas, the sea is equally depressing: sloshing onto the shore begrudgingly – ugh, not again – bleached litter swashing about its sickly, milky-blue surface. I swim nonetheless, fully clothed because I think I have lost my bikini.

After my 'swim' (treading water, fully clothed, wishing to be somewhere else), I wander over to a distressed looking hut plonked on the shingle. Inside it, a few men are reading bad news in Times New Roman, lips pinched around miniature cups. There is just one woman in here, the barmaid. Chin sinking into her hand, shiny black ringlets tumbling down and gathering in pools on the bar, she glares at the empty space between the men. Then she glares at me and begrudgingly heaves herself upright.

'Prego,' she snaps, bright red lipstick retracting back to its unimpressed pout, matching red nail varnish tapping impatiently.

'Um...Can I have...That?' I ask, pointing at a glass cabinet of beige things.

'Questa? Foccacia?' she says.

I nod, 'Merci.'

'Un euro,' she bares her palm and looks the other way.

'Oh and um, a...' I squint at the menu above her head, '*café?..* Mer–...Th–Thank you?"

'Due euro.'

I swap a two-euro coin for a greasy bread thing wrapped in a napkin and a thimble of coffee.

To increase its volume more than anything else, I drop a sachet of sugar in the coffee, then park myself down with my weird lunch, empty belly and a chest full of sigh. Maybe I should just cut my losses and go back to France. Then a thought occurs.

'Bonjour!' Auntie Penny's voice chirps through my phone.

'Ciao!' I correct.

'Oh goodness! You're in Italy now?'

'Yes! I've accidentally fallen across the border and I don't know any Italian. I'm kind of stuffed here and instantly thought of you.'

'Have you got a pen?'

For the next five minutes I jot down a good twenty words and phrases: numbers one to five (Penny says I won't need more than five things), sorry, please, toilets, can you help, this, why, excuse me, help and (most importantly) thank you very much.

'Anyway, how do you like Italy?' asks Auntie Penny.

'Well...' I sigh, 'I've been here an hour, and everyone seems so pissed off. Like, I met these two Italians but they just told me to go back to France.'

'That's rubbish!' she laughs. 'Italians are the most friendliest people in the whole world! Just wait, you'll see.'

I look down at my notes, '*Grazie!*' I say.

'*Bene!* My pleasure. Ring me again if you need any help. Oh and by the way, we all think your amazing.'

'Pah!'

'Really! You are! Anyway, good luck!'

I put down the phone.

'The most friendliest people in the world. You'll see...'

I sink my teeth into the focaccia. Crisp salt grit pricks my taste buds, soon soothed by a basting of olive oil and then a bready flavour, as deep and resounding a pebble hitting the bottom of a well, draws through me. *'Uuuunctuous'*: with Gregg Wallace's sexy 'I'm a geezer' voice resounding in my head I lick my slick, salty lips, roll my eyes, and recline deeper into the chair, moaning. Then I take a sip of espresso. Or rather, an offensive blast of burnt toast, petrol and chocolate. I savour every, vicious, delicious sip, wincing.

I set a euro on the counter.

'Una ancora?' asks the barmaid, impressed.

'Sì, grazie!' I reply.

As she hands me my fourth consecutive focaccia, her bright red lipstick thins into a motherly smile.

'Prego,' she says.

I scoff my new favourite snack and pedal onwards. Where to? Does it matter heck! My limbs are supple from all that olive oil, my blood vibrant with sugary espresso. I charge up the cliffs, melt back down them, whizz through sepia tunnels that drip and echo, alongside beaches, more cliffs, more tunnels, more bars. Past Italians that roar, drink, chat, knock back espressos, congest ice-cream shops, smoke, swim and sunbathe, like it wasn't 2pm, like it wasn't a Monday. Italy has stolen me. It's under my nails, made translucent by olive oil; in the blush of my sunburnt cheeks; in my intestines, clogged with focaccia; the sand between my toes. A message beats in sync with my caffeinated heart: *'I'm home, I'm home, I'm home'*.

'Ciao!' a voice echoes in another sepia tunnel, followed shortly by its owner: a man cycling with one hand (his other is holding a lit cigarette).

'Ciao. Um...' I consult my hand. 'So-no ing-lese...'

'Yes I see dat,' he laughs. 'Wat are you do ere?'

I again consult my palm of blurred notes.

'Pedalare! Hey, can you teach me some Italian?'

He chuckles and takes a drag of his cigarette. 'Yes. Sure, what you wanna know?'

The smoking cyclist teaches me: 'il bagno', 'ciclista', 'dove' and 'scusami' (though he insists that in Italy you never exuse yourself or beg a pardon, you simply make demands).

'Hey dis is where I stop,' he says. 'Maybe you geev me your nuamber?'

'Grazie but...' No Alice, no more men. 'Ah, my phone doesn't entirely work all of the time,' I say.

He shrugs, lights another cigarette.

'What is your name?' he says.

'Alice.'

'Ciao, Aleechay,' he says, then pedals off, ash and smoke falling behind him.

'*A-lee-chay*. Aleechay.' I repeat, as I roll onward under a sinking sun.

An hour or so later I stop, famished, in Imperia. What a con! The only thing remotely *imperial* about this town is a refurbished McDonalds. Although to be fair, McDonalds has gotten so fancy these days: it's all 'flat whites', 'table service' and muted décor. Just ahead of the fancy McDonalds a tree, sparkling with black mulberries finds me jamming on my brakes perhaps a little too enthusiastically. My phone leaps out of its mount, flies a bit, and meets the ground with an upset clatter. I dash towards it, flinching as The Insect clatters behind me and then flinching again as I reach for my phone (well, mum's on loan), hoping to high heavens it hasn't broken.

'Hmp. Ah, bollocks.' I say to the mangled, epileptic disaster in my hands.

I tap its fractured screen a couple of times, to no avail, so I dust the sugary glass from my fingertips, stash my phone away and lean The Insect against the mulberry tree. As I step onto his crossbar and reach for the first branch, my heart flutters with friendship. Now, I'm not materialistic (I stand by that as a principle) but I would say, proudly, that I am completely in love with my bicycle: we fit as one with the satisfying latch of two magnets meeting. Downhill he carries me, uphill I carry him and on a flat we find our perfect unison. When Loic left me in the desert, he was there to carry me away and offer a mudguard to cry on. He always listens to my mad ramblings, and I listen too. To his graceful whirring, his creaks, his clunks, his operatic screech when I pull his brake levers.

Because there are fewer places more comforting than up a tree I stay for a long while, watching the sun drop behind the sea, chain-eating mulberries, wondering where on earth I might sleep tonight. With my phone smashed to smithereens, there was no hope for Couchsurfing or Warmshowers. Suppose I could camp, but where? I assess my location, watching through the lattice of branches as people start gathering around bowls of crisps. An idea.

I sidle up to the party, revising the notes on my palm one last time.

'Ahem, scusa?' I say, entering a circle of beer-drinkers.

About twelve faces look at me and I present a bag of mulberries to them. One of the men grabs a handful, says 'grazie'.

'Posso ai-ut-ar-me?' I ask. 'Sto cercando un pos- Ur...I'm looking for a place, to camp...'

'DISPIACE! NON. LO. SO. NON CAPISCO,' says one of the men, eyes wide with the effort of shouting.

A woman, suddenly inspired, grabs me by the arm and marches me to the buffet.

'Mangiare!' she demands, lifting a bowl of crisps.

I pick up one crisp.

'Sì! Mangiare, mangiare!' she insists.

The woman rushes off, leaving me squeezing a mulberry onto the crisp, but returns before I'd had the chance to eat it and says again, even more excited, 'MANGIARE! MANGIARE!' waggling a brown paper bag at me.

'Grazie.' I say.

By the time I've returned to my mulberry tree the entire party, about one hundred and twenty eyes are glinting at me.

I peer into the sandwich bag. Ugh: ham. Vegan or not, I have no idea why anyone would eat these perverted, creepy, fleshy flaps. Perhaps I can feed it to the fish. Spotting a silhouette on the dusty shingle, I instead give them to a Russian fella.

'Oh thanks, sure....' he says, tweezing the paper bag nervously, as though it contained organs.

But I mean, it could well. Who the fuck knows what they put in ham these days? Ham is pink. And so are lungs, hearts, lips and balls.

'Can I swim with you?' I ask him.

'Um...Sure...'

After an awkward swim I wish I'd never suggested, the nice Russian boy (who proves as useless a knight in shining armour as I am a damsel) wishes me luck and scurries away. The first star winks at me. Well, I guess this'll have to do. I toss Loic's sleeping bag on the jagged stones, lay my tent above it as a make-shift pillow and there we have it: a bed. I sleep naked (because it's hot), a couple of metres between my head and the lapping sea (as I have learned, the Mediterranean Sea is too lazy to have a tide).

What a night. I slept poorly, thanks to a series of unidentified screeching noises and a gang of pervy mosquitoes. Also, according to my neck, using a tent as a pillow was a terrible idea: I feel like a giraffe on a long-haul flight (Loic? Loic who?). Naked, sunburnt, hair twisted in salty knots like an unwatered Pot Noodle, I crawl out of my packet. Sticky beige things are usually great (donuts, cake, jam tarts), but not this sticky beige thing. Yet I feel rather pleased with myself.

Dragging the mess that is I into a café, I order a coffee and a slice of focaccia (then another), take my phone out, set it on the table, go 'hm' and switch it on. It panics the same as before, flashing green, white, pink. After shaking it, hitting it, swearing at it, speaking to it very nicely, I resort to my instincts and ignoring the mild electric shock and distinct feelings of guilt, I stick my licked finger in the cracked hole of its screen. One more flash, then it magically settles itself. Fixed! I look left, look right. Did anyone see that? Brilliant! Although, I do feel like a bit of a sexual predator.

Admin time. I log onto warmshowers.org and send a message to a guy called Pietro politely requesting a place to clean my once crisp, then floppy, now rigid, socks. He replies 'Yes but I no speak English'. Next I penetrate the many sockets of the café with electricals, then I skip into the toilets, brush my teeth, flash myself (one tit bigger than the other, as per), and scrub the cog stains off my calves (even though I quite like them). Two euros well spent. Now for a shopping mission. God bless those European supermarkets with their lack of staff and strange systems of weighing things. I exit with a box of chocolate covered dates. Bad idea: I eat them all. Round two: I pass the dates, the crisps, the bread, the jam, the biscuits, anything within the category of 'cor, go on then' and pick up two much more sensible things. Some of us souls cannot have our cake and eat it. Some of us must eat tinned beans and dusty muesli.

The sea keeps me company all day as I twist up and down Liguria's cliffs and mountains, the smooth roads yielding beneath my tyres as if it were they, not my wheels, that spun. Fifty miles of hilly glory check-pointed by fully-clothed runs into the sea, Italian note taking (I can now say 'strabiliante', 'campeggio' and 'quanto'), intestinal-clotting focaccia sessions and intestinal-loosening espresso sipping.

Pietro acts strangely upon my arrival in Celle Ligure, kissing my cheeks nervously, then dragging me about with much head-scratching bewilderment apparently looking for somewhere to put me. The kitchen? The living room? On a deck chair? In the end, he chooses a ledge on the patio. Which is unfortunate because to get to the dining area (which the strange pick'n'mix of hovering characters seem to suddenly want to do), they have to pass my ledge of shame.

First of the torrent of weirdos is a bald guy who pauses, hands on hips, looks down the length of his nose at me and says, 'So Pietro say you're vegan. Does dis mean you look at us like we a piece a sheet?'

'No! Not at all!' I say.

Second in the spurning line, a distinctly non-Italian, porcelain-skinned woman brushes past, squinting at me. Then her toddler, who copies her. A couple walk by but are so dizzy in love, they miss my existence completely. Lastly, and worst of all, a lollipop of a woman: skinny, high-heeled and pregnant. She, actually cringes. And all the while a very nervous Pietro runs back and forth with rice. Honestly, I have no idea who on earth all these people are but oh Christ, my leg is bleeding.

Noticing my predicament, Pietro scoops me up and drives me into the house, down the stairs and into an impressively regal-looking room with an emperor bed thickly layered in emerald green sheets and far too many cushions. Stacked neatly on its edge are a collection of fluffy white towels for every occasion imaginable. Because *of course*, this is an en suite. What a bizarre upgrade from my miserable ledge! What to do first? Eat? Charge things? Shower? Plan tomorrow? Roll my sticky self up in the sheets like a really disgusting jam roly-poly? I check my broken phone: still working and with a text, from Becky.

'Alice. We're coming out to see you, me and Carol. Can you be in Genoa by Thursday?'

I reply 'OMG OMG OMG REALLY? YES!'

Floomp: I face plant the bed and writhe with joy. This will be the second-best thing those two flower-power women have ever done for me, though they're probably not aware of the first.

Carol's singsong laugh and Becky's endless technicoloured outfits appeared in my life thanks to a leaflet that landed in my lap on my 19th birthday. It read 'Hailsham Vegans meet up May 25th'. And there was me thinking I was the only vegan in the village (though Hailsham is technically a town, ten miles from home). Attending was a big deal to me because I had a dwindled number of friends after hospital and because to me, food was still to do with guilt, denial, excess, control and anxiety. But in I went regardless, parking my nervous skinny butt on a table of twelve others. It worked better than I could've imagined: yoga with Carol, brunch with Becky, skinny dips with Dave, bike rides with other Dave, pub nights with Liz. We even went on holiday to a haunted house that one time! Forget they're twice my age, they might well be the reason I'm alive (albeit kicking and screaming sometimes).

Grey liquid swirls down the shower's plughole as I do a joyful stamping dance on my socks. Note to self: must learn the word for 'dirty' in Italian. Now for dinner. Remember that bland bag of muesli I bought? Well, here I am eating it. All 500g of it, face-planting fistfuls upon fistfuls of the stuff like a horse. No, a donkey.

An oat. On the pillow next to me, lit by morning. I eat it, then sidle into the kitchen gearing myself up for an awkward goodbye. Pietro and his bald friend who made that vegan comment stand in the kitchen, crossed-armed, leaning against the counter.

'Buongiorno,' says Pietro, uncrossing his arms then handing me a slice of focaccia, 'ti piace?'

'GRAZIE! Foccacia is my favourite thing ever-ever-ever!' I say.

His bald friend smiles cheekily at me and says, 'I'm sorry for yesterday. We all look at you like you a piece of sheet.' He puts his hand on his heart, 'It no very kind of us.'

'Ah, no problem,' I chuckle, cheeks muffled by focaccia. 'But who were those people?'

'You don't know? You don't know dis is a B'n'B?' says Baldy.

'OH! Riiight, I was wondering.'

'By de way you left blod were you seet yesterday.' Baldy starts to laugh, 'You no wanna know what dey tink.'

I was about to defend myself and point at my leg, the culprit, but Baldy continues, 'So dese are de famous socks?' he points at my feet. 'You're right, dey disgusting.'

I was then about to defend my socks which I'd very expertly cleaned with shampoo, but–

'You like boats? I tink you come on my boat. Yez? We go on my motorbike. Yes, lez go.'

As instructed, I pull the helmet over my head, hop aboard and grab on for dear life. A ripping noise tears through us and after many months languishing at 10.2mph (my average speed), the experience of riding on Baldy's motorbike was like being catapulted.

We eventually pull into the harbour. Furiously excited by the whole shebang of whipping up and down the cliffs, I hop off, de-helmet, and leap up and down, whooping. But I lose my footing, and crash into Baldy.

'YOU FOOL! YOU CUD AVE KEELD ME!' he shouts. Then he says, 'Lez get a drink.'

Into the bar, he grabs two bottles of water and two cartons.

Baldy slumps under a sliver of shade and hangs his head. He keeps it hung as he passes me a carton of juice. Oh no.

'Grazie,' I say.

My stomach twists into a hard knot.

Me and my fellow inmates had always considered her a kind of evil villain, which perfectly fitted her neat silver hair and pursuit of stalking.

'Alice?' She's found me. 'Can you come into my office?'

Damn you Yvonne. And damn the curtain fitter who left the bottom end suspended above the carpet, exposing my odd socks.

'Fine,' I exhale, stepping out from behind the curtain.

The other girls throw me sympathetic looks as I follow Yvonne into her lair: another carpeted room, conveniently situated on the ground floor (not that we could jump out of the locked windows anyway). The nervous sweat of her last victim is still lingering in the air.

'Okaaaay...' says Yvonne, clicking and tapping on the computer. Up pops my diet plan. Fucking hell, it doesn't even fit on one page. 'You're due an increase. How about we add another juice to every meal?'

'But I'm already on five cups! That's...God, that's a whole litre!' I say.

'Yes. But your BMI is still very low and your weight this morning hasn't changed since last week.'

'Yeah well, I'm fat enough anyway.' I drop my head into my hands and start to bawl. 'The fattest one in here.'

Yvonne carries on clicking and tapping, obviously used to (and bored of) this sort of thing. The printer chugs, spits out my new fate: three more cups of juice and another bowl of bran flakes at breakfast. That brings me to 3,700 daily calories.

When I leave this place, I will never, ever drink juice again.

'It's so facking ot,' says Baldy. He takes a long, crackling slurp of juice, then continues, 'Too facking 'ot.'

I stare at my straw, mangled by anxious gnawing – deep breath – then take a cautious slurp. A sweet, sharp, cool rush of pear gristle slips down my throat. I pause, I smile, I finish the carton.

'Let's go,' says Baldy, crunching the empty carton in his hand.

This does not make him look tough, or cool.

A racket like a blender full of nails blares from the boat's engine, completely in vain. Noisy and hot, without really getting anywhere:

like man, like boat.

'DIS IS GREAT NO? EY! NO SHOES ON DE BOAT' yells Baldy over the engine.

He whips off his shirt, revealing a slack chest the colour and shape of a walnut and I kick off my shoes. After a full hour of ear-blistering racket Baldy finally turns the engine off, pulls the ropes and we 'sail'. Or rather, we drift aimlessly out to sea.

'Look at dese,' he says, pulling my pink socks off my feet. 'Dey are *dizgusting!*'

'Ha, like me— OI!' I quickly peer over the side of the boat. 'Those were my only socks!' I yell, watching my two pink socks sink into a turquoise oblivion.

'I am sorry but you can't wear dem. DEY TOO DISGUSTING. I will buy you new socks. I promiz,' he says.

'It's alright. Oh, by the way, who was that pregnant lady from yesterday?'

'Oh, dat bitch is Pietro's wife. She look to you like you a piece of sheet, no? Pietro wants to be like me, without a wife and without kids. I am 'appier. I don't need no family. I am like you...' he pauses for dramatic effect as the boat slowly drifts a little further out to sea, 'Wild.'

A while later, we drive the boat to shore to pick up Pietro, who looks so confidently buoyant that at first, I don't recognise him. Perhaps his wife really is a bitch: he so suits her absence.

The afternoon whittles away with ease: me, Baldy and Pietro, three unlikely musketeers, diving off the boat, laughing, guzzling blueberries far out at sea. Then we head back to land and Pietro buys us falafels. Baldy rebuffs them, saying he's not hungry but occupies himself by dousing my dinner with olive oil, salt, pepper, vinegar, ketch- I start to scream.

Ketchup. Ugh. Even the word tastes sour to speak. The flatulent noise as it is ejaculated onto food, the smear on plates, the sickly tang that intrudes the noses of even we who refuse to eat it, its arrogant presence on tables, its stale-blood colour: that godforsaken squelching matter seems to have haunted my whole life.

'Sorry, I just...hate ketchup.'

To my utter amazement, Baldy shuts the hell up, puts the ketchup down and behaves himself, for the first time all day.

After lunch Baldy says, 'I gunna go back. See you guys at the B'n'B. Oh, Pietro, if you buy er socks, dey mus be pink!' He dashes off still shouting, 'IZ VERY IMPORTANT DAT DEY ARE PINK!'

As the bus quietly bumps me and Pietro back to Celle Ligure I turn to Pietro and say, 'Grazie mille Pietro.'

'No,' he says, glossy-eyed, 'No Grazie. You are here and you are *you*. You always smiling an dat is enough. You not to say tank you.'

I smile at him then stare out the window, repressing the tears.

Off the bus we amble up to the cliff top, pushing on our burning thighs.

'I sorry,' says Pietro, taking off his shirt. 'I like to be nude.'

'Hey, it's no problem. And me too, it's freeing! I actually did a naked bike ride a couple of years ago for charity, it was great fun.'

'Wow Aleechay, dat so brave and so free. Cool. Hey, you'll stay again tonight, sì?'

'Sure.'

At the top of the hill, Baldy is waiting for us, grinning wickedly.

'Iz forre you,' he says, dumping a pink bundle in my arms. Eight pairs of socks. Light pink ones, dark pink ones, thick ones, thin ones and one bonus item: a pair of frilly pink knickers.

'To match your socks,' Baldy winks.

'I *love* them!' I say, admiring my one and only pair of pants.

'Do you want to come out for another ride on my motto, to get some drugs?'

So that was my day: juice, boat rides, pants, and a drug pick up in the indigo of twilight. Not bad.

It's today: the day of Carol and Becky. Dare I believe it? Not yet. Anyway, my head is so full of Pietro, of the tearful, two-minute, goodbye hug he'd given me. The way Baldy had smiled over his shoulder and said *'you will come back, yes?'*. And the way I'd nodded, knowing in my heart of hearts that I'd never see them again.

'Una focaccia e un caffè, grazie,' The sound rolls off my lips naturally, as if a breath or a sigh, as if I had always said 'focaccia' and 'caffè'.

Bum to chair, focaccia turning the napkin into a stained glass window, espresso with its thick, creamy top, my new routine: scribble new words, sip espresso, and dunk the focaccia in it. This was my third time, but felt as familiar as the nine-hundredth. There is something so right about it all.

Grabbing me by the heart strings, music pours out of the radio. English music. The Verve, 'Bitter sweet symphony'. I start to shake, fat tears plonking in my espresso, soaking my focaccia. Not a nice, graceful, steady stream of tears but a demented eruption, rendering the whole café uncomfortable.

50 miles later, the claustrophobic battle of Genoa's narrow and congested streets springs up in front of my eyes. The cars and footfall and noise and ever-ignored red lights thicken the hot air, which is sticky in the mouth and lungs. And here we are: the station.

Sticking out like two strawberries in a packet of crisps: Becky hauling an enormous suitcase, Carol clutching the padded straps of her backpack. I start to bawl again.

'Alice!' says Becky.

'Oh Alice,' says Carol.

'Sorry...It's um. PHEW,' I sniff, 'an emotional day. I'm just so happy to see you.'

Becky sits down next to me and Carol in the cafe, 'You look great Alice, really happy,' she says, handing us our ice-creams.

'I am.' I lick my ice cream, 'The best I've been in a long time. I'm... *better*.'

Becky smiles, knowing full well the extent of 'better'.

'And guys, thanks so much for coming. You're the best friends ever. I don't believe it. I just don't believe it.'

'Pft, we just flew here, you bloomin' well cycled!' chirps Carol.

'I don't think you're destined to stay in one place, Alice. Umm...' Becky looks around, 'do you think there is anywhere we could buy some crisps and Chardonnay?'

Back at the apartment, Becky hands me a steaming cup. Stiff hugs, newspapers, Saturday afternoons, oak trees, *unbelievable* weather, Radio: these flash through me one after the other.

'Ahhhhh,' I sigh. 'Bringing the teabags was a really great idea.'

Carol giggles and we three vegan witches clink cups.

'You know, it was hilarious seeing you guys at the station. Carol, you've packed so frugally, and Becky, *Jesus*, you've brought your whole bloody house!' I say pointing to the pink elephant in the room.

'I know! But choosing my clothes was like asking me to choose between my children!'

'But you hate kids!'

'Ugh! Yes.' Becky shudders. 'Horrible things. Oh, I almost forgot, here, this is for you' Becky lands an envelope in my lap titled 'Alice' in Dad's capital handwriting.

Inside the envelope is a note from everyone: Mum, Dad, Billy, Louis, Joel. Telling me they're proud, amazed, rooting for me. My tear ducts yet again spring into action.

Me, Carol and Becky: the three vegan witches spend the day at the beach, fuelling our incessant chatter with focaccia and ice creams. By night time we are collapsed in chairs awaiting pasta.

'Cheers!' we yell, clinking glasses (Becky and Carol's full of wine and mine of sparkling).

We eat our pasta and chat, though I'm not aware of quite what. I'm too engrossed in this feeling of staring into the faces of home and realising I feel no urge to go back.

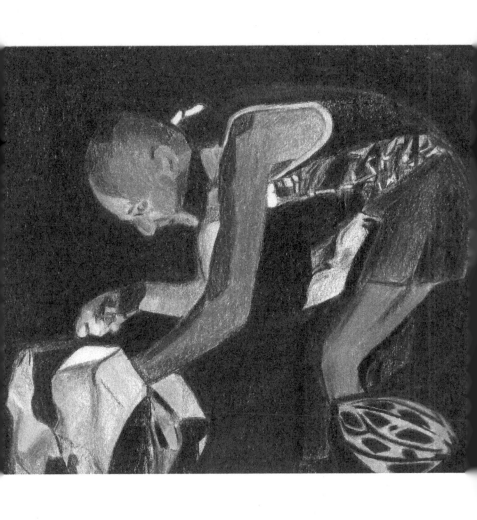

14

Happy Aaron and the carrot

'Have you got any baked beans?' Becky had asked this morning when we sat down to a goodbye breakfast. And though our final group hug was hours ago, I still find myself laughing at the thought. But a voice interrupts my daydream.

'ARE YOU MARRIED?'

'Huh?' I say, turning around.

'ARE YOU MARRIED?' the sweaty blob on wheels yells again.

'Um,' I take a quick glimpse at his shiny face, now at my side, 'No.'

Pedalling with suspicious ease, the man foists a cornetto at me.

'EY!' he insists.

'No thanks,' I return, confused as to where the ice cream had come from and why it hadn't melted.

'You all alone. I elp you–'

'NO! NO, THANK YOU!'

The audacity! How dare his fingers brush my ass, moreover, how *dare* he touch The Insect.

'Okaye. Bai.' He lets go of my saddle and carries on ahead, suckling his cornetto.

As the electrical whir of his bicycle recedes and his blobby silhouette shrinks up the mountain I start to cry. Not about the man, or even about Becky and Carol. Just crying for the sake of mountains, standing forever big and agonisingly beautiful.

But all this mountain and all this bawling has its consequence: I realise mid 'Ciao' as my host Georgia approaches that I haven't got much voice left, just the ragged wheeze of a winded Phil Mitchell.

'Are you tired? Your voice sounds bad.' says Georgia.

I nod, gripping my sore throat.

'You must rest, de forst ting to go when you're too exhausted iz de troat. Ere, come meet the guys. Dey work for me, Wooffing. We are making my uncle's old ouse into a yoga retreat B'n'B. Ah, dere dey are,' she gestures behind her as a couple of men emerge from the garden, muddy and sweaty.

'Hello! Nice to meet you, I'm Shayan,' says a pale man, sticking out a rigid hand.

English, oh so very English: the clammy handshake, the fleshy complexion, the charming irregular teeth, the foreboding sense of apology. God! I just want to projectile-cry into his lovely self-conscious face. I think I love him.

'Oh! And this is Aaron,' says Shayan, shifting politely to one side.

'Ello! I am a cyclist like you!' says Aaron. 'I cycle from Milano. Georgia say a cyclist iz coming an I wait for you, to meet you. Where are you go to next?'

Aaron's eyes are a scorching blue, fiercer than a gas flame. He has no hair, and no body fat, both blasted away by his sheer voltage.

'Maybe...' I think for a moment, where *am* I going? 'Rome?'

'OH MAI GOD! ME TOO!' Aaron bursts, 'We go togetter to Roma. I teach you Italiano, you teach me Engleesh. Iz perfecto!'

'Tandem learning!' says Georgia.

'Oh!' I croak, 'Right, yeah.'

An hour or so later we congregate around a long oak table in a stone-floored kitchen. We being Georgia, Shayan, Aaron and about ten other faces. Some Spanish, some Italian, young, old, boys, girls. Apparently I've met them all, but I don't recall: it is very hard to think or remember anything beyond the coarse agony of my throat. One of the faces though, the unquenchably jolly Sebastian, is impossible to overlook because he keeps laughing at nothing at all. Hands permanently clasped in interesting shapes, face unable to settle, Sebastian has a very enchanting type of special needs that I can't quite put my finger on.

'Ere, you will need it.' says Georgia, insisting I take more chickpeas, 'for strength.'

'Grazie. I eat so much these days' I croak, 'it's day four and I've eaten *nine* pieces of focaccia!'

Everybody laughs, Aaron especially.

'Me too. I eat so much with bicycol. We are de same,' he says, snogging a greasy chicken wing. He looks up at me. 'I know you are vegan, but my *God*, dis meat is so good!'

I stare at the meaty, orange lip-gloss circling his grin, trying to work out if I was okay about accidentally adopting him.

'Oh, don't worry, leave that,' he says, as Georgia starts clearing plates, 'me an Aleechay can wash up.'

A little resentment twangs in my gut. Wash up? My head is too heavy on my shoulders, my throat too raw, my brain too fogged, to *wash up*. Aaron washes, and I dry, firing aggressive thoughts to the back of his head about how unfair it was, about how, *actually*, I never wanted to adopt him anyway. These thoughts are cast aside, however, as soon as the first twinkling strum of a guitar silences the room.

'Look! He's going to sing,' Aaron whispers, gliding a sponge over a greasy plate, nodding at the Spanish guy, 'E make me crai when e sing. I crai a lot on bicycle.'

'Me too! I cried into my focaccia today!' I hiss, throat suddenly a little springier.

Aaron laughs.

'Aleechay.' He shoots me those flaming blue eyes. 'We are going to ave fun.'

Maybe Aaron is right.

The next morning, I wake up and nobody is around. Every single room: empty. Except for the kitchen, where Georgia stands, looking surprised.

'Ch-' I begin, but nothing comes out but rasping.

'Aleechay, your troat! Iz worse! An you sleeped so long dat you miss yoga! Ere, take dis for your troat.' Georgia hands me a mug billowing with citrus clouds. 'An ere take some pano and marmelada.'

'Mar-me-la-da.' I repeat, spreading the jam onto a slice of bread. Aaron skips into the room, 'Morning!' he says, 'What time you want to go today Aleechay?'

'Now?' I say.

'REALLY? But iz so ot! I normally only cycol in de evening. But okay, lez go den!'

Our smiles grow wide outside as we admire our steeds, side by side.

'Wow. Look. Dey are de same!' Aaron laughs.

And he's right. Our bikes, both hilariously haphazard, could well be long lost siblings. Mine with its bulging panniers and sock-bunting (my laundry) and Aaron's, with its also bulging panniers, and clumsily attached bin bag (he says it contains a tent). He is definitely no Loic. Although, I really ought to singe that French boy from my memory, to spare myself all the little heart-attacks of remembering his big green eyes and fluffy hair.

'Aaron!' I croak over the whir of our wheels, ten miles in.

'Yez?' he says.

'How do you say 'hungry' in Italian?'

'FA-MAY.'

'Aaron I am FA-MAY.'

Aaron laughs, 'Me too, we stop at de next supermarket, yes?'

Foreign supermarkets are the dream. Forget the fact their one and only staff member doesn't like you by default and won't therefore show you to the 'marmelada'. Forget the flies, the complicated weighing systems, the narrow aisles, the non-existence of very normal foods like peanut butter and brown rice. Ignore all that, because they are cheap, novel, and the food, unlike the uniform, sci-fi specimens of home, is real.

'Look!' Aaron points to a bunch of carrots, proper ones, muddy and long, a mass of green foliage exploding from their heads. 'Iz you Aleechay! All skinny an tan an all dat corly har. You such an appy, strong carrot.'

After sharing 'Blimey, the best apricots ever!' and 'de best bread in de world wit de best jam ever dat is too expensive', we hit the beach.

'In England,' I say as we plonk our bags between a monopoly of sun beds either side, 'there is basically no such thing as a private beach. I just don't understand why there are so many here.'

'Iz terrible! No? So many, many privata beach here. Some people, all dey care about is monay.' Aaron dips his first toe in the water, 'Ahhhh, dat is better. De sun is so ard today!'

Leaving Aaron to relax in the shallows I swim further out, enough so his golden head is a mere dot, then yet further still, racing towards a blue oblivion until I can't see him at all. Not because I want to be away from him; a little perspective, that's all. Maybe Aaron doesn't exist; maybe it's just me and The Insect: the dream team. A horribly delicious thought.

Back at shore, Aaron and I lie belly first in the miniature pebbles, propped up on our elbows, cool waves lapping over our sun-burnt backs. Aaron laughs as I make a pillow from the technicoloured beach gravel and sink my chin into it. Then I laugh as he scoops himself an even bigger pebbled pillow and bits of technicolour gravel stick to his face. Like babies with bath foam, we play like this a long while, digging, scooping, pouring, communicating in soft laughter.

'I don't think we're gunna make it to Levanto today,' I say to Aaron, scooping pebbles in my toes and catapulting them onto my back.

Aaron laughs. 'No, Aleechay. I no tink we will.'

It becomes apparent as the day goes on, the sun beating harder, Liguria's mountains rising in front of us, that travelling with Aaron is a brilliant mistake. Everything is fun and everything calls for a whoop, despite the ever-worsening scrape of my throat. Aaron teaches me *macchina, sogno, stella, cielo, cibo,* and our favourite: *'siamo liberi'* (we are free), which we shout at every bend in the hairpin road. Up and up and up: the scenery is so excruciatingly beautiful, Aaron and I actually scream. We scream at the freckling of towns which had seemed so enormous a few hours ago and we scream at the graceful carves of green and purple mountain, going on forever and then abruptly stopping at the glassy plane of sea. The whole thing is wonderful torture.

Aaron and I stop at the tip-top, to jump for joy, then fly back down to sea level, eyes streaming, cool wind pouring over our tired limbs. Our excitable cheers, however, diminish at a sign. A sign I'd seen the likes of before.

'De man, e say dat de tunnel is maybe seven or ten kilometre, an we ave ten minuti before de cars come from de otter side,' says Aaron.

'So...' I say, staring into the mustard mist of the one-way tunnel, 'We just have to go, really quick?'

'Yes. Very quick. When dat clock say go, we wait until oll de cars are in de tunnel, den we go, so fast. Before de car come from de otter side'

'Siamo forte' I say, squinting at our mission.

'Ha! Yes, Aleecahy. Siamo forti,' he corrects, 'Do you ave lights?'

'No.'

'Okay Aleechay, when the light go green we go very, very quick...'

We wait. First for the clock to tick all the way down to '0.00' then for the impatient queue of traffic to funnel into the narrow tunnel. The last car disappears, and Aaron screams, 'GO, GO, GO!'

The clock warned us on our way in that we had 8 minutes and fifty-eight seconds to make it, though I'm sure nine minutes of arched bricks and pollution have zipped by. If a car comes the other side, that's it: kaput. Because the tunnel is so narrow that there would be no room to cower and so dark that the cars would only see our panicked faces too late. An enormous groan floods through the tunnel and a faint light blooms ahead of us, lighting the bricks. Fuck. Suddenly, a shard of light pierces the right side of the tunnel.

'ERE! GO ERE, QUICK!' shouts Aaron.

We swerve right, out of the tunnel to a checkpoint. Just in time for a great WHOOSH-WHOOSH-WHOOSH, of cars to paint the tunnel.

'Blimey,' I say, staring at the blur of speeding traffic.

'Oh mai God,' Aaron agrees.

'EY! You wan play some golf?' asks a guy stood behind us.

I turn around, confused by the glitzy 'MINIGOLF' sign going on. Minigolf? Who the hell is going to play minigolf here, stranded at a tunnel checkpoint? Italy is so bizarre.

'No, grazie,' says Aaron, calmly as if this were a very normal thing indeed.

The last car whooshes and we complete the remaining 2km of tunnel.

Wild on the adrenaline of the perilous tunnel, Aaron and I trample through a corner shop, filling the tiny aisles with our loud voices.

'I love these! Sesamo!' Aaron beams, gathering fistfuls of sesame snaps.

'Yeah! Sesomo, sesamo! I eat all the sesamo!' I agree, grabbing more.

Bum to gravel we munch our sesamo snacks with all the gleeful ease of young siblings.

'What the hell is that?' I ask.

'Ah, dey Goji berry Aleechay, you wanna try?'

Aaron chuckles at my crinkled face as I chew the bitter, salty, soapy specimen (they taste as they look: like earwax), then goes to put our litter in the bin. But he hesitates, hovering above me as I eat my yogurt with a fork.

'Aleechay... You are de strongest girl in de world.'

Watery-eyed, Aaron ruffles my hair: a platonic gesture, I'm sure. Although the way he looks at me from the bin is unnerving.

It's dark. And we are still pedalling. Our second, third, fourth wind had kept us so enthused we hadn't really noticed the sinking sun. No doubt the view is astonishing, as we have been climbing a good few hours, if only we could see it. But the night has erased everything but a twinkling cluster, a town, perhaps. We bomb down towards it, a black wind combing my hair and probably running like water over Aaron's scalp, I imagine. The cluster is Levanto.

'We made it!' I croak.

'Woo-woo! Aleechay! You are so strong! Te strongest girl in de wurld. Even hours we climb and you always smiling. Hey, watch this,' Aaron unhooks his panniers and tosses them over the railings onto the beach, 'BAI, BAI!'

They land on the beach fifty feet later with a duff.

'Yeah! Let me try! HUP!' I toss mine too. And we laugh and laugh and laugh our way down the steps to the sand.

10:40pm. Aaron cooks pasta on his gas stove which, lit only by a tiny haze, rumbles dark and glossy like a saucepan of oil. We season the pasta with crushed Taralli biscuits, then dump our heads on the sand.

Sleeping on sand is great. Though it infiltrates every intimate nook and cranny, it's soft as icing sugar and pleasingly infinite. Aaron's eyes ping open, even bluer somehow.

'Do you think I can go buy a focaccia? *Ho fame.*' I say, voice still croaky.

'Aleechay, iz too orly for focaccia!' Aaron laughs. He closes his eyes then sings, '*Wake me up, when focaccia's done...*'

Aaron was right. But the man at the bar says he can have it ready in '*vente*' minutes, which I'm hoping means less than five.

A while later, I return with one espresso (it looks so funny in its takeaway cup complete with a lid) and two focaccia.

'Tadaa!' I sing tossing a focaccia on Aaron's sleeping bag.

'Tank you,' he says, unfolding himself, wincing.

'Are you okay?'

'Um...Just my legs a beet stiff. But after stretch dey will be strong. You no stretch after oll de mountain Aleechay?'

'Naaah,' I say, voice muffled by focaccia.

After focaccia, Aaron cooks us a bonus breakfast of porridge, 'for de bad troat.' I eat it and thank him, even though that whole knob of ginger he'd seasoned it with made it taste like a burned down charity shop.

'Such a strong carrot...' Aaron mutters as I lick the spoon clean. He gives me a strange look, the sort of look you might give the last biscuit: a savouring look.

Two hours we've been pedalling and my legs still make no fuss against the strain of mountain. Strain, though, does not seem the right word. Not when mine and Aaron's spirits are so light and the drop of the precipice we've earned is so thrillingly vast. My still ruined throat does nothing to deter from whooping. Until that is, we happen across a woman, crying madly into her hands.

'Er boyfriend an er ad an argument, so ee leave er behind,' Aaron whispers as the weeping woman presses buttons on Aaron's phone. Then a car pulls in, which must be her boyfriend because after a brief exchange of angry squints, she hops in and they drive off. I look at Aaron as the sound of the engine diminishes.

'Oh dear!' I say.

'Sì!' he returns.

We shrug it off, do a few excitable jumps then continue climbing.

Apart from the slow ticking noise of bicycle wheel and the odd excitable exclamation from me and Aaron, which are now becoming more like small gasps, it is startlingly quiet up here.

Olive trees rib the cliffside, row after fluffy row, the odd backpacker meandering peacefully alongside them. And way down below, next to the sea, as severe a blue as possible and infinite in its lake like stillness, a perfect ripple of red, yellow, blue and white buildings.

'IZ DE CINQUE TERRE!' yells Aarron.

'THE WHAT?' I yell back.

Aaron explains that the Cinque Terre are a set of five historical villages strung along the Italian Riviera. We sail above each of the five villages, huddled and clambering in tiny pockets. There is just something about seeing an entire village from an aerial view, looking so harmlessly miniature that breaks my damn heart. This place is so different from the bustling, vigorous Italy I'd come to know. It's almost too much, the severity of peace, the overbearing mass of the sky, the neat rows of olive trees, the charm of the- HONK. HONK-HONK-HONK.

'WOO WOO!' yells Aaron, again squeezing the red balloon of his horn, looking over his shoulder at me.

Then again: HONK-HONK-HONK-HONK.

A couple of hours of climbing pass us by, check-pointed every ten minutes or so with a definitely-not-annoying honk from Aaron's red horn followed up by another last-biscuit smile thrown over his shoulder. Meanwhile, I am denying myself a thought. A thought so detestable, I keep spurring really loud thoughts like '*WOW I LOVE ITALY*' and '*OH MY GOSH I WONDER HOW MANY CALORIES ARE IN FOCACCIA*' and '*AARON IS SO NICE, ISN'T AARON SO NICE?*'. But still, the thought slips underneath, gentle but unmistakable: '*I have to leave Aaron behind*'.

It doesn't seem fair. Why should I have to say goodbye to Aaron? I *like* Aaron. Stupid thoughts, stupid, horrible thoughts.

'You arre so strong,' says Aaron. *Again*. 'De strongest gurl in de world. We climb up, up, up and oll de time I look, you are smiling. You arre so strong, so smiling.'

I don't feel strong. I feel upset. A crumbling husk, a fraud. Oh how I wish Aaron would stop banging on about how strong I am.

'Olways wit smile,' he continues. 'Hey Aleechay, you olways like dis? Dis appy? Olways?'

I can't remember why I did it, whether I planned it, what I hoped would happen. My blood seems to be hot and curdling: too late now.

It all started as a fun game, I think. Did it? Wait in queue for your miniature paper cup, take the multivitamin first, open mouth wide to the nurse, then the Mirtazapine, open mouth wide to the nurse, then briskly (but not too briskly) walk to your room before the latter pill melts under your tongue –oh wait it's locked. Tuck it in the bra for later. A sly smile.

As the weeks went by my sequinned purse, tucked stealthily in my pants drawer, began to bulge with my collection. It was then more than a game. My 'just in case', my secret, my...something. I sure as hell wasn't getting out of here anytime soon, not after the sock incident, and I'd been dumped, so I needed a 'something'.

But now it's done. The staff have no idea what's gotten into me, why I'm behaving myself, why my skin is yellow, why (much to the bemusement of my fellow inmates) my head is in my dinner, why my legs and arms are completely flaccid, why I'm –fuck I'm gunna be sick.

I heave and heave and heave into the bin, HCAs gathering around me whispering things like 'sickness bug?'. Sorry Mum, Dad, but I'm going to die in here, and that's just fine.

Aaron's eyes seem to pierce more than ever, so I look away.

'Sì,' I lie.

15

Cold porridge

Cheerful but depleted, Aaron and I laugh our way around a supermarket, tossing pasta, beans and carrots into a miniature shopping trolley. Dinner sorted, we then weave through the many tourists of La Spezia, park up our bikes, and plonk ourselves in the sea. However, being much less generous than the enormous zone reserved for yachts, and heaving with tourists the 'swim zone' proves a bit of a bumper-car mission. For someone like me who likes to swim underwater this is a nightmare. But I do it anyway, to wash away the sour words beating through me *'Aaron go away, Aaron go away, Aaron go away.'* All the while that lovely boy floats on his back, smiling at his fate. I must be the worst person in the whole world because this bothers me.

The pot of pasta that we've set up on the rocks bubbles away as easily as the chit-chat between us. His funky accent makes everything sound poetic and beautiful and his laugh is so true and so ready, you can see it in his mouth and eyes basically all the time. In my heart of hearts, I love him. But not like that, not like the last biscuit.

'Ah! Aleechay! I find us a place to sleep tomorrow! In Lucca wit my–' Aaron stops to laugh and puts a hand on my shoulder, 'wit my friend. Ee cook and let us stay an ave shower.'

'That's great,' I say.

'Oh!' Aaron laughs, 'Aleechay!'

Aaron is touched. He thinks I'm crying because of some kind of relief. But the exact opposite is true. Falling asleep is difficult tonight; I feel trapped.

'Morning,' says Aaron, snivelling. 'You sleeped gud?'

'Molto bene. Are you okay?'

'Yeah,' he sniffs. 'Iz juz... look!' Aaron shows me the screen of his phone: a picture of me, sleeping. 'It make my crai. You look so niace. So appy.'

Uh oh.

You can smell the anticipation, of something unsaid, pending, overdue. An air dense with too much to say and a voltage looming in the heavy clouds above our heads.

'Arre you okay Aleechay?'

'Sì. But my stomach doesn't feel good. I feel... a bit sick...'

The dark and static sky begins to rumble. A fat drop of rain lands on my forehead.

'Quick, lez go ere,' says Aaron, swerving right.

Ducked under the shelter of a grim-looking petrol station (a really grim one, it doesn't even have a shop) he asks me again, 'Aleechay, are you okay?'

Suddenly, the heavens bust open. Raindrops clang around us so noisily, they almost completely obscure the sound of my weeping.

'Aleechay!'

I can feel him want to put a hand on my shoulder but Aaron, feeling my prickling overwhelm, does not.

'God...I'm so sorry,' I say. 'It's just...I think I need to travel on my own.'

Aaron says nothing.

I continue, staring into the blurred shapes of my anxious fingers, 'I don't know why, but I know I have to be on my own. And God, you are just the best person in the world to travel with. But you see, back home in England, I'm anxious, and...poorly. Maybe this is why I am here, because I have something to fix. And I'm getting better, every day, all the time. But it's not done.'

Aaron starts to cry.

'I understand you Aleechay.' Aaron pauses for breath. 'Because when I was twenty-two like you, I was de same. An so I make travel alone. But now I am twenty-forre and I want to travel wit you. You are de strongest girl in de world and I am so, *so* appy to meet you. But I know what you feel like, I do.'

He sniffs. I sniff. We laugh.

'I will miss you,' I say.

'I will miss you so mauch.' Aaron chuckles at our haphazard bicycles then looks at me and says, 'we are de same Aleechay.'

'But hey, maybe one day we travel together again, when I'm better?' I ask.

'I ope so. Very mauch.'

'And maybe tomorrow we can have a day in Pisa together like we said. And then I go away. Okay?'

'Yes.' He inhales sharply, as though wounded, 'I am so sad. But so appy that I meet you.'

Shoulder-to-shoulder, we stare at the rattling veil of rain, communicating only in sobs. It carries on for just the right amount of time (ten minutes) then the weight of the clouds lifts and the sunshine makes a timid appearance.

'How you feel now?' asks Aaron.

'Better, actually... Completely better!'

Just like magic, the sun bursts through, cooking that lovely musky smell into the tarmac.

The slick ground and resolved tension make the journey such a breeze we arrive with time to spare in Lucca, a town entirely circled by a 40ft wall that was once a rampart but now a pedestrian promenade skirted by a grassy bank. We lean our bikes against the bank and climb aboard the grass which has enough girth for us to lie on, but only lengthways.

'You like, how you say... Robbie Weelliams?'

'Sì!' I gasp.

Nobody likes Robbie Williams these days and I could've grabbed Aaron by the shoulders and shaken him with excitement. With glorious Robbie serenading us through the tinny output of Aaron's mobile phone, Aaron scribbles passionately in his diary while I lie on my back, thinking about my imminent freedom with equal measures of glee and regret.

'I'm gunna do a Roly-poly,' I say.

Aaron looks up from his scribbling, first to me then over the precipice and says, 'Okay, but you must go EZACLY STRAIGHT.'

'Yeah, yeah, sure...Wahey!' I yell, tucking my chin, pushing against the balls of my feet.

The world distorts to an upside-down sweep of colour. One of my feet lands with a thump, the other lands on something invisible:

the precipice.

'Oh fuck,' I gasp, shimmying away from the edge.

Every ounce of Mediterranean caramel drains from Aaron's face. 'Do not ever do dat again,' he says.

Aaron's friend Geoff is a little man from Singapore. Permanently frantic, great polka dots of sweat brewing on his starchy white shirt, he races about, talking without pause, 'Here is shawa. You can wash. And sink. And dis is where you can ave rest. OKAYE? Iz okaye. I make speshaw dinna for you. Okaye?'

Geoff is strange. I wouldn't say that I didn't like him but for some reason, I can't help but wish he was someone else. Rustling around in that white shirt from filthy room to filthy room, panting, eyes beady and glistening: there is something insatiable about him. Now his continuous stream of chatter has transferred onto a mobile phone.

He cups his hand over it and says to me and Aaron, 'my nine-year-old son.'

This is strange because there is not a single trace of the boy's existence in Geoff's flat, despite my thorough eye.

Showered and rested, watered and fed, we thank Geoff and offer to clear up.

'Yes, yes. Aaron you elp me and Aleece,' Geoff pulls up a stool to the centre of the kitchen. 'You sit there. Women don't know how to wash up properly.'

I do as I'm told and sit propped on the stool, feeling especially uncomfortable.

'After wash up I massage you both, yes?' says Geoff.

'No thanks, I'm too tired,' I say.

'YES PLEASE!' Aaron says.

'Is okaye. We go quick. Hurry, hurry. And ten just a very small massage. Yes?' says Geoff, showing me his wide eyes.

'No, thanks, I'm just too tired,' I say.

'Okaye so we do a little one. It will make you much better for cycling.'

'No thanks,' I repeat, rubbing my eyes.

'Leave her! She's tired! We can do tomorrow,' says Aaron.

'Okaye. Tomorrow. Tomorrow I massage.'

A bright white flash and a shrill splitting sound yank me and Aaron out of sleep.

'WOAH!' me and Aaron say in perfect synchronisation, staring at the surprise in each other's face.

More flashes, more shrieks continue through the night, filling the room in pure white, the sound seeming to crack in our heads.

The next morning, me and Aaron wander to the train station. Yes, of course I would have wanted to cycle to Pisa but Aaron wants the day off and life is about compromise so fuck off and leave me alone.

'Aaron, que questo? What does that sign say?'

'It say a man was hit by lightning last night in Lucca.'

'JESUS!'

'Iz okeh,' Aaron shrugs, 'Ee survive.'

Little did we know that the screams and the flashes jabbing our ears and eyes last night were striking a victim. I wonder, if we'd bothered to look out the window, if our legs had not been so happily horizontal, whether we'd have seen the fellah get hit.

After a rickety train journey, a sweltering plod through the city and after collecting a French couple I really didn't like all that much (Aaron seems to like them though), here she is: the leaning tower of Pisa! An underwhelming spiral smaller than my local church, leaning not quite far enough left to be entertaining. I take back the exclamation mark. All right, all right, that's not entirely fair. Suppose it is quite a beautiful thing. Though perhaps more so without the technicolour spittle of tourists in and around it, making stupid forced perspective poses for photos, clattering their trinkets, drinking their diet cokes, fanning themselves. And yet more so, if I wasn't in such a bad mood.

'I 'ate it when peepol pet my dog,' says the bratty French girl we'd adopted, 'Zey come up to 'er and zey make ull zeese stupid noises. Zo I do it right back in zere faces.'

What with her bohemian superiority and 'I don't need to shower cos I'm so pretty' presence, I sort of hate her. Her boyfriend is silent and I take my revenge on the French girl by secretly fantasising about him.

Dragging my stupid grumpy arse alongside Aaron, we make our

way back to Lucca.

'Okay, iz okay I leave you ere and go see my friend?' Aaron asks, opening the door to Geoff's empty flat. 'She says we can ave coffee at her house but I tink you are too tired? I wunt be long. Only an hour? Geoff won't be back for a while so you can rest ere alone.'

'Of course! Yes! Go! Uh- yeah I mean, I guess I *am* quite tired...'

The door click clacks behind him. I wait, breath held for about ten seconds and then yell with delight, collapse onto the bed, convulse with joy and fall into a glorious, juicy nap. The sound of the door latch wakes me up.

'Ciao!' I say.

'Yez,' says Geoff looking both nervous and delighted all at once, 'You be resting, I see. Your eyes, dey are brighta now. Sit, sit! Where's Aaron?'

'He's gone to see a friend but he'll be back really soon. Can I read this?'

'Naturally!' says Geoff.

I take the pocket Italian-English dictionary from his shelf, sit myself down on his sofa and thumb its thin, brown pages, trying to ignore the unnerving fact of Geoff's absolute absence of chatter. Geoff walks up to me and puts his tiny fingers over my shoulders, clamping them tighter, then looser; my muscles stiff and clunking under the pressure.

'Oh you tight, tight muscles,' says Geoff.

And I should tell him again that I don't like massages but something stops me; it's like my voice box is covered in glue. Geoff's hands move over my face which immediately screws into a pinch. *'Tell him to stop, tell him to stop, tell him to stop,'* my brain begs and yet I do nothing as clammy pressure continues about my forehead, my cheeks, my neck. Geoff's hand slips under my dress and skims over my breasts, then over my belly moving from hipbone to hipbone. Maybe this is just what a massage is like. Maybe I'm being ridiculous and uptight. I'm a Brit, after all. But his fingers, his stubby, greedy, maggoty fingers, again find my breasts. At first, he pretends that it's all part of the massage, skimming over them, continuing with my back. But then his greed overtakes him: he slips his other hand under my dress and grabs both breasts, one in each sweaty hand, hard, breathing hot condensation over my neck. Then he lets go, feels again over my stomach, my face, then plunges lower, finding the pink frilly rim of my knickers – the lucky ones, given to me by Baldy after he threw my socks in the sea. I crunch my eyes shut, frozen stupid as his hands feel over the trim. Just tell him to stop Alice! And Aaron, where the fuck are you? How could you leave me with this man, this *friend* of yours?

The door click-clacks, and in the second it takes for Aaron to say 'ellooo' Geoff's hands are off me and I am off the sofa. Aaron's face is uncomfortably happy and I feel two things towards him: utter disgust and stabbing guilt.

'Ah, I ad such a good time. Phew!' says Aaron, 'You ave a good rest Aleechay?'

'Yeah!' I say, with surprising conviction.

'She has good rest. Hey, let's cook, come, come,' says Geoff, scuttling into the kitchen, nervous, guilty, unsatisfied.

We cook. Or rather, Aaron and Geoff cook while I stay propped on that stupid, stupid stool again, chatting, joking and laughing as though nothing had happened. Maybe it didn't?

'Ah, I will miss you,' says Aaron, stirring a sizzling pan of onions.

'And me...' I reply, staring into nothing.

The sight of Aaron's ignorant face sickens me.

'Let's do massage after dinna,' says Geoff as I try to swallow the last slippery slice of aubergine. Goddammit, aubergine used to be my favourite.

'No, thanks,' I reply. 'I'm too tired.'

'We go quick. It's okay. Hurry, hurry.' Geoff yanks Aaron's unfinished plate from under his nose.

'EY!' says Aaron, mouth full, fork loaded.

Geoff storms into the kitchen with the plates and Aaron follows.

I escape to the spare bedroom, and pretend to sleep until nasty footsteps scuttle towards me.

'Leave er, she's tired,' whispers Aaron.

'ALEECE! ALEECE! WE DO MASSAGE!' Geoff shouts.

'SHH! She's sleeping! Leave er alone,' Aaron insists.

'ALEECE!' says Geoff again.

'Uuughh...' I toss a little.

'Leave er!' says Aaron.

Finally, they leave me. And I spend the next five hours stuck behind the dark of closed eyelids, pretending to sleep, trying to forget the feeling of fingers.

Finally, finally, morning comes. Aaron is fast asleep so I make every effort to disturb him: shuffling around the insides of my bags, stomping clumsily about the room.

'DO YOU WANT PORRIDGE?' I hiss.

'I don't–'

'I'm making breakfast now and then I'm leaving.'

'Yez. Okay.'

I keep my movements in the kitchen light and delicate because I do not want to wake Geoff today. I make some coffee, pour the porridge into two bowls, set it all down on the table and then peer again into the bedroom.

'Hey, it's ready!'

'I come,' Aaron groans.

So we sit, me sipping very strong coffee and feeding myself spoonfuls of porridge. Nervous porridge is never much fun but I know once I've finished spooning in the starch, I can leave. Porridge then freedom: that is how it goes.

Aaron sits down opposite me with his hands on his lap, ungratefully *not* eating the porridge I'd taken the care to bash together and undercook. He's just sitting there, curdling the atmosphere with his sad, sad un-eating face. One fat tear hits his porridge with a wet slapping noise. But I look down, into my own bowl and continue shovelling, thinking, *'don't cry, please don't cry. Just eat your fucking porridge so I can get the hell out of here'.* No use. Knowing the enormity and blueness of Aaron's eyes, I shouldn't be so surprised how torrential they could be. Maybe I'm not surprised, just plain pissed off.

'Uh-huh-huh-huh,' Aaron hiccups tears upon tears upon tears into his porridge. 'I sorry. Iz jus... I never meet a girl like you,' he chokes. 'And I tink, when I cycle, I will torn around, dere–uh-uh-

uh,–' Aaron stops to hiccup more tears. He takes a breath and continues, 'Dere will be no-one smiling at me anymore. You are de strongest little carrot.'

I stare into Aaron's bowl, at the pit-pat of tears denting his porridge and think about how rude he's being. After all, we're not in Scotland, and I so wish he'd gather a shred of decency and aim his salty tears elsewhere. That wouldn't be so hard, would it?

'I'm so sorry to leave you,' I say, finally. 'We'll meet again, I'm sure.'

'I ope...God I so appy to meet you. You are the most perfect person I ever meet in my life. I write this oll in a letter. Ere,' Aaron hands me a folded sheet of paper, 'And ere, I want you to ave dis.' He hands me his fancy lemon jam.

'No, Aaron, that's your fancy expensive jam!'

'Please, I wunt you to have it.'

So I take the stupid jam, and finish my stupid porridge. Then Geoff walks in the room and hands me his pocket Italian dictionary. All these men giving me all these things and I just want to get out.

'Okay, bye.' I hug Aaron (a stiff, guilty hug) and step outside.

But his damn lovely face follows me out the door.

'GOODBYE! BYE! BYE!' Aaron shouts, his voice still wobbling with tears.

'ARRIVEDERCI!' I scream back.

16

Jump over your shadow

I pedal on with unnecessary velocity, pulling on The Insect's handlebars, pushing on his pedals, squinting ahead at nothing. Pisa whizzes by and I barely notice. But eventually my legs go rickety with emptiness and I take a pit stop.

'Un espresso e una focaccia. Grazie.' I set two euros on the counter.

The barman smiles cheekily and hands me, the strange English girl, my usual: one espresso, as thick and sweet as treacle, and one piece of focaccia both salty enough to dry the lips and oily enough to balm them again. Perfect. And of course, there is no need to drink the coffee: the focaccia does that for me, much to the bemusement of the bar staff who point and gossip about the sacrilege that is, *dunking*. I have been told, here, the only acceptable occasion for dunking is when in possession of croissant and cappuccino and that one can only drink cappuccino in the morning. This is too narrow a dunking window to an English girl so I persist, guzzling sodden clods of focaccia pausing only to read the newspaper aloud or to jot new words in my pig-eared notebook.

'Per-ic-o-lo-so,' I say, tapping each syllable with my pen.

Eighteen speedy miles later I stop in Livorno, urgently excited to mark my lonesome territory. A nervous release, a thrilling gush, a primal ceremony: there's something innately satisfying about eco-weeing. Although, even if you're quick, as soon as the pants drop, people *will* appear out of nowhere (they've *smelt* you). Air flowing between the legs, release already begun, there's no going back now so I do all I can to avoid eye contact and apologise under my breath as a Niagara of relief falls between my knees.

With the bushes fertilised, I pull out a box of fibre flakes and admire my picnic area. Horrible! How wonderfully, wonderfully horrible. Horrible enough to only feature limp trees, historical litter and a creepy old couple sat on a bench, petting each other.

'Posso restare, qui? E...Mangiare cibo?' I ask.

'Certo! Certo!' says the man, keeping one hand on his lady's thigh and using the other to flap in welcome.

'Grazie,' I return.

I sit beside them and face plant a handful of cereal.

'Prende!' says the man, dumping a bunch of cherries on my lap.

'Per me? Veramente? Ah, grazie mille. Troppo gentile,' I say.

Next to him, his woman stares ahead, knees splayed apart, dress riding a little too high up her thigh, smacking her glossy, red lips. Hopefully she's wearing pants, though she seems just like the type who wouldn't.

'Lei é bella. Mia bella ragazza,' says the man, patting his woman's thigh. She giggles. He turns to me, 'Sei un angelo! Guadra! Con I tuoi capelli biondi Sei un angelo, sei un angelo! Sei tutta sola? Niente ragazzo?'

'Grazie! E sì, tutta sola. *Meglio* sola,' I smile.

'In Italia, c'é un milione di ragazzi per te. Con tuoi capelli Biondi!' he says.

I laugh and thank him over and over. Then he strokes his woman's thigh and tells me once she is *'morto'*, (dead) he will finally have it off with her sister who is, apparently, much younger.

I scoff the cherries then head on my way.

As I cycle on, the penny finally drops: I've just held a conversation, in Italian! It's been just over a week. A week of words, people, dangerous roly-polies, sandy sleepovers, one molesting, seventeen focaccias, sixteen espressos, mountains, and there we have it: by some force of magic, I've absorbed some Italian. Probably the magical fault of magic Aaron, which reminds me... I pull over, and unfold his letter.

'Dear Alice,

I write this as we sit on the grass: dirty, tired, happy. And I see you lying down with eyes closed and smile. You are always smile. All my life I dream I meet a girl like you. All my life I look for this girl. You are so strong, so wild, so happy. The strongest girl in the world. And we are the same.

I am so sad that you leave but so happy. All my life I dream that I meet this girl. And now I so happy because this girl I always imagine

I meet her. SHE EXISTS! And I will always be happy to meet you.

I hope we meet again sweet carrot,

Aaron.'

'Wild' and 'happy' start to bleed. I flap my tears off the letter and pedal on. A swim. Yes, a swim will wash the guilt away.

Oh, here we go again.

'SCUZE! Questa é una spiaggia privata. IL SPIAGGIA LIBERE É LÁ!' A taut-arsed man clad in tippex-white shoos me away, pointing furiously to the 'Spiaggia liberé', the free beach.

Incredible. How they've managed to separate the black sea of the free beach with the turquoise sea of the private beach, is beyond me. But it might have to do with that ginormous charred tree dumped between them. Now, I'm not a picky girl but even I, a girl whose regular lunch is tinned chickpeas followed by the thick, cold juice they sit in, a girl who sleeps on the sand, a girl who washes herself in sinks and considers pants for the most part redundant, will not swim in this black soup. It has sharp objects in it! The real cherry on the cake through is that on the posh side, nobody swims. Too superior to splash, they just lie caramelising in rows like sardines on a barbeque.

Bearing all this in mind I take my chance and peg it, fully clothed, past the snobs cradled by sun beds shouting, 'MI DISPIACE! TROPPO CALDO!' as I splash into the designer sea.

60 miles down, ten to go: it's late and quiet. Quiet, save for a lumpy looking silhouette on the coral horizon that seems to be shrieking. I close in. The shrieking noise is coming from a rusty bike that appears to be, according to its every-which-way wobble, held together by a single piece of string.

'Ciao!' I say.

'Hi!' says the boy.

A great celebration of freckles turns to face me, his whole body in fact, glittering with them. Beneath the shadow of his baseball cap, his eyes glow a piercing blue, smaller and sharper than Aaron's. His face is whittled, his arms long and freckled too. Then, noticing the frayed ends dangling from his crossbar, I realise his bike really *is* held together by a piece of string.

'You're German?' I ask.

'Yes,' he says.

'Where are you going? Your bike doesn't sound very well,' I say.

'Oh, I bought it off a friend in Milan so I could cycle to Grosseto, zen Rome. I gafe him fifty euros.'

I laugh, then say 'No offence, but your friend has *way* over charged you.'

'Yes,' says the boy, matter-of-factly. 'But I like a challenge. And Vhere are you going?'

'All over the place. But eventually somewhere with a ferry. I promised Mum I'd join them for a family holiday in Greece.'

'That's so cool. And you come all ze way from England? Alone? As a girl? So cool. I'm Eric.'

'I'm Alice.'

'But don't you get bawd?' Eric asks. 'Cycling all day?'

'What? No! Not at all! Why, do you?'

'Yeah. Every day is ze same, cycle, eat, camp. Just me and my music.'

Eric's cheap music speaker tries to get a word in, but manages only a slight metallic buzz as it bashes around in his front basket, buffered by a half-eaten loaf of bread. Amazing, even riding that string-away-from-collapse donkey of his, Eric carries himself with such grace, slow-galloping along with his long legs. And I so enjoy him: the plunge of his vowels, the static edge of his S's and Z's, the spread of his perfect teeth as he smiles. He speaks precisely, sentences crafted acutely, about ice-cream and parties and aperitifs in Milan. I ask him what an *aperitif* is but Eric, so shocked I didn't know, never quite gets around to telling me.

'You sure it's okay?' Eric asks, as we pull up outside Learte's flat.

'Oh yeah, course, I'm sure he won't mind,' I reply.

'Ey guys, I'm Learte!' says my host, opening out his arms either side, as though for a hug, then swiftly re-pocketing them.

'Ciao!' I say. 'This is Eric, can he stay too?'

'Sure! Course! Come on in!'

I have never met an Italian to excuse himself quite so much as Learte. Everything, it seems, is something he ought to be sorry for.

'You can put your bikes here. I'm sorry there's not mauch room. I haven't got much, but I will try to cook. Sorry guys. I so sorry, I'm shy, I'm really shy,' Learte says.

Me and Eric look to one another, even for us two Anglo-Saxons, this is too polite. Really, I wanted to tell Learte to not be so sorry because he is in fact a bit of a solid gold hunk of man angel, what with his brilliant smile, sexy laughter lines and sweeps of shiny black hair. But given how shy Learte keeps telling us he is, I think better of it.

Learte cooks. Well, he said he'd cook, but distracted by absolutely everything an hour goes by and he has only managed to put a courgette on a chopping board and open the pasta cupboard. In the end, the pasta and courgette never make it any further so we take the blood and body: wine and focaccia. Pretending to myself that I actually like wine, I take a few rancid sips here and there feeling equally cultured and nauseous. Meanwhile Learte tells me and Eric about his job as a graphic designer, then teaches us gesticulations and swears.

'CAZZO! CACA CAZZO!' I yell, flapping my arms. 'Did I get it right?'

Learte laughs, 'Yez.'

Then bedtime. Two beds, three people: uncomfortable maths.

'Ey, iz okeh we let Aleechay have er own bed?' says Learte to Eric, 'She is a lady.'

So Learte puts on a film and shares his bed with Eric. Meanwhile I lie in the bed next to them, utterly touched (in a good way, not literally, like yesterday), Tom Jones's 'She's A Lady' spinning over and over in my head.

'I'm hungry,' I whisper to Eric who, like me, is awake early.

'Me too,' says Eric. 'I might go out to get breakfast.'

Learte stirs. 'Morning guys,' he says. 'You want breakfaz? I take you to a cool place, de best place in de *world* for breakfaz. You gunna love it.'

Learte drives us among the valleys to a little town, apologising over and over that the best place for breakfast was closed, promising us he will find an alternative.

If *this* is the alternative, then Learte's first option really must have been the best place in the world. Perched on the hilltop, overlooking the lapping of valleys studded with neat rows of fruit trees, we sit around the one and only rickety table of...well, I guess this is a fruit shop. A fruit shop which also serves coffee, if you know the owners well enough.

No salt, no oil, no onion, no garlic: these were my base rules back at uni. Along with a few other sub-rules that I would pick up for one reason or another. Like, no bread because Steph doesn't eat bread. Or no lunch, because Alicia had said once that she doesn't eat lunch (though I later found this to be a lie). Of course, there was the no sugar rule after the government went ballistic about it, that raw diet I went on, then the Japanese diet, the intermittent fasting I played with. Perhaps the worst of all my food phases was the five-day mono diet: porridge being my mono of choice. That was a gloopy, white mistake if ever I did try one.

Today's breakfast, breaking just about every rule from this first bite, blows my little head off. The unctuous squish of focaccia, the grassy tang of just-picked tomatoes doused liberally in olive oil, gravelled with coarse grounds of salt that pinch and leave you wanting, all washed down with the delicious slurry of sugary espresso. It was as though my whole life had been leading up to this point, this breakfast. It signals freedom. And all the while Learte talks about his experience of gang bangs.

'Good for you!' I say. 'I was offered a threesome once, but we never got around to organising it– are you not going to get that?' I ask Learte, as his phone rings for the sixth time.

'Ah, iz okay. Iz jas, well, I was supposed to go to a wurk meeting dis morning.'

'Oh jeez! I'm so sorry!' I say.

'Iz okeh, I like you guys and I really wan you to av a great breakfaz.'

'It was *strabilliante*. Il meglio in mia vita,' I say.

Learte lets out a coy laugh.

'Yeah. It was *a–mazing!*' says Eric, in a tight English voice, mocking me.

And we all laugh like three best friends.

'I ope I see you guys again. You olways welcome,' says Learte.

I think I love Learte. How could I not? He's shy and kind, artistic, built like a Roman athlete and with the manners of a prince.

'God, he was too nice,' I say to Eric as we pedal on together.

'I know!' he returns, 'He kept saying sorry to us and I didn't know vhat to say because he vas just so nice! Hey! Can you do no-hands?'

'WAAAAH!' I scream, reaching out my arms either side.

Neither of us had actually said the words 'let's travel together', but it seemed about right. I am glad of his freckled company, his hilariously practical sentences twisted up in his funky accent. Yet I can't deny the flashbacks of Aaron crying into his porridge, the prickling of guilt as Eric and I career no-handed down the empty roads. Then it happens: something I'd been waiting on for weeks.

'FIGS!' I yell.

Man alive, you wouldn't have believed it. As far as the eye could see, trees beaded with peaches, apricots, nectarines and what I'd been looking out for since I'd met Loic: figs. Eric and I dump our bikes in a clumsy heap and fill our bags, our arms, our baskets, our mouths until an eighty-year-old rhino, one hand holding her floral dress up to her knees, the other waving a stick, pelts after us.

'AIE!' she yells. 'AIE, AIE AIE, AIE!'

I vow here and now to never again steal fruit: you never know what earnest hands or what furious cretin may lie behind those trees. Pumped with adrenaline and stolen fruit, Eric and I spin away to a beach, where we flop and chat.

'Can I ask something?' says Eric.

'Yeah?'

'It's very unusual to meet a girl like you. You trafel fery far and camp completely alone. And your attitude...Are you always zis happy?'

'Yes.' I think about Aaron, how he had asked me the same question, 'Well, I am now. But back home, in England... Well I guess I had some struggles. But these days, everybody gets a bit lost and crazy.'

'Really? What happened?'

'I...Well... Long story short, I ended up in a mental hospital a while ago.'

'Wow. How did that happen? Like, why did they put you in there?'

Eric stares at me, interested but somehow unsurprised.

I um and ah for a minute, realising I hadn't told anyone I'd met so far about my incarceration. Mind you, even some of my very good friends don't know of that 'nothing' space in my life. Fellow students often ask where I went on my gap year and I'd either change the subject or say quite frankly 'hospital'. And most of the time that is enough to inspire the tumbleweeds and changes of subject. I guess they assume it was cancer or something. Or maybe they know and maybe doing time in a crazy place is actually a little bit frightening to others.

'I was...distressed. And I starved myself. The doctor said to me I'd gotten so thin that she was going to put me in this psychiatric hospital but I didn't believe her until I was there, in that strange place with windows that opened only this much.' I make a pinch, an inch of air between my thumb and forefinger.

'For how long?'

'Just one final question,' Doctor T. frowns at his paperwork then looks up, 'how long do you think you'll be here?'

I think about this question for a moment then say, quite cheerfully, 'Two weeks?'

'Hm,' he replies.

'Six months,' I say.

'Woah,' says Eric.

'But d'you know, I wouldn't have changed it? In a way, I'm probably the luckiest girl ever because having your freedom taken away like that, God... You know, I've never quite gotten over the thrill of being released.'

'I *knew* zere was zomezing more to you. I just knew it. What was it like? In zere?' he asks.

'Three hundred and one, three hundred and two... and three... and fo- are you okay?' Georgia completes squat number three hundred and four, then whispers, 'Shall we stop?'

'No,' I hiss back, grabbing the bedside table. I pull myself off the floor onto my rattling knees, shake away the dizziness in my head

then whisper, 'It's okay, I'm fine. Let's finish this.'

'Okay. We'll go from two hundred and fifty, yeah?'

'Yeah.'

'Two hundred and fifty, two hundred and fifty-one...fifty-two... fifty thr- Fuck! Alice!'

'What?' I ask in a nasal voice. 'What is it?!'

A tapping sound beats on the floorboards and suddenly a taste like paper clips floods my mouth. I raise my hand to my wet face. Blood.

'Shit. Should I call someone?' Georgia says, no longer whispering, the threat of a giggle on her lips.

I burst into hysterics, blood Jackson-Pollocking my face, pyjamas, bare toes, the floor. Georgia laughs too, louder than her tiny little body should allow, loud enough to disturb the nearest HCA who thunders down the corridor and bursts in.

'What appen?!' he says, gripping the door handle in case he should faint.

Georgia and I laugh louder and More blood spatters the floor.

I have never seen his lovely Caribbean skin look so pale.

'Often hilarious, other times very dark,' I say.

Eric's eyebrows arch, probing me to go on. So I tell him, about the rules, pills, staff, 6am weigh-ins, about dance therapy, the net overhanging the stairs (to stop us jumping, though we just jumped into the net instead), the dreaded Big Portion Karen and the much-adored Small Portion Karen. Eric listens intently.

'Wow... That's insane,' he says, impressed.

'Lunch?' I say.

'Sure,' he smiles.

Between us, our lunch selection features: figs, cereal, baked corn, stale bread, dried fruit, nuts, Aaron's expensive lemon jam and a 500g block of marzipan beaded with ants.

'I accidentally bought this thinking it was some kind of fancy Italian snack,' I explain, chopping off the ant portion, which Eric didn't seem to mind.

We tuck in, trying every possible combination of things. The best, we decide, was the lemon jam, marzipan and cereal sandwich.

Then Eric buys me a granita – he says *I must try granita* – but I tip it away when he's not looking because I suddenly realise, I don't know how many calories are in granita.

'Eric?' I ask as we heave uphill, cycling parallel to each other (Italian drivers don't seem to mind this like English drivers do). 'What's your dream?'

'I have zis idea...I want to travel with stickers of my face and paste them all over the world.'

'Dude! That's so cool! You'll be famous! I think you should start now before someone gets there first.'

'It's on my to-do list. I have lots on there. Do you have a to-do list?'

I laugh then say, 'I think you might mean "bucket list". What else is on your list?'

'I vant to go to America, I vant to try couchsurfing and – hey, we did couchsurfing yesterday! I can cross it! And...I vant to try *wwoofing*, that's vhy I'm going to Grosseto. Oh and I vanted to try efery flavour of ice cream on the menu, but I did that one.'

'Wow.'

'Yes. There vhere sirty flafours and ze lady she put a teaspoon of each in one tub. She vas not happy, but ze sign said you can try as many flavours as you like. What would be in your list?'

'Well...One day I'd like to write a book, maybe. Oh and I'd love to travel all over the place by bike and sell paintings as I go. Oh! And, I tell you what, I'd love to cycle *all night long*. To watch the sun set and pedal and pedal and pedal until it rises again.'

'That's so cool. You should do it. Soon. Here, in Italy.'

'Maybe I will.'

As the sky mellows to the grungy rainbow colours of a gothic shop, a second wind swoops through me and Eric. Maybe because it's cooler. Or maybe it's Eric's company, or the tinny tunes coming from his speaker, or the mass of sunflowers, pitter-pattered as far as the eye can see either side of our empty silver road.

'WOAH!' I shout.

'Let's stop,' says Eric.

We stop at the top of the hill to stare at the fat nectarine sun, brewing all sorts of colours into the sky as it falls behind the sea.

Blissful idiots we are really, watching the last piece of light dissolve, wilfully forgetting our lack of bike lights.

Twilight offers a little sympathy, enough for us to just about see navy shapes.

'I sink we can go through here,' says Eric, pointing at a forest.

So we rustle our way through the thick band of trees, until finally our wheels hit sand. We lean our bikes against two bins, dump our sleeping bags on the sand and eat beans: borlotti for me, chickpeas for he.

'Let's mix this shit up,' I say, crushing a handful of cereal into the sloshy mix of cold legumes. 'You want some?'

'Sure. Vhy not,' he says, grabbing a handful and tossing it in his tin.

Then we add marzipan, jam, peanuts, corn, and raisins. After our Heston Blumenthal dinner, we shuffle into our bags, too knackered to bother taking off our dirty clothes. Or maybe too shy, who knows.

Above us the sky is dense with stars, the mist of the Milky Way sweeping over our heads. We stare at them and witter on about stuff like kids at a sleepover, until at some point the last word is said.

BEEP-BEEP-BEEP-BEEP!

'AAAAH!' I scream, squinting at the stab of white light. I stumble in my sleeping bag to my feet and again scream, 'AAAAAAH!'

The truck stops, its bright lights still thumping at my retinas as Eric wakes up, startled and confused.

'Ciao! Scusami!' says the driver, jumping out of the truck. 'Sono–Oh, ey! Sorry about dat. Where are you guys from?'

Me and Eric exchange a great 'what the fuck look' then, too polite to leave the question unanswered, reply.

'England,' I say.

'Germany,' says Eric.

'Ah, cool! An you cycle. Niiice. Well, nice to meet you,' the bin man walks behind me and Eric, picks up the rubbish from the bins behind us, jumps back into the truck and yells, 'BYE! BYE, BYE!'

'Woah...' I say, staring at the diminishing light of the truck as it trundles through the sand, 'Well that was bloody close.'

'Veird,' says Eric.

By some magic, Eric and I fall asleep fast, though I do have recurring nightmares of bright lights, tyres and beeping.

'I can't believe it didn't wake you up,' I say to Eric as we pedal into town in search of breakfast. 'They almost ran us over. Thank God I'm not as light a sleeper as you, otherwise, we'd be toast!'

Probably more like jam sandwiches, I think to myself, smushed and crushed with bits of sand sticking to our guts.

'It was pretty funny zough. He gets out saying "Oh hey guys! Sorry about zat. Where are you from? Nice to meet you!" So random.'

'Crazy,' I agree.

'Hey, let's stop here.'

Coffee, focaccia, a table to rest our notebooks on, a bathroom to wash in, full charge on our phones, free tap water: two euros well spent. Dad rings, and I duck away from Eric for a moment to answer.

'How's it going with your Italian fella Alice?'

'Oh yeah, well I'm actually with a German guy now, long story.'

'Blimey! You're trying out all the flavours!'

'Yeah, I guess so! But I reckon we're going our separate ways soon, so I actually can't talk right now, can I call you back tomorrow?'

'Sure! Have *fun*.'

I roll my eyes, hang up and join Eric. We say nothing for an hour, both scribbling things, perhaps about each other. Then Eric closes his notebook and says, 'Ready to go?'

'One sec...' I finish my sentence with the word brilliant', thump a little full stop on my page then say, 'Yes.'

I'm going to miss Eric. Not in the pained way I miss Loic, or the guilty way I miss Aaron, but I will miss my freckled compadre with a smiling heart. Though I know, deep down in my deepest Spidey-sense, that I won't ever see Eric again unless by some miracle we meet by chance, somewhere strange (like a Norwegian prison or Australian bakery, I imagine) but never as the result of a plan. This was it. Perhaps this is why we've both gone so quiet, only the gentle whir of our bicycles filling the silence as we bump down a dusty track.

'I lofe how you liff,' says Eric.

'Man! I love how *YOU* live. You are one of the *coolest* people

I've ever met. It's been wild and fun, even though we nearly got squished to death last night. I hope you feel less bored now.'

'I do,' he says. 'Definitely.'

'You know when we both go back home, we have to stay with our free spirits. We can't lose it we have to stay crazy and fun, yeah? Brave and wild, even if everybody else is being serious and normal.'

'YES!' Eric bursts, 'YOU'RE SO RIGHT! We have an expression in German for this, "*über seinen eigenen schatten spingen,*" and it means to "jump over your shadow". Like, to ofercome somezing with courage.'

'Woah, that's absolutely perfect *über se…?*'

'Ü-ber sein-en eigen-en schatt-en spring-en,' says Eric.

'Über seinen eigenen schatten springen,' I repeat.

'Perfect. You got it.'

Maybe I have got it.

'GROSSETO,' reads the sign. Our end.

'Shall we get lunch? If you have time?' Eric asks.

'YEAH!'

We exit the shop with lettuce, beans, nuts and plums, toss them together and munch away until all that remains is a sentimental silence.

'Okay,' I sigh, 'I best head off. Thanks for everything, for being so fun. You're going to go far, and I don't just mean on that pile of rust.'

'Aw man, it's been awesome. Ah, come here!'

To my amazement, Eric opens out his long, freckled arms and folds me into a brotherly hug.

'CIAO!' I wave frantically behind me, probably to dispel the stupid tears trying to fill my eyes. I do not let them.

Eric will be '*wwoofing*' soon. Actually not a sexual thing, *wwoofing*, I've reason to believe, is a euphemism for 'cheap labour'. Sort of like an apprenticeship but without a minimum wage or qualification. But maybe I'm wrong. I'd like it if I was.

17

A long night

Two days with Eric had felt like two years. I'd grown so fond of his every freckle; his Germanic instinct for practicality; the elastic intonation of his sentences; the sentiment disguised behind every seemingly logical observation and of course, his eagerness in trying weird food combinations. I even miss the ear-rinsing creaks of his bike.

At night I dump my head on the sand of Monte Argentario (a peninsula separated from mainland Italy by A five-mile strip over a lagoon) and Eric's freckled face seeps into my dreams. "*Über seinen eigenen schatten springen*," he says, just as he had in real life. What a beautiful phrase to carry in my heart as I wake this morning. And to think, Brits can be so quick to piss all over the German language. 'Brutal', 'masculine', 'crude', they say, 'not like those nice Latin languages'. Well, in actual fact, of all other European languages, it is the one that sounds the most like English. Sure, their robust phrases don't trickle off the lips like Spanish, French or Italian but you can't deny their sentences have thump.

Anyway, the decision is made, to jump over my shadow. Or rather, to pedal all night until my shadow reappears, long in the first light of morning. So I spend the day on Monte Argentario, waiting for night to fall.

This mostly entails sleeping but I also finally charge my lights, scribble down new words in my red notebook, eat too much beige food, read an Italian newspaper and write postcards. Posting them, however, proves to be a bit of palaver because apparently post boxes don't exist in Italy according to *everybody*. In the end, they fall into the hands of a guy who knows a guy, who says he'll post them. Hm. Then I ring Dave, weeping into an espresso, telling him how he's my best friend, that I just wanted him to know that he's my *best* friend. Dave laughs and tells me I've gone nuts. And I suppose as a twenty-two-year-old girl perhaps knighting 'best friendship' to a fifty-something-year-old man is a little off-beat. But I really do like Dave. 8pm rolls around and so, with caffeine zipping in my veins, charge in my lights and zest in my spirit, I set out on my quest, first crossing the lagoon, then heading south.

Ten miles in, the golden hour strikes in a gorgeous assault of bronze: the trees brassy with their blue shadows stretched and softened. The air is marshmallow soft, best taken in long, smiling sighs.

'DOVE VIA?!' shouts a man from his car window.

'ROMA!' I yell.

'ROMA?! QUESTA NOTTE? YOU ROCK!' he yells, punching the air with his fist, beeping his horn furiously.

20 miles done. With the sun set, the golden hour relays to another hour, not yet given its deserved name but I call it the pink hour. The sky deepens, and the last colours of the day glow purple and rose-gold.

30 miles. Twilight. In an effort to avoid a dual carriageway, I take the bumpier road paralleling it, which has found me pedalling through what looks like a 'Call of Duty map'. Now I am stuck here, locked behind a six-foot tall gate, kept company by derelict buildings, one creepy office chair missing a wheel, a few violated mattresses, scattered broken glass, warning signs of various severity, and one boy on his BMX. I ask him how to escape but he just shrugs, which looks like an effort to his shoulders, burdened by the weight of adolescence.

40 darkening minutes go by and still I'm stuck behind this Goddamn spear-headed gate, cautiously wondering whether to try and surmount it. Tricky, the last time I tried to scale a fence like this I was in London Trafalgar Square (attending a vegan protest) and ended up – after a couple of excruciating seconds hanging from one of the fence prongs – on the concrete with shorts torn in two pieces. And yes I went commando that day.

'SCUSA!' I yell, clutching the gate poles.

I catch the attention of a French couple who manage to haul me and The Insect over to their side. No wedgies, no social faux-pas, shorts still intact. Phew.

35 miles in and I stop at a night market, hungry and sleepy. My wander around it yields a handful of free Taralli but these remind me of Aaron and so the biscuity deliciousness is undermined by bitter regret. Still hungry, I enter a bar to try for an 'aperitif' which, if I have understood Learte and Eric correctly, means access to free beige food if you buy a drink. We used to have this sort of thing in England in the form of ashtrays of nuts on bars, but then somebody somewhere said something about germs and they mysteriously evaporated. The 'aperitif' hack works a treat though: I am now three hundred calories stronger.

50 miles down and it has just gone midnight.

'YEEHA! BEANS!' I scream, cracking open the tin.

They go down the hatch no problem, I even sip the gluey bean-juice too. Battery in lights: check. Eco-wee: check. Sense of wellbeing: massive, off-the-page, red-sharpie tick. And off we go again.

With the roads empty and the moon bathing the road in enough silver light to just about make out ahead, I switch off my bike lights. Which proves about as reckless as it does thrilling.

60 miles. Things are becoming frightening. Rustling bushes, threatening animal calls, the distant grating of grit: these ambiguities are a cause for concern. Therefore, I start to sing:

'Cycling in the dark, and it's 12 o'clock at night. I'm a little frightened, but otherwise alright. And I can hear lots of animals, the stars are above my head. Cycling in Italy while everyone's in bed.'

A car slows beside me. Its window moans its way down and as the smell of perfume, clang of jewellery and the girly titters flood out of it, I breathe a sigh of relief. The women ask what's wrong with me, if I need help but I just yell that I'm just a crazy girl going to Rome.

'SÌ. PAZZESCO!' agrees the driver. 'CIAO!'

And off they go. God bless women.

70 miles. Dual carriageways are not for the faint hearted of cyclists, particularly at night. Perpetually luminous from the endless sweep of cars I wobble along, withheld by massive concrete barriers, a little too tall and thick for my liking.

'Calm and strong, calm and strong, calm and strong,' I say this aloud, resisting against the jet-stream of car, after lorry, after truck. Then finally, I veer off and laugh with relief. Relief, or maybe delirium.

3am: 75 miles down. Following the sickly haze of something open, I enter a corner shop. One might wonder how a shop like this makes any money opening at such a ridiculous time stocking only toilet roll, tinned things, and pens (none for less than two euros). Needing all three of these things, and being too tired to protest at the rip offs, I just so happen to be their ideal customer. Yet I buy only one tin of beans (toilet roll and pens, like razors, are free to those with a keen eye).

80 miles down, 4am. The delirium has worsened and it seems as though my mouth is saying things without my brain's consent, things that don't even make sense, things like 'I don't wanna lose my head!' which, I have now worked out, is a line from Toy Story 2. Then, lit by the lazy haze of streetlights, a massive, lumpy silhouette steals my attention, a silhouette that splits in three as I near it: a man, a bicycle, and a gigantic pile of rags tailored to it.

'Hi,' says the man, a nasty bite to his voice, 'why are you ere?'

His cruel eyes point out of his dirty skin like glass in mud. And he smells. Like a urinal. Or maybe the smell is coming from that pile of rags.

'Well, I'm cycling all night long to get to Rome.' I say.

'Why would you do dat?'

'I like a challenge,' I say, quoting Eric. 'What's under there?' I point to the 5ft high rag pile.

'Animals,' he says. 'By the way, I don't agree with your way of life.'

'Okay...' I shuffle backwards, 'I'm gunna go now. Nice to meet you!'

He sticks out his hand, thick with dirt. I take it, and as he shakes it Jesus Christ that pile of cloth starts meowing.

'Don't get raped.' he says, still gripping my hand.

'Okay.'

'I wouldn't say dis if you an ugly girl. But you pretty so you will probably get raped.'

'Ur, thanks. See ya!'

I wave him goodbye and continue my quest, feeling quite flattered by the rape comment.

85 miles done.

'OI! MOVE OUT OF THE WAY!' I yell at the puddle glistening with a herd of impressively noisy frogs. I thought frogs 'ribbit' but these guys are practically roaring.

'MOVE!' I scream, stamping my feet.

The frogs scream back, making guppy noises as they eject themselves out of the way.

90 miles down. The very first notch of the day's volume is turned to a very subtle navy light. All of a sudden, something lifts and a golden sliver peeks above the horizon. How mesmerising: the sun had fallen behind me and is now rising in front, like I'd chased it down, like I'd spun all the way around the world. A wonder, a treat, a joy, enough to overlook the industrial sweep of cars going on to my left and crash barrier to my right. Not quite inspiring enough though, to overlook the inner carve of hunger, curling like the twist of this roundabout bend.

I pull into the side and rest The Insect against the crash barrier. Probably not an ideal picnic spot as aggressively indicated by the suspicious confetti of toilet roll in the hedge. Ah well, I have my magic and expensive beans. I toss the can in the air, catch it in my palm, and give it a vigorous shake of joy. €2.14! But €2.14 well spent.

'FAGIOLI FREDO!' I cheer, then, 'No. Please, God *no*.'

The metal piercer, detached and stuck to my thumb like some sort of stupid ring, winks at me. I try to put it back on. But alas, once something has snapped, it'll never be the same again. And what does that say about me, eh? I am so, *so* hungry.

'AHHH!' I scream, slamming the tin can into the road barrier.

It clangs. I pick up the tin, which is now dented and beaten, to no avail. No doubt the €2.14 I spent on them went on bullet proof packaging. Clang: and again. Another dent, but no luck. I scream and hurl and clang and scream, over and over lorries whooshing by, until I have only enough energy to whimper at the beaten tin and suck two tiny beads of bean juice from a pin-prick hole.

'NOOOOOOO!' I wail, collapsing to the floor in anguish.

I throw the tin into the hedge of tissue and continue, lamenting loudly.

96 miles. A heavenly 'ahh' noise blasts in my head: even more inspiring than the sunrise, the saccharine glow of a service station dilates in front of my crying eyes. Fuel your car and yourself! Maybe even have a coffee while you're at it. Even a wee! In a *real* toilet! In I stumble, jerking involuntarily like a deranged chicken. They say a person can survive longer without food than sleep: sitting here, without a brain cell left unpickled, sitting here with eyes aching with such heaviness I'm convinced they're sliding down my twitching face, I could believe this. I don't actually think anybody else has ever felt this tired. Ever. I feel sick.

The bar lady, hair shiny, black, cut in a razor-sharp bob, hands me my request: a bag of popcorn and small pizza. How come she looks this sharp at 6am while I look like a mangled turd.

100 miles spent now and my body seems to have dissolved, leaving just my weary head hefting through space while the ground zips beneath me and the scenery reorganises itself. Things which had always been faithfully solid like the ground, trees, and buildings are nauseatingly fluid, and noises lose their integrity too, fluctuating from muffled to suddenly shrill, as though I'm repeatedly diving underwater then back to the surface. Death seems like a lovely, sleepy idea.

'Alice... Don't ever do this again, okay?' I say aloud to the spinning tarmac, 'you might one day think, oh remember how I cycled a hundred miles without sleeping, maybe I should do that again. Well, DON'T. Don't. Ever. Do. This. again. I feel... SICK! I FEEL SICK. UGH!' I shout, above the racket of a headwind pummelling my poor delicate ears, zapping my speed.

My knees crack, I'm sure I hear them crack. But I'm nearly there, I can taste it in the salty wind. I lift my hanging head to read a sign: 'WATERMELON.'

What the hell am I doing? I don't even like watermelon (I ruined it on another mono-diet once), yet here I am, pink juice gushing all over my top, devouring a fat wedge. The man gave it to me for free, for a reason I now cannot remember, insisting I sit on a stool (just as creepy, awful Geoff had). If the melon wasn't so sweet and if I hadn't been so utterly, utterly shattered, I'd have felt rather uncomfortable.

'Give me a kiss,' Says the melon man, pursing the tiny lips of his plump face.

When I don't respond, he shifts his pucker to the right side of his face and points determinedly to his left cheek. I guess there really is no such thing as a free lunch. Because I had eaten his melon, because I lack the capacity to say *no*, because I am so achingly weary, I kiss his slippery cheek. It tastes like onions.

107 miles. And then I arrive in the glorious, glorious (albeit chocked with people) Ostio Lido. I lock up The Insect with a hazy, clumsy fumble, find a patch of shade and collapse onto the sand, softer than any sand any person has ever happened across. I did it. I fucking did it.

Two unconscious hours later, the hullabaloo of beach shenanigans wrenches me out of the cosy depths of sleep. Hot and hazy, I squint and groan at the jabbing sun then curl up tighter, tucking myself into a diminishing sheet of shadow. My eyelids fall again and the last thing I see is a cigarette butt, orange and white, crinkled and crushed at its end. It makes me smile for some reason.

Quick as a blink, sleep swallows more hours and I wake up more exhausted than ever. You know that flustered, sickened, confused feeling post-nap? Well times that by about seven million. Oh, and push the heat up to 40°C.

'Ciao! Ello! Inglese ragazza?' asks a man.

Through squinting eyes I look at his cheeky face hovering above me. The classic middle-aged specimen. And forty-year-old men are usually my favourite, but I am not in the mood. I groan something about being tired ('stanca') then turn over and close my eyes.

Half an hour later another smack of heat and nausea jolts me awake. So I go for a swim. Although, not quite a swim: disabled by lethargy I kneel in the sea, rocking and swaying as the waves crash over my shoulders. With the same counter-magnetic power of a turd in a swimming pool, the water around me clears of people. I think I'm making people uncomfortable. Lunchtime? Lunchtime.

The doughy man hands me a piece of pizza, the most beautiful thing. Could I possibly explain the beauty of these mushrooms winking olive oil at me? The confident grace of crimson tomato puree? The landscape of its stone baked crust, with its volcanic charred bubbles? Or the emerald garlic dashed on its surface, warming the back of my throat before I'd even taken a bite? I chew, gasp and sprint back into the pizzeria to yelp at the man (in Italian, may I add) that this is THE BEST PIZZA I'D EVER EATEN IN MY LIFE. He almost, almost smiles yet seems most displeased when I re-enter ten minutes later and request another.

For pudding (because in my exhausted state I had forgotten I don't eat pudding) I waltz into an ice cream shop and ask about vegan options. I leave with cinnamon ice-cream! Perverse? Or just plain genius.

'Ah!' I yell, 'Help! What? What's happening? Oh...'

This must be the fourth time I've woken up screaming into my soya cappuccino and so perhaps it is time to go to Rome and meet Marco.

Ten miles is not really a long way. But ten miles when one has been up all night, ten densely trafficked miles when one's legs are 107 miles indebted, is a painfully long way to go. Especially with such a sour smell puncturing the air. What the hell *is* that smell? Whatever it is, it's getting worse. Manic laughter quite annoyingly begins beating in my ears. My own, manic laughter.

Rome breaks my heart. Not in the usual, inspired way, but in the way of utter pity. Because that strange smell I'd noticed six miles away, it's unbearable here. And the source? Rubbish. Piled in mounds the size of army tanks, warming the air with an enormous rotting smell. All throughout the city, a pile here, a bigger pile there. A city whose cobbled roads, fountains, Coliseum and ruins that might have found me otherwise gasping in wonder, leave me sighing with sympathy. Shallow sighs, because of the smell.

Marco is a lanky fella, a little older than me, a lot cooler than me and definitely stoned.

He sits me down with a glass of water and bowl of fruit then switches on the Tour de France. I fall asleep in an instant, a sleep intermitted by my own confused yelling as I wake with a start to those whippets on screen followed byy Marco's stoned laughter.

I wake up to fresh white sheets and a fresh white brain. Well, not quite. But I am certainly feeling more human after yesterday's 117 miles in 24 hours without sleep. Must put that on my CV when I get home.

'Morning' Says Marco, less stoned, 'Breakfaz?'

'Yeah!'

That was really all that was said between us.

For my second breakfast I go to a pizzeria. The coffee slips down a treat, the pizza however goes catapulting off its tray, landing face-down in a gory mess.

'Bollocks. Er, mi dis–' I start.

The pizzaman grunts, much displeased, and slams a roll of paper towel and a kitchen spray on the counter.

Now used to the smell, I decide on another night in Rome. Simply because my nerves, muscles, brain and sinews are fried to a crisp. Too much motion would surely make them shatter and crumble into dust. But I switch hosts, to a guy called Claudio.

'Hey! Aleechay! Tink I came just in time.' says Claudio as a small bunch of men, who had been leering about me, skitter off.

And so begins a six-hour continuous stream of chat, checkpointed only by the odd toilet trip, snack or shower. Claudio is as beautiful a specimen as his name might suggest. His eyes are big and glossy and interested, his face relentlessly smiling. We go to Decathlon, because Claudio says they sell portable solar panels there. I buy one, and a three-euro blow-up pillow thinking my neck probably deserves better treatment than the poles and plastic of my tent.

'What appen to your fon?' says Claudio, as we wait in line for a hold-the-cheese-pizza and beer.

'Ah, yeah. It flew onto the floor when I stopped to pick mulberries. See this black patch? It gets bigger and bigger every day. Sometimes the whole screen goes green, but I just stick my finger in this hole here and it seems to sort it out' I say.

'Ere, I have a spare at ome, you take it. An I ave a gas cooker, it leaks a bit but I tink you can use it.'

We eat our pizza, and wander.

'Claudio?' I ask, as we amble alongside the Coliseum, the ruins, the fountains, 'Why is there so much rubbish everywhere here?'

'Ah, yes. It iz very corrupt ere. Iz the mafia.'

Claudio goes onto to explain a convoluted story of corruption, poverty, government complacency and ransoms. But still, I have no idea what the mafia have to do with bin day.

'Goodnight Aleechay. I've left a bag of special focaccia crackers on the table, if you get ungry in de night you are welcome to ave some,' says Claudio, flicking the light switch.

That night, still dangerously hungry, I doze off cuddling his snack bag of focaccia brittle. I like Claudio. His eyes are fiery, and I feel heat in mine too. We will always be friends. Even if I never see him again.

18

Never trust a bin man

A girl stared back at me in the mirror today. Not the brittle, pallid, raccoon-eyed thing of before. No. This girl, soaked in tanned skin, hair a silvery-blonde, bright-eyed, bra-less breasts showing their Taj-Mahal shape beneath a thin shirt that reads 'something odd yet beautiful', she's different. The swelling of her glands has gone, the cuts on her arms sinking beneath her bronze skin. Her smile holds truer, lasting in the eyes when the mouth collapses. I've finally come home.

Beguiled by the novelty of *Claudio's mirror,* I stand a little while in front of *Aleechay,* curiously at one. She's bigger too. Not just in the blooming fat and muscle cells but dammit, she's actually taller. Amazing, after five years of stalling at 5ft 5" I've grown an inch and a half.

After a sprint of enthusiastic chatter and marathon of thank-yous, Claudio sends me bumping down 'de oldest rrod in de world'. Fascinating. Only thing is, cobbles and wheels do not suit a lady whose bra is lost somewhere in Spain and whose breasts (thanks to ample focaccia) have augmented. To give them a break, I stop for a coffee. This time however, I'm given two shot cups: one full of espresso and one with fizzy water for 'palete cleansing.' I knock it back feeling supremely cultured.

Up the mountain, down the mountain, eat too much focaccia, go back into the focacceria and again eat too much more. What's amazing, is that despite eating too much basically all the time, I haven't yet gotten fat. Bigger, perhaps. Stronger, definitely. Fat? According to the keyhole between my legs, the very slight jut of my hipbones, and militant, anxious, over-feeding of just about every Italian I'd met, certainly not.

The last twenty miles are straight, smooth and all downhill. In fact, the only slight exertion I endure is jamming on the brakes for red lights, or to wave apologetically as I zoom through them.

Though this is a little over-polite and unnecessary: it seems red, amber and green lights are one the same to southern Italians.

There she is! *Il mare*. After a short trudge through essentially a giant ashtray, I dump my ass on the sand, and cook using the camping stove Claudio had given me. Yes, everything in my left pannier stinks of gas. Yes, my spinach has gone slimy and my mushrooms fishy, bruised and sandy, and yes, it is indeed quite the challenge bringing fire to life using a novelty lighter in the shape of a miniature toilet. Still, lark at me cooking al fresco like Bear Grylls or something (only without an appetite for lizard heads and posh hotels when the cameras are off).

While my pot of rice and veggies rumbles, I think about something Claudio had said to me: *'Watch out. You in de south now. People are more crazy in de south'*. And he hadn't been the first to warn me. Even more than the patriotism of region to region, the split between north and south Italy has proven distinct. Maybe this is why I had been told, over and over, to keep a sharp eye for the roads, the men, the food, the people. But we shall see.

Then my attention slides onto a couple, fondling each other in the dark. Aw, how sweet! I love, love. Though I do wish they'd pause their PDA to appreciate this impressive set up of mine: for the steaming bowl of rice and hummus nestled between my thighs and for the improvised bed I'd made using a deflated lilo some idiot mistook for rubbish. Anyway, the couple never do acknowledge Alice self-sufficient Lushington, even as they pass my side, leaving me with only the moonlight for company. Hold on, where the hell is everybody? Why are the bars closed? Where are the drinkers, the late-night ice-cream gorgers? Spooky. Ah well, at least I have the moon, which glows as full, sad and lonely as a silver marble, bathing the sand in silver, throwing jittery streaks of light onto the sea. Between the moon and the sea, a collection of clouds beat with red, pink, orange, purple colour: nature's angry disco. Then a pink stem of lightning zigzags down from the clouds seemingly in slow motion, hits the water, and fades, shortly followed by a sonorous rumble.

Feeling subtle prickles of doom, I send a text to Dad asking if he thought lightning out at sea was dangerous. He replies 'nah' and I stash my phone away.

'Tchu! Dinner *and* a show!' I say to The Insect, laid down next to me like a faithful lover. 'Nu-night pal.'

CRACK!

I sit upright, jerked awake by a shrill noise taking up the whole sky. Not just a loud noise but a big noise, a hurting noise, the noise of a sky breaking. Panting hot breath I look around at the furious and shrieking sky, scarring in rips of red lightning, throbbing with white light. Thunder thumps through me, undermining the beat of my heart, which stops cold, then thumps harder.

'I don't know what to suggest,' says Dad, on the other end of the phone, 'I don't know what to do either. Can you ask someone for help?'

'Urrr. Well no one is around. But where should I go? I'm on the sand, completely alone, and –AH! There? Did you hear that? It's screaming at me. Fuck-fuck-fuck-fuck.'

'I think you should go and find someone, knock on someone's door, ask for help.'

Suddenly, the urge to hang up overwhelms me. I'm tougher than this and quite cross I've stooped to such an level as crying to Dad like a baby.

'Actually, I'll be alright Dad,' I say. 'But thanks for the chat.'

'You sure?'

'*Absoludo,*' I say, stealing his catchphrase.

One erect idiot on a flat empty beach, I stand alongside The Insect, wondering if it was possible to be more seductive to lightning and yet never feeling more grateful for the company of my metal companion. A bin lorry appears, crunching through the dusty, grey sand. Out hops a man, his smell overtaking him as he storms towards me.

'VIENI,' he shouts over the thunder, a wicked look brewing on his face, a dull face, given no shine despite the full moon.

He wheels The Insect across the sand and I follow him into the shelter of a beach bar where he settles my bike down on the wooden floorboards, then he begins prowling the empty bar, dragging chairs and tables around. This is spooky because the shriek of thunder mutes the clang of the furniture and the violet-white pulse of lightning gives the bin man the jarring animated look of an old cartoon. He takes my sleeping bag from my arms, lays it inside the den of tables and chairs, and points. I crawl in.

'Grazie! Perfecto!' I say, actually quite impressed with my den.

The binman says nothing but stares at me, a little too keenly. I hold his gaze and wait.

'Dormito, dormito,' he says.

I stare at his face, occasionally lit by flashing white light.

'Dormito, dormito!' he insists, clasping his hands in prayer and pressing against his cheek.

'No,' I say.

To my surprise, that was enough, he mutters something and walks away.

As if replacing the discomfort of his presence, the storm rages harder. First in retina-searing white flashes, then comes the noise, so quickly afterward my thudding heart isn't given the chance to thump. Thunder in my memories is suppose to rumble, but here it seems to scream right in my face as though the sky is splintering. Even the torrential rain sounds like a modest 'sh' under it.

The creepy binman returns, only this time carrying a heavier stench of cheap cigarettes.

He crouches down, cocks his head to one side and says, 'Che bella,' stroking my cheek with his damp fingers. 'Dormito. Dormito, bella ragazza.'

'No,' I defy him.

His yellow fingers hover above my eyes, which instantly water under the smell of piss and ashtrays. He presses on my eyelids and draws them downwards.

'No!' I say, opening my eyes, sitting up. 'No,' I repeat.

The creepy binman stares a while longer, souring the air, weaving creepy whispers into my ear about how beautiful I am, how I ought to sleep. I do not sleep. I wait, bolt upright in a staring competition with the creepy binman. He loses and I am left to the company of the lightning. This is going to be a long night.

Gentle hubbub: what a lovely thing. Scraping chairs, soft early morning chat, the lap of the sea, the rumble of coffee machines: Did the lightning fry me in my sleep, did the binman finish me off? Have I died and gone to heaven?

'Ciao,' says a man, a beautiful man, bald, thin, voice full of sunshine, peering into my den of chairs and tables.

'Ciao. Buongiorno!' I say.

He laughs: a lovely sound.

'You are Engleesh, yez?'

'Sì...How–'

'You look Engleesh. Dere are not many Italianos wit blonde corly har! You wan breakfaz? Caffè?'

'Oh sì, sì, sì, grazie!'

He grins, and helps me to my feet.

'Dis is your bike? You arr a cycliste? Me too. Oh, I am Orlindo,' he says.

Orlindo buys me pizza and a coffee, draws another chair among his circle of friends and sits me down.

Morning melts away nicely in the company of Orlindo, his wife Paula, a large man swollen with the promise of a chortle, his wife, and another man who shuffles cards. They laugh lovingly at my wonky Italian, teach me the word for lightning, 'fulmine' and pour me beer.

As my pizza crust absorbs the pissy fizz, I say to them, *in Italian*, that beer and pizza make you strong, that – I tap the crust on the side of the cup – pizza and beer are a good combination. An earthquake of laughter and disgust rocks the table.

'NO! MAL COMBINAZIONE!' yells the card shuffler.

'YOU ARE TOO ENGLEESH!' roars the chortling fellah.

'SÌ,' I announce, proudly.

'Aleechay,' says Orlindo, 'you will stay with us? Sì? You can riposo? An come to my mother's birtday? She eighty-seven today.'

'Really? I'd love to!'

Paula (Orlindo's wife), shoots me a small smile. Up until now, she hadn't said a word but after an encouraging nod from Orlindo who she'd been whispering to, she finally asks, 'You really come ere in bici? Dall'Inghilterra?'

'Sì, con bici.'

Her cheeks puff up, impressed, while the whole table fills with the collective 'Oo' of kudos. After then, Paula's shyness billows away with the smoke of her cigarette.

Paula is a curious character with ruffled, auburn, sparrow-like hair stopping just below her ears. Indeed, she is bird-like in all manner of ways: nimble, slightly frightened, dainty, big-eyed.

'Sei coraggioso,' she says, touching my arm lovingly.

Orlindo and Paula's flat is glossy and cool on my feet. I take a shower, leaning pathetically against the wall, unable to lift any of the lotions and potions by the plughole: the espresso of this morning has worn off and I feel like a bag of raw sausages.

'Riposo,' says Paula, dragging my sagging self into a bedroom.

The bed slams under my body. A breeze floats from the balcony and washes over me.

I wake up heavy, a pile of clothes to my side. One by one I inspect them: a brown shirt, shorts, frilly knickers, a jumper with the word 'believe' on it, a leopard print bikini top offering as much coverage as a pair of Doritos hung on some tooth floss and one other top. This one was electric blue and had the words 'Ci molto stelle in nel cielo come ci fosse molta sabbia sulla spiaggia' which means, 'There is lots of stars in the sky, like there is lots of sand on the beach.' Even though I don't get it, it's my favourite. I slip it on.

A gust of garden herbs, tomato and garlic sweeps into the room as Orlindo opens the door.

'Dey for you. You like? Paula is cooking. Shall we go fore a walk?'

They really do have a shop for everything: a shop for pizza, a shop for vegetables, a shop for focaccia, a shop for cheese. How very European. Back home you only need to walk into Tesco to find anything from butter to high heels, mobile phones to condoms.

'Che questo?' I ask, pointing.

'Pizzeria.' says Orlindo.

'Che questo?'

'Gatto.'

'Che questo?'

'Cane.'

'Che questo?'

'Carne.'

A pause.

'Paula gets very tired,' says Orlindo, saddened. 'Paula has had cancer.'

About now, I should say something. But lost in the drop of my heart, I stall a few seconds before I ask, 'Is she better?'

'Yes. She has had treatment. But she still gets very tired.'

'Paula is strong,' I say, staring straight ahead.

'Esattamente,' says Orlindo, staring straight ahead.

Back at the flat, Paula is still stirring that same melding pot of tomatoes. The smell makes me woozy. It smells like Saturdays, bouncing on my little heels, eating the triangle of cheese too small to grate, snapping the spaghetti, going *'Uergh!'* as Dad stops chopping to bite into a raw onion as if it were an apple. Never was a child as happy as me.

'Spaghetti alla pomodoro,' says Paula, piling three plates with crimson squiggles, pebbled with capers.

Once I had a Hare Krishna friend (believed in fairies and all sorts) and she said she could taste when something had been made with love. Now, as I take a first mouthful and the world blows away, I know she was onto something. The slosh of spaghetti, richly coated in a velvet of tomato, the electric-shock burst of capers, the seductive haunt of garlic: the whole thing is so moving, I barely say a word. This is the best thing I will ever eat in all my life.

'You must remember dis, see dis bread, you go like dis.' Orlindo mops up the red residue with a hunk of bread. 'SCAR-PE-TTA. It mean little shoe in Ingleesh.'

'Scar-pe-tta,' I repeat, swiping the bread sponge around my empty plate.

Italy has reached its climax.

Party time!

A racket of 'Ciao!'s commence. Kiss after kiss, hug after hug. Women, children, babies, mothers, brothers, friends. It is impossible to know who knows who and for what reason because these Italians all treat one another like their favourite brother. Except me, who is treated like Kylie Minogue and hence subject to 'Complimenti' after 'complimenti'. I don't quite know how to tell them they've got it wrong, that really I'm just a strange plonk of curly hair whose progress is the result of a free bike, free food, free shelter and the limitless kindness of others. Such misdirected credit. So I shrug my shoulders and say 'Facile', the Italian word for easy. Which might have accidentally made me look like a cocky prick.

A woman called Eva, a caramel creature with buttery curves and a buttery voice seems to be overwhelmed by me.

'I'm in love,' she says, grabbing my face in her hands, 'Your Italian is bene, you slept on the beaches, not afraid. You tink everybody good and nobody bad, you trust everybody. I'm in love! I'm in LOVE!'

Before I've the chance to laugh, she dashes off, caramel hair flopping behind her. But she boomerangs quickly back, dumping a mass of dried figs in my hand. Typical Italians.

Then another woman, wearing a toddler on her hip takes her turn and gives me a book. An Italian novel titled 'un posto nel mondo'. So I've had the gold, frankincense, now where's the myrrh?

Hushes and whispers. We funnel into a kitchen where the victim of eighty-seven years, wrapped up in a floral apron, sits expectantly.

When there is occasion for singing, be it a happy birthday or a hymn, there's always one who goes a bit Whitney Houston, a bit OTT. Here, everyone is *that Whitney*, flexing the full potential of their voice boxes as the cake is presented. Once the singing and applause fades, the old lady rests her hand on her heart and blows out her two candles: just enough to be plural and for the veins of her neck to stick out like noodles, but not too many to cause her old heart to pack in. We clap at the feat, and then amble outside to look at the yellow moon.

19

Don't judge a book by its paperwork

Rustling noises wake me up. I follow them out onto the balcony where my panniers lie unrecognisably tidy, a hands-on-hips Orlindo stood sweating above them.

'Dey a mess. So I clean dem for you. An I put some tings inside,' he says.

'Goodness! Wow, thanks I–' I shuffle through them, realising my collection of toilet paper, diary entries, snacks and Aaron's heartfelt letter have been mistaken for trash and replaced with inner tubes, a puncture repair kit I don't know how to use and a carefully wrapped sandwich. 'Grazie, troppo gentile,' I say.

'An dis. For de *zanzara*,' says Orlindo, handing me a bottle of mosquito repellent, '*de zanzara tigre*.'

I look down at my leg, scarred and buttoned thanks to those damn tiger mosquitoes, then back up at Orlindo.

'Grazie, grazie, grazie mille,' I say. 'They've been absolutely eating me alive.'

'Oh yes, dey orrible. Ey, Aleechay, my zizter an er uzban wait for you outside dey wanna cycle wit you, bene?'

Orlindo and I peer over the balcony and wave at the two arrows glazed in fluorescent Lycra, the studs of their shoes matching the clips of their pedals, their bicycles kind of mean-looking.

As predicted my new friends are painfully faster than me, advancing in leaps with each casual stroke while I heave hard against the pedals, trying to conceal my panting breath as we exchange the odd bit of Italian chit-chat. Most of it I manage to understand, and when I don't, I just laugh and shout 'SÌ!', which seems to work a treat.

Finally, after two breathless hours we stop for coffee. But even then we don't sit, but instead join an erect line of Italians, knocking back their thimbles as if they were cars and this was a petrol station. Freshly caffeinated, me and Orlindo's rellies part ways. How long until I can stop without them seeing me? Call it five miles.

Four miles later, I find myself a little cove to lunch in. The sea draws gently in and out, circling rocks, filling their pools. And punctuating my centre of vision, a slight dash of bum, belonging to a man reading the paper in his trunks. For some bizarre reason, I take a picture of him. Is that creepy? I think he noticed. I scoff the best sandwich of my life and leave the poor guy to it.

More tinned beans, more dusty sand, more pizza but no lightning: I sleep like a baby.

Today has so far been full of men. Inviting me for lunch (PRANZO! PRANZO!), buying me coffees, dousing me in compliments (Bella ragazza, *che Bella ragazza!*), insisting upon selfies, tooting, shouting from their cars. At first, I'd been polite and stopped to chat to each bachelor, explaining my too-busy-for-lunch predicament. But as middle-aged spread number five looms behind me, collecting behind him a queue of traffic, my patience wanes and I begin ignoring them. Besides, I'm on a mission. A mission to reach Napoli.

Towards the city centre, a great mass of exhaust pipes cough, grilling wavy patterns into the dusty air. Furious Italians toot at nothing, yell at each other, overtake, undertake, brake abruptly, while suicidal pedestrians do their worst to get in the way. Can't they see? They're only making it hotter. Despite the thick air and towering buildings, I trudge through, right to the centre. And you wouldn't have believed it.

This, I think to myself as I glide over the glossy mosaic roads, is like a better version of heaven. Bust through the tumult of its thick urban belt and Napoli is the perfect amount of quiet. Quietly warm, quietly busy, quietly lit and...just quiet. The only sounds being gentle ones: the odd flap of a rug from a balcony, buzz of a moped, babble of the Fontana del Nettuno, and my own humble gasps.

I pedal slow. Slow enough to lose balance, so I walk: alongside the clutter of pizzerias, osterias, focaccerias, every kind of 'ria' you could imagine, squashed next to each other with the closeness of teenage sweethearts. I walk between ladders of balconies occupied by chatty neighbours, past gossiping old ladies sat in a huddle of rickety chairs, past men smoking cigars together. I'd been warned time and time again to keep my wits about me in Napoli (unless I should want to be made into a leather coat by the mafia) yet I let my few wits melt and wander calmly, feeling quite at home among the textured chaos. There's even a bloody volcano towering just behind it all.

I turn a corner and there stands my host, so meaty looking I have to double check my eyes haven't lost their sense of perspective.

'Hi,' he says, a whipping sound.

'Ciao! Pete?' I ask.

'Yez. Ere, I take your bags.'

Pete, having more strength in one pinkie than I have in my whole body, makes my bags look as light as two packets of crisps. He opens the door and dumps them on his sofa while I heave behind him, making constipated noises as I try to surmount the last two steps of his apartment with The Insect on my shoulder.

'Ere. You can sit ere.' Pete waves a tattooed hand at two high-chairs and finally looks at me, for a jab of a second. 'You wanna drink?' he asks, clicking some things on his laptop.

I jump a little as a deafening chafing noise beats out of the enormous speakers in Pete's tiny flat.

'JUST WATER IS FINE!' I shout over the heavy metal.

Pete sets down two glasses of water (the bass making them shake slightly) and sits opposite me, looking as though he was trying to shrivel away from his enormous shoulders. His eyes dash about the room, deciding on what might be safe to look at and eventually settle on a fluffy cat that begins purring around his feet. Pete smiles and the cat jumps on his lap.

'SHE'S SO CUTE!' I shout.

Pet's lips flutter as though he'd spoken, but his mumble is lost to the murderous screams of Metallica.

'PETE, HOW COME YOUR ENGLISH IS SO GOOD?' I ask.

Pete's face lights up, and he mumbles, 'English is easy... four years in Englan... pubs an...I ad to come back... some stupid reason... go back someday... Ere! Wait dere, I show you someting.' Pete whips out of the room.

While Pete faffs about his cat jumps onto the table and stares into my face, her eyes as enormous and glossy as marbles, her nose twitching. 'TSCHE!' She sneezes, covering my flinching face in cold snot. As I wipe my face with the back of my hands, Pete returns holding a framed certificate.

'Look ere,' he says, his voice stronger than before. 'It say "*dark haired BRITISH male*".' He props his criminal record on the table, and stares at it adoringly. 'I got dis in England an I was so appy because de guy taught I was a real Brit. So I kept it an put it in a frame.'

'TSCHE!' his cat sneezes on me again.

Pete's eyes, full of pride, transfer seamlessly from the words '*offence*', '*British*', '*aggressive*' onto his cat. He ruffles her head tenderly with a hand weighed down with rings and says, 'Sorry, she as a cold.'

'I don't mind,' I laugh, 'She's so unbelievably cute!'

'Yez an she very smart and– Oh wow! She is usually so shy! She likes you. Dat is a really great sign.'

Pete is a great example of not judging a book by its cover. Actually, Pete is a great example of not judging a book by its paperwork, which is good news for me: my cover is a mess, and my paperwork a little frightening. Not quite a criminal record, but I've done my own sort of time and the documents will tell you disturbing things like: 'low BMI', 'hyperactive', 'distressed', 'sleep troubles', 'risk', 'suicidal'.

'People don't understan,' says Pete, audible because his screamo playlist has ended and now out from his speakers pours the glorious nonchalance of Noel Gallagher. 'People call me *Pietro* but I no wanna be called Pietro, I wanna be called Pete. I don't wanna be Italian.'

'Why?' I ask.

'Because I like de English. Dey ave de best sense of humour and de food is much better den ere.'

'You've got to be joking! Italian food is the best in the world! I've had the best food of my life here!'

'Nah, I like de fried food and de gravy and de meat.'

Another hour goes by.

'But you are brave travelling as a young girl, all alone. Be careful,' says Pete.

'Ah, but everybody has been so kind to me! Except, well. Sometimes the men can get a little much and, well, there was this one guy... touched me a bit. He was a couchsurfing host, like you.'

'That's disgusting! What an arse-ol! Next time, remember dis: don't ever leave your bags in someone's ouse until you are absolutely *sure* dey are safe. Because if dey ave your bags, you might not be able to escape. Yeah? Remember dis, you're my little sister. No one hurt my little sister.'

Another chit-chat hour dissolves into the delicious soup of my life; it's 11pm and Pete is stirring a pan of couscous and peas.

'Yeah, she leave me dis note,' Pete points to a crumpled note, pinned to the wall. 'She was a prostitute an I let er sleep on de sofa. Den she came back because she said she mizzed me. She say to me "ey, you an arse-ol but I loves you a bit anyway." Ere, eat up. You need to be strong. Carbs will make you strong.'

We eat a while and by the time bedtime comes, Pete's desperate shyness has melted, proven by the deceleration of his darting eyes and his voice now more sweary, no longer muffled behind his fidgeting hands. I like Pete.

'You look sleepy. Go to bed. Oh! But have this,' Pete gives me a speaker, 'For music. An ave this,' Pete gives me a charging cable, 'an this,' Pete gives me a water bottle, the words 'PROTEIN' stamped on it. 'Goodnight. See you tomorrow. I'll make you breakfast.'

Pete's tiny sofa is the comfiest, safest bed in Napoli.

'TSCHE!'

A wake-up call: a cool spritz coating my face. Two marble eyes protruding from a mass of fur glare at me and a gigantic bogey, glistening in the morning light, dangles dangerously close to my lips. Pete's cat sniffs the cold bogey back up its nose and jumps off.

'You!' I begin, my wet face still cringing. But Pete's cat is too cute. A quick peach smoothie made by Pete, then I'm on my way.

Now, here is the million-dollar question: is 11am too early for pizza? Perhaps by the time I've scoured the menu, asked the waitress if this exact pizza is definitely vegan, ordered, waited, it'll be about 12am: an acceptable time for lunch (although 12.30am is technically perfect: that was lunchtime in the unit). Anyway, I don't have the luxury of choice now because by some curious form of jiggery-pokery, I've found myself on *maybe* a date. Maybe. A twitchy kind of fella with hair in shiny black ringlets as tight as his un-smiling face is sitting opposite me, firing accusatory questions like 'why you ere?', 'why you sit like dat?', 'what you want? Order someting.' He's short too. At least, I think he's short: hunched in a bad mood, it is quite hard to make out his vertical potential. And because Ringlet-Man speaks so aggressively, I haven't the courage to protest as goes ahead ordering me a pizza at 11.15am.

My pizza arrives, nearly as big as the table itself.

'Can't we share it?' I say.

'No. Dis is too early for eating. You eat it,' says Ringlet Man.

Obeying the commands of my date, I eat it in front of his thick frown while he points out all the places which have been recently ransacked by the mafia. The whole scenario is so uncomfortable (eating while being so sternly watched of course reminds me of hospital), that I'd forgotten Neapolitan pizza was supposed to be the best in the world.

'Grazie. That was *delizioso*. I'm...' I look around for an excuse to leave. 'I'm gunna go...' then I spot it, lurking in the hazy distance. 'Climb the volcano.'

The Ringlet Man, for the first time in our hour together, cracks a smile so sudden and true I could've almost (*almost*) loved him for it.

'You should take a shower forst. Come to mine for a shower, an fill your bottles.'

Red alert, red alert, man-down, mayday: do not go into this man's home.

'Pete... I didn't do the bag thing!' I whisper into the streaming hot water. Showering directly after lunch does not feel nice, especially when a slightly creepy man waits outside for you and you have been an idiot and let him lock your bags, your bike, your everything in his basement. I look down at my bulging bread-belly and try to flatten it with carving motions. No luck.

'MEGLIO!' I sing, walking into Ringlet Man's living room in a cloud of steam.

He smiles dangerously and pats the empty space next to him on the sofa. I sit. Is this a bad idea? Our hips are touching and that certainly feels like a bad idea. The room tightens with metallic anticipation of a thunder storm and I start to hum a tune. But Ringlet Man finds this endearing, so I start a speech about how *great* his tap water tastes. This makes it so much worse.

He laughs, an elongated, seductive laugh, and then says, 'You're too pretty to be English.'

I laugh, secretly pocketing the compliment forever while also trying to calculate an escape route.

'I like you,' he says.

'Oh! Um yeah, I'm actually not that great, really,' I shrug.

He reaches out his index finger and strokes the fluffy hairs on my thigh and dammit they prickle up in response.

'Hm,' Ringlet Man smiles, 'I like your leg hair, iz so funny.'

'Oh!'

The air turns itchy and we sit in silence.

'Can I kees you?'

'Um... I think maybe not? Sorry.'

'Iz jus I really wanna kees you.'

Hadn't I learnt from the melon incident? There is no such thing as a free lunch! Maybe I should just kiss him. Kiss and leave. Just a couple of seconds on my lips, for the sake of courtesy. A fast, hard press, rushed but romantic, then pull away, tell him something theatrical and leave. I mean that's all good and well, but I'd sooner eat my own fingers. Is that an option? It'd put him off, for sure, not to mention it would be more palatable than his glossy, hungry, lips. Only I like my fingers: they pick me my berries and paint me my pictures.

'I'm sorry, I can't,' I say this to the plastic octopus I'd made out of a disposable cup. 'I just can't.'

'Why?' he asks.

'I... I' – think Alice, think! – 'I don't want to like anyone like that. I have a journey to complete and... *I must go alone*,' I say, feeling quite impressed with my cinematic delivery.

'Okay,' he sighs. 'Okay...Buuuuut, I-will-kees-your-back.'

He smacks a hard kiss just below my right shoulder blade. It sticks like a bruise.

'Can I go climb the volcano now?' I say.

Who the hell decided 6pm was an appropriate time to close a volcano? It's taken me four hours to climb up here. Four *heaving* hours! Bloody hell. And anyway, how does one even go about closing a volcano? That's like closing the sea, which I suppose actually, they kind of do here. I sit like an angry toddler at the precipice, maybe laughing or maybe crying into the space between my knees.

'SCUZE!' says a man, 'I zorry iz clozed, take zis.'

The man hands me a bottle of iced tea and a bag of croutons then scuttles off, just a little afraid of my wilful neurosis.

That line from the Snickers advert *'You're not you when you're hungry'* blasts in my head as I crunch my expensive croutons (I know they're expensive because the packaging is thick) and sip my iced tea staring poignantly (at least this is how I imagine myself in third person) out to the juicy amber of a ripe sun. It falls behind the horizon and the timid spittle of evening lights scattered below start to glitter. Didn't need to see that poxy volcano after all.

Then I descend: past the youths (apparently volcanoes are a cool hang out spot), the charred trees, the pizzeria whose customers had given me a standing ovation on my way up, the house of the man who invited me to bed as I was pedalling my way up. I stop halfway down, famished, and trot into a restaurant. Yes, yes! I *know* three pizzas in one day is ridiculous. Look, if spaghetti hoops count as one of your five a day according to the UK government, then I too shall count pizza. Tomato, innit.

'I make you a pizza.' says the pizza boy. 'You no worry about cost. Don't worry. I tell you, don't worry.'

After free pizza number three of today – which curiously had no tomato on it – I bolt towards the sea.

Just in time for dark, I pull into a seaside town, pulsing with an "oomph" of club music and occupied by partygoers of all types: Grannies wearing sticky perfume and gaudy earrings that worsen the problem of their pendulous earlobes; teenage girls in fluorescent crop tops; clip-clopping women, slim and handbagged (sigh, I haven't owned a handbag since I was 14); boisterous lads waggling their booze about like trophies.

A small free beach, dirty enough to be empty of everything but grey sand and neglected row-boats, offers a little respite if one ignores the blaring Justin Bieber disco going on to my left. This is actually a blessing, however, because Justin is undermining the petite squeaks of vermin that are coming from somewhere behind my head. Luckily also, I have a brain full of dough to muffle out all of this hullaballoo.

Morning comes and people filter in, displacing the mice and rats. Among them, a Pakistani man is dragging his trolley of tacky plastic things behind him, waving oversized red sunglasses to each and every beach-goer, one at a time. Each one but me. Not a good sign at all.

'Sono sporco,' I mutter to myself, cringing at the feel of my own dirty skin. 'WAH!' I yell as a dead seahorse lands in my lap.

'ZZZZ!' Says the man who must've dropped it there, he has one of those robot-voice-tracheotomy things attached to his throat. 'ZZZZ, PERR TE, ZZZ. È BUONA FORTUNA' he says.

My fingers shake as I nurse the corpse in my palm. Just a tiny little creature, no bigger than my pinkie, torn from his underwater home. Someone has burrowed his poor wee eyes out. The man tells me through the clunks and whooshes of his robot breath that dead seahorses are good luck, but I'm not so sure. I mummify the hapless creature in a napkin and study the map. *'The Amalfi is beautiful. But full of tourists.'* Claudio's voice rings in my head. Beautiful will do me fine.

And beautiful it is.

'I'M FLYING!' I yell, ribboning up and down the cliffs.

I peer over the precipice at the infinity of blue, speckled with little boats ruffling up fluffy white trails. Just imagine hurling off the edge, a grand finale while at my peak happiness. End on a high. I've had a good innings. It would mean I didn't have to go home, back to university, back to the agonising war zone of my 'smaller than average' head.

For as long as I can remember I've always thought of death in two ways: seduction and sadness. When I was four, I realised that I too would die and I still remember the weight this put in my heart. Then when I was fourteen, I realised I could choose to die, and though I did nothing about it at the time, this kept me company. These days I get both feelings, often at the same time. But today I don't want to die. Actually, I want to live forever.

At the tip-top of Positano's cliffs I almost buy a banana. But it is too expensive. The fruit shop lady must have understood this perfectly because she gives me ten euros (for pizza), a bunch of Japanese biscuits, a cup of granita, and *'de best ting you ever gunna eat in de world.'* She turns around, pours water over a piece of bread, douses it in olive oil, then the final touch: some kind of red dust.

'Here.' She hands it to me: a wet flopping piece of bread, leaking oil between my fingers. 'Dis is the most delicious ting you ever eat,' She repeats.

I take a bite and Jesus Christ she was right. I daren't ever try to describe it.

'An take dis.' She hands me a packet of the red dust. 'Dis will make everything you eat delicious,' she says.

I thank her five different ways and she laughs, hugs me, and takes my picture before I'd had time to get the bits out of my teeth.

The town bellow is chock-a-block with very white tourists wearing very white clothes. Trinkety things, embroidered dresses, mosaics, ceramics, all pretending to be authentic glimmer and gleam from under-stocked shops, beguiling the tourists, teasing the money out of their jangling pockets.

It isn't easy changing into your jammies on a beach, especially with a man hovering and peering. And yes, maybe I did accidentally flash him a bit. Anyway, the feel of my jammies against my skin is heaven, a cool, crisp relief from the clothes of today which had been made limp and sticky and gathered a bit of a nasty tang. Surely the cool of night will wash away their pong...

Night did not wash away any pong. But between you and me, I actually quite enjoy festering in my own filth. It makes me feel raw and real and protected from men.

20

Men, dogs and flies

I leave Sorrento with haste, back up the Amalfi cliffs, back to rural beauty. Gosh it is so, so, so hot. So hot my saddle, in its melted, mangled state, has glued itself to my arse. I unstick myself with a sweating wince.

'CIAO!' shouts a man, hosing his cliff-top olive trees.

'PER ME! PER ME!' I yell. 'ACQUA PER ME!'

Understanding me immediately he hoses me down. The gush of it, the punch, the whiplash kicks the air out of me and I feel so suddenly violated I could burst into tears.

'Grazie,' I slur, soaked.

'Niente!' says the man, his smiling fat cheeks squishing his eyes into slits. 'Vieni, vieni!' he says, calling me over.

The waitress sets down two panna cottas, 'È vegana. È fatto di soia,' she says.

I thank her and sink my spoon into it. Typical, you ask a guy to hose you down and he goes and gets the wrong idea. Still, dessert was delicious. At least I remember thinking that, but thanks to just one shot of lung-burning, stomach-aching, head-hammering limoncello, I've forgotten exactly what flavour it was. Courgette? No, fuck, that was the pasta.

'Andiamo!' says my sweaty not-date, 'Piace Beyoncé?' He squeezes his fat cheeks into his motorbike helmet: just like a birth, only in reverse.

'Sì! Perché no!' I yell, straddling the seat behind him.

With Beyoncé's caramel voice gushing from his speaker, we catapult off, a midnight wind battering my ringlets. The stars, the lights of towns far below, sparkling like embers. 'YOU'RE THE ONE I LOOOVE!' Beyoncé howls.

I wake up on top of a double duvet with my legs spread like a pair of open scissors and my dress bunched up at my hips. Weird dream, probably. I close my legs, yank my dress down and shuffle into the kitchen and there he is, weeping with sweat: my chubby little fan.

'Per te!' he says pouring me coffee.

'Grazie,' I return, sitting down on the very edge of a chair.

Triggered by my company, his soggy state deteriorates. He crosses his arms, uncrosses them and prowls the kitchen, making the whole kitchen made humid as I sip my coffee.

'Per te! Per te!' he says, pouring a bag of stuff all over the table, 'Per te! Guarda!'

He unboxes my gifts, fumbling and slippery, announcing them one by one – a flask, charging cables, coffee, bottles of water, a fan, a torch, snacks, cola – piling them in my arms. There ain't no way I'm drinking that cola, but I thank him anyway and start packing up to leave.

'Restare! Restare!' he pleads, 'Hai bisogno reposare! Buono per le gambe! Restare oggi, andare adomani! Restare, Aleechay!'

'Mi dispiace,' I apologise, mounting the saddle.

'Oh, Aleechay.'

I click into first gear and spin my pedal to 1 o'clock (like Mrs Edmonds had taught us in our cycling proficiency. Or, wait, was it supposed to be 2 o'clock?). 'Arrivederci,' I say.

'Aleechay!' he bursts, grabbing my face with his sweaty hands, kissing my cheeks in many slobbery smacks.

As soon as he is out of eyes reach I wipe my slimy cheeks and pull over. Feeling dreadfully nervous that it might explode, and even more nervous I might accidentally drink it, I leave the cola by the kerb. There was a time, back in 2015, when diet cola was the only thing I let pass my lips. It zapped my taste buds with insincere sweetness, fizzed like faulty electric wires down my throat, made a terrible fuss in my empty stomach and then the finale: I'd have these electric-shock burps explode in my brain. It was my favourite poison (cola cleans pennies, don't forget). Four years on from my last swig and my inner chemistry has only just about recovered. So I have taken an oath to never touch the stuff again.

The day goes as predicted: cycle, focaccia, swim, espresso, read the paper, focaccia, cycle, another swim, snack (more focaccia), cycle. Evening sweeps in, which I am very glad of for it means night is near, after which there will be a day's space between me and my sweaty fan. If only he'd stop texting me. 'Alice, send me your location. I want to come and say goodbye,' reads the most recent.

I ignore it and go into a shop to buy apricots. Apricots, because if I'm to eat any more wheat, I'll be too doughy to pedal. Fate has a different plan however, in the form of free pizza given to me by the man at the till. No matter my efforts it seems pizza is inevitable. That's one more line on my 'free pizza' tally (eleven, so far).

Another text:

'Alice. I come to Salerno to find you. There in 20 minuti. Send me your location.'

Dammit! Lesson learned: never tell a sweaty man your trajectory. Pretending the ceaseless ringtone wasn't going on in my pannier, I push uphill, until Salerno diminishes to a haze of light pollution.

A church sits at the top of the hill, enormous and isolated, complete with – get this – a working tap outside. I knock, hoping for a God-loving man to answer with plastic cups of squash and rich tea biscuits, and the promise that I'd be all right. My knock echoes a long while... No squash, no safety but at least I have the company of water on-tap.

'You'll be okay, it's alright. Anyway, he won't find you.' I mumble to myself benignly, as I fill my saucepan with water. And then a little more aggressively, as I unroll my tent, *'Fuck's sake.* I already have a stalker at home and I don't need an Italian one. Fucking men. Stupid fucking men.'

On a positive note, Camp is looking very sophisticated. My plastic house is furnished with: a sleeping bag, a blow up pillow and a torch, strung to the ceiling like a real light bulb. I've even laid my solar panels on its roof (they barely work during the day, but I thought it would be fun to put them on my tent like a real house). Outside my tent I've assembled the kitchen: a bubbling saucepan of rice, a plastic pot containing one thin strip of aubergine, a flask of stale coffee and a bottle of even staler iced tea. Then we have the garage: my bike, leaned against a tree. And last (but by no means least), the toilet: clumsy handfuls of napkins fostered from bars and one sandy bottle of antibacterial gel. Receipts too, just in case.

Seven new messages and five more missed calls later, the rice is ready.

'I just want to say goodbye,' reads another text.

I rub my fork against my thigh: my effort at cleaning it.

'Send me your location.'

Yuck. The courgette was a slimy mistake: my dinner tastes of swamps.

'I love you.'

Swallowing hard against emotional indigestion, I turn off my phone and stare out at the navy cliffs, pink sea and amber city lights. The sky melds deep reds, purples, oranges, telling me about its day.

'It's okay Alice, you're fine. You've always got me,' I mutter.

A motorbike engine rips through the air, fraying the few nerve fibres I have left. Heart pounding, I drop my empty bowl and scamper into my tent, pulling my sleeping bag up over my head, curling up like a woodlouse. Surely that's him, that's him on his motorbike out to get me. I'm not afraid, just alert. My heart is ticking fast because it's alert. A good heart, ready to pump blood into my legs, ready to have them sprinting. I talk myself to sleep.

Morning comes and I greet it by fist-bumping the air. Alive. Alone. Untouched. I peer out of the tent flap, a warm blanket of lazy sunshine coating my face. This is going to be a good day. To the Apennines!

Lesson learned: do not attempt to climb mountains without an adequate supply of water. Despite the rhyme, Alice is not a camel as my pasty mouth, buffering blood, withering brain and peeling lips will concur. But wait, is that a mirage, or...

There's a man at the fountain, face split by a toothy grin. He laughs at me as I hurtle towards the fountain, stick my head under the tap and shriek at the agony of brain-freeze.

'No! É fredo! Troppo Fredo' he yells, cupping water in his hands and hurling it at me.

Once was funny, twice was also *quite* funny, third time was a bit *alright, fuck off now*, then on the fourth, he lunges towards me, and gropes my left tit, hard.

'NO!' I shout, smacking his hand away.

'Che bella ragazza,' he says, smiling stupidly at the two nipple targets of my translucent t-shirt.

'NO!' I repeat, storming off.

'LEI BELLA! BELLA RAGAZZA!' he yells.

Off I chug, wondering whatever happened to foreplay. Barren mountains are a good place to be in times like these, although that meaty looking dog just ahead does not look friendly. He stands as frozen as a statue, until I near him, then his head begins following my spinning legs. As I pass he lunges for me, dismembering my eardrums with his hollow bark. I pedal faster than I knew I could, my whole body taut and powerful as the dog's furious jaws snap behind me. It is only when I outpace him, turning a sharp right up the zigzagging precipice that I start to shake. But I do not cry because I know in my deepest spidey-senses there's more trouble to come and that I will need my strength.

My instincts were correct. Up 4,000ft I've just survived dog chasing number five and have decided if the next dog kills me, then so be it: to my scorched adrenal glands, death might be lovely. Yet still I push on, driven by something I'm simply too shattered to understand.

Just as things were looking hopeless, a perfectly horrible picnic spot presents itself. Strewn with litter so old some of it has already started biodegrading, it has no men and no dogs, only some barbed wire and a bad smell to keep me company. I sit beneath the bridge, sighing the sigh of a blow-up mattress as you squeeze the last lumps of air out of it: a defeated 'floof'. Alone at last.

A fly lands on my thigh, a juicy one with iridescent wings.

'Go away fly, please,' I say, shivering him off.

He (I'm sure it's a he) whizzes around my head, then lands on the opposite thigh.

'Please? Look, this is *my* leg. Get off.'

A couple of his friends join in, harassing me, buzzing from one limb to another, crawling along my legs, rubbing their hands together wickedly.

'JUST LEAVE ME ALONE!' I sob, 'STOP TOUCHING ME AND JUST FUCK OFF AND LEAVE ME ALONE!'

Tears shed, focaccia eaten, throat hoarse: onward. The day dwindles fast and the first star appears. A car pulls in beside me.

'CIAO!' shouts the driver, 'EY!'

Just as I had done for every angry dog, I stare ahead and ignore him.

'Ciao, you are Engleesh?' asks the man, 'Sì?'

'Sì,' I say.

'Ey you wan some elp?'

'No, grazie' I smile, heart lunging in my throat.

'Ere,' he sticks a note out at me, 'Take it. Take it!'

'NO, GRAZIE.' I shout.

'TAKE IT!'

'NO!'

He revs off, tossing the note behind him, 'FOLLOW ME ON FAZEBOOK I am called Mu...' his car and his voice, disappear.

I pick up the twenty euro note (that's twenty focaccia) and watch it flap in my trembling fingers. My trust, my irrational optimism, it's dissolving. Soon I should be a bitter mess, soured by fear and hate.

I make it to Potenza and it is too dark and I am too hungry. Hungrier than hungry, porous for it even. My legs are bendy, because the hunger was so enormous it ran out of room in my belly and took over my limbs. Too urban to camp, too rural to yield an open shop, I trudge through Potenza scratching my hungry head. Outside one of the villas, three old women are sat on plastic chairs, pecking conversation at each other, cackling like Macbeth's three witches. I stand staring at them.

'Prego?' says the central witch.

Silhouetted by the light flooding from the kitchen, it is impossible to know what sort of mood she might be in. You'd think from her sharp sentences she was cross. But remember, this is Italy, Southern Italy, in fact. We exchange a very quick ping-pong conversation which ends in the kitchen.

'Mangiare,' she demands, sitting me down to a table adorned with plates of beige things.

'FORMAGGIO? CARNE?' she says, flapping a piece of ham about like a dusty rug.

'Um, no grazie, sono vegana.' I say.

'Sì,' she says, putting the ham back in the fridge. She slam-dunks a loaf of sourdough on the table in front of me says, 'PANE,' and scuttles back outside.

Hungry, exhausted, hunched alone in a dimly lit room with food piled around me, I laugh the laugh of an evil villain.

All the other kids have left the table to play, to bounce on the bouncy castle. Idiots. They've left all this food.

Cubes of cheese impaled on cocktail sticks, half eaten bowls of jelly made cloudy by melted ice cream, the crusts of sandwiches, mini sausage rolls, pink panther biscuits: I gather them around me, a queen with her banquet.

Teeth sinking into cocktail sausages, cool puddles of ice cream lapping over tongue, the satisfying snap of a Party Ring, the juicy smash of jelly, the cheesy tang of Wotsits turning lips and fingers orange, sticking to teeth: ecstasy. My feet bounce beneath the table.

Across the room two women, one with flat, brown hair, the other wrapped in too-tight jeans, whisper about me. They think I don't know just cos I'm a kid. I do know, actually.

'You've got an impressive appetite! Where do you put it?' asks the brown-haired lady.

'In there!' I pat my little belly. 'I eat and eat and I don't get fat. I just stay skinny.'

The women laugh and I smile, delighted with my small body and gigantic appetite. I'm special.

My arms hinge rhythmically in front of me, grabbing and devouring: boiled potatoes, raw onion, croquettes, grease dripping off my elbows. Tangy, salty, soft, greasy, quenching. A dopamine rush, a glorious feast. Watery-eyed I move onto the sourdough, ignoring the fluffy blue spores thriving in its craters. I chew, lustfully, with my eyes closed, my head bowed and fists lightly banging the table as every single fibre holding me together sears with whole-body gratification.

Meanwhile the witches, like true witches, hiss, snort and squeal outside, thinking I can't understand them. But I know exactly what they're saying. They're mocking me.

Gravity is intense this morning. Too intense for standing, so I fall to my knees in surrender and send a message on Warmshowers.org to a guy called Rocco, asking if I can stay. What did those witches put in that bread? Five minutes. I'm allowed to be tired for five exact minutes. Ugh.

Despite my five exact minutes of lying on the floor like a dead body, despite knocking back two espressos that, I had been warned by the barman, would be '*like rocket juice. You no sleep for six nights after dis*', still my legs refuse to yield. And the sun, holey moles of Jesus on bicycles, it smites me as though I had no skin to protect my organs, which seem to be caramelising by the second. Don't even ask about my arse, or rather a raw stump that used to be an arse fused to the melted mess of what used to be a saddle. A car overtakes. If only it would hit me, then finally I'd have an excuse to lie horizontal.

And, oh no. Not again, please not again. Maybe he won't notice me, if I pedal really quietly. Smelling my unwashed socks, his meaty head turns with a jolt and he bounds after me, dust kicking, jaw snapping, barking my ear drums to shreds.

More dogs. More dogs. More dogs. To think, people actually *love* dogs. '*He's not usually like this!*' they'll offer as their precious gremlins dismember your ankles, sexually assault your leg, maul your shoulders and snog your knees. Dogs are evil, worse than flies, almost as bad as men. These dogs are particularly gruesome because they have been hard-wired to murder and spend all day waiting for such an opportunity. You could imagine then, how a lump of young curly-haired meat, barbequing in the sun will send them livid.

Another two hundred pounds of pure meat comes tearing towards me, paws thumping, bark watery with drool. That's it. I'm ready, I'm ready to die. I slam on my brakes.

'WHAT DO YOU WANT FROM ME?' I shriek, voice echoing across the mountains.

The dog stops with a jolt. We both stare at one another (even though they tell you to never look a dog in the eye), panting.

'WHAT IS IT YOU WANT?' I sob.

He bows his head and walks back to his spot in the shade.

21

Rocco

Thirteen. That is the number of dog chases for today. One more, I swear to God one more, and that'll be it, I'll die. I'll collapse into a miserable, dying heap of–

'ALEECHAY!' shouts a voice.

On the dusty horizon, a tremendous smile riding a bike advances towards me.

'Rocco?' I ask, as our bicycles meet.

'Yes!' says Rocco, bursting from his own grin which, according to his deep laughter lines, is quite permanent.

'Boy am I glad to see you. Molto, *molto* cane attacko,' I say.

Rocco laughs sympathetically then says, 'Ah, de dogs, dey are orrible. Well, see dis road we're on? It az many more mountain to climb. And many, many angry dogs. But dat road dere,' he points to a road, running parallel, 'iz flat. No dogs. Andiamo!'

Rocco bolts off and I follow behind. Even his back and shoulders are smiling. What a nice guy.

The final hurdle of the day: Rocco's drive. Well, 'drive' might be a little ambitious; it looked like a quarry that had recently undergone an earthquake: not good news for my arse which is currently bleeding and fused to my bike seat. But the excruciating bump down Rocco's drive is totally worth it to get to his 'L' shaped house.

'Welcome! I give you a tour,' says Rocco, gesturing me through the front door.

We walk through the kitchen, stocked only with sugar and coffee, then Rocco shows me his 'stuff room' (containing a jumbling stack of guitars, furniture and dusty photos) then the daddy long leg hangout zone (a bathroom with only two sheets of toilet paper left). We walk back outside, up the exterior steps and Rocco shows me his bedroom of two beds (one bed to sleep in, one bed for more guitars et cetera). It is all powered by solar. Or at least it was, until the battery packed in.

'I sorry is so dark, I ave been meaning to get it fixed but ave no time recently. Ah!' Rocco jumps back from the sight of his watch. 'I'm late! Sorry, I ave to go teach. You stay and rest. I come back later an we go get pizza, yeah? Oh, an my shower, iz...an unusual shower.' Rocco quickly gestures to a bottle of shower gel next to a hose pipe, then pelts off.

There is something innately degrading and satisfying about hosing oneself down like a car.

Rocco returns after sunset with a box of Earl Grey tea.

'Ey! *Phew*,' he pants. 'Sorry I'm late, I stop by de shop because If I'm aving an Engleesh girl stay, I must ave tea. Lez go get food.'

We hop into Rocco's car, hit the town, order two pizzas. I hope Rocco doesn't pay because it doesn't look like the poor fella has much money.

'Rocco, how did you learn English so well?' I ask. 'Your English is amazing.'

Rocco's face warms to a deeper shade of bronze and he says, 'I lived in Yorkshire for nine years to learn an I stayed with a man called Michael an iz wife an kids. Dem kids where great. Dey elp me learn English de best because dey laugh at me when I'm wrong.'

'Jesus, that's so impressive! Even *I* can't speak Yorkshirian, the accent is an absolute nightmare.'

'Ezacly! When I first come I undezand nutting. Nutting at oll. And I work in de keetchen and de boss ee shout at me, "YOU IDIOT! WHY YOU DID DIS!" And I can't tell im "IT WAZ NOT ME! IT WAZ IM! IT WAZ IM!" cos I no speak Engleesh. So I juz cross my arms an take it. But I learn. Michael and his family elp me learn.'

'NINE years!'

He nods, a slow, smiling, nostalgic nod. Pizza arrives.

'And the English food?' I ask.

'Oh god. It was ORRIBLE.' Rocco squirms in his seat. 'Day one I work on Michael's farm and he makes me dis breakfaz and oh my god I tink I would be sick. It was dis pile of greasy bacon and eggz and dis orange beans. Oh my god, I could not eat it. Day two come an I so ungry dat I eat de disgusting breakfast. I get used to de English food... eventually.'

'Wow...Nine years! Why did you leave?' I ask, holding a slice of pizza, floppy with lashings of aubergine and olive oil, with two hands.

Rocco sighs, then says, 'Michael was de most craziest, stubbornness, difficult man you would ever meet. He ate too much, an e drank too mach and we were always getting into trouble. We always drinking. One time we drive to a party and get drunk. Den Michael says he needs his medication which ee leave at ome. An I'm so drunk but I drive us ome for Michael's medication and I lose my licence. It is den I realise, it been nine years and we are not getting anywhere in life. So I go back to Italy to teach English to refugees. Ey! Maybe you come with me to class tomorrow, be a perfect, real-life, English example.'

'I'd absolutely love to!'

Rocco smiles, delighted with my empty plate. 'Ey, lez go get ice-cream,' he says.

Of course Rocco pays the bill and we join a stampede at the ice-cream shop. Apparently midnight is ice cream rush hour.

'Oh! EY! Rocco!' says a fatherly man, certified by a black and white collar.

He smooches his chocolate globe, giving himself a brown lipstick of sorts, wild-eyed in sugary euphoria. Oh Italy, you are the best thing to ever happen to me.

On the drive back home, Rocco slows down and says, 'Oh you see that man dere?' he points to a lump, sleeping on a bench, 'Dat's my Dad. He likes to sleep outside iz ouse.'

'Like a dog!'

'Esatto. My mum, she scream at him to get inside but he juz say *"shut up woman I like de fresh air!"'*

'That's crazy,' I laugh. 'I like the sound of your Dad.'

'He's blind too!' Says Rocco.

Back at Rocco's middle-of-nowhere pad, well away from the slightest haze of a street light, it is pitch black. So black that the full beam of Rocco's car seems to cut a hole out of the air.

'Er, you no ave a light, do you?' he says, hesitating in turning the ignition off.

'Ur, just this,' I pull my rear bike light out of my pocket and flick it on.

We crunch down the gravel, ascend the stairs, over the patio.

'Ey,' Rocco whispers, pausing outside his bedroom door, his face looks so ghoulish lit by the red haze of my light. 'I ave a spare bed if you want it. But Maybe you want some privacy an maybe you camp in de kitcheen. But I warn you *not* to camp outside. Dere are wild boars.'

'Just here is fine,' I whisper back, pointing into the dark of Rocco's bedroom.

I fall asleep on top of rugs, a guitar, books, a harmonica and some other miscellaneous objects, too tired, too satisfied, too relieved to bother moving them. Rocco is restoring my faith in men.

A mocha of strong coffee, a pot of tea, lashings of sugar and a bag of biscuits: breakfast. The biscuits have a curious taste, sort of breasty, sort of unvegan. But I am simply too hungry and too exhausted from the tsunami of men, dogs and flies of this week to bother checking the ingredients. Not like me at all, and I kind of like that.

'You still wanna come to my class today?' Rocco asks. 'Today I teach dese African girls Italian. But juz to warn you, dey can be... difficult.'

Difficult was right. Only two of them have turned up, but their attitude stinks like they wish they hadn't. Particularly Jamila, who is so explosive the whole classroom, which should've felt big with only the four of us in it, is made to feel quite claustrophobic. The other girl, her sidekick Efia, offers the odd titter every now and then but nothing more.

'Okay, so.' Rocco points at his whiteboard. '*Sono andato* or *Io vado*, which one iz-'

'WE AV A DROG IN AFRICA AND YOU TAKE IT, YOU FORGIT YO OLE FAMILIE,' shouts Jamila.

Efia giggles.

'Okay, okay, but let's get back to this,' says Rocco, 'what is the differ-'

'YOU FORGIT OLL,' Jamila roars. 'YOU FORGIT YO MUM, YO CITY, YO FORGIT WHERE YO COM FROM, YO FORGIT YOSELF. YO TAKE DE DROG, YO AH FINISHED.'

A lady clip clops into the room, talking in short, crisp sentences, and gives us each a mint. Jamila crunches her mint loudly, crumples the wrapper into a hard pellet and flicks it in front of her. Efia is very entertained by this. I thank the woman for my mint, eat half, and tuck the other half into my purse for later. The class ends and Jamila swings down the corridor, bangles clanging while her loyal sidekick scuttles behind.

'How do you do it?' I sigh.

'Oh I know dey are so rude and dey act like monkeys but dey very smart gorls. So smart. You know, de exam board messaged telling me they aced the exam, some of the best in Italy on dis programme an dey say "how you do it Rocco?" An I tell dem, it wasn't me. Iz de girls! Dey so smart.'

How could I tell him? How could I tell Rocco that he was the best person I'd ever met.

The next heroic quest of Rocco's is to hunt down all his students that hadn't made the class.

'Is so annoying. De government no geev dem money if dey not make my class,' says Rocco, banging on a peeling door. 'An some of dem ave kids. Dey need de money. EY! EY!' he shouts across the road to a woman, leaning over the gate of a park, hands tucked defensively into her coat pockets.

The woman is staring anxiously at her son, a tiny thing sandwiched between big trainers and big hair, climbing the wrong way up a slide.

'EY!' Rocco repeats, dashing across the road.

The woman jolts in her own skin but seeing that it was Rocco, relaxes a fraction.

'You weren't at class today. Why?' he says.

Her reply was too feeble to make out.

'ROCCO!' yelps the little boy careening towards him in those massive trainers.

Rocco pats his afro and the woman smiles.

On the way home I ask Rocco about the woman. Turns out she'd escaped Africa while bloody, blue and pregnant thanks to her husband. One way or another she landed here, in one of the Apennines' many 'nowhere' towns hiding and attending Rocco's

Italian lessons: a new beginning for her and her baby. It was Rocco she called when her waters broke, Rocco who drove her to the hospital, Rocco who kept her and her baby boy protected.

Then one day, with not an anxious nerve left to keep her going, she committed a suicide of sorts and revealed her location to her husband who came at once to finish her off. Though he didn't quite manage it, and is now imprisoned. But her face, her broken, anxious face, will tell you that he is still coming for her. Rocco tells me all this while cooking lunch, then quickly changes the subject.

'We ave a special cheese ere in Italy, an illegal cheese,' he says, stirring a pot of soup perched precariously on top of a fire, 'Is shame you vegan because I could get you some. But you ave to know a farmer really well to get it. Iz worm cheese.'

'As in, fermented?' I ask.

'No. Worms. Live worms, you can see dem white and squirming in de cheese.'

'ALIVE?'

'Yep. Dey alive until dey crush in your mouth. But iz really hard to find dis cheese, iz illegal,' says Rocco, proudly. His expression changes to panic as he removes the pan from the fire and says, 'Oh! We are burning!'

Comatose by warm soup and a terrifically hot day, we spend the afternoon singing 'in il mondo che', me swaying in the hammock, Rocco strumming his guitar. When it comes to singing, I am unashamedly grandiose, operatic, provocative, experimental: a hybrid Britney-Simone. When alone, that is. But in company I lose my powers and manage only a dithering whimper, like a new puppy lost in the woods. Every now and then though, me and Rocco harmonize and it feels like coming home.

'I have an idea,' He says after a fifth round of *Il mio canto libero*. 'If I get you some pencils, and some paper, will you draw a picture for me?'

It's been a while since I did any kind of drawing. Three months ago, to be exact. Just me in my empty student house, accompanied by the soulful tunes of Billy Joel: my safe and lonely world. And yes, I know, I know: I should have been at uni that day. And the day before that, and the one before that. But I couldn't go back. What if I ended up howling in the toilets again? I was sick of toilets. Sick of the sparkly galaxies of their grey floors, the brain-piercing stench of bleach, the hollowness of doors which never, ever go close enough to the ceiling or floor, the passive aggressive 'wash your hands' posters, and the guilt-tripping charity posters. Unless it was a disabled toilet: since (they assume) you are already compromised, they usually omit the sad faces of African girls, and give you a full-length door.

Following the contours of Rocco's laughter lines with my 4B pencil, it comes to mind that September is only a month away, that my life as I left it is only one month away. Tears prickle behind my eyes.

'Aleechay!' Rocco bursts in.

I quickly obscure my drawing with pencils, blushing.

'My students are coming ere soon!' he says. 'Will you join my class? I'm teaching dem Engleesh dis time an dey not refugees. Dey very well be-aved. You can be my perfect example!'

'I'd love nothing more.'

'Maybe you could write your story of your bike journey on dis?' He hands me a sheet of paper. 'I ave a idea.'

While I sum up my journey in a paragraph, Rocco gets to work on his patio: a couple of extra chairs, some blue tarpaulin tied with string to his house (an improvised white board), a stack of paper and hey presto: we have a classroom.

In filter the students, each one a different degree late though keen and polite, ready with their pens and exercise books. They're all about forty (my favourite age). Rocco begins by tearing my story up into little sections and asks the group to piece it back together and read it aloud.

'Den I wen-T to Spain,' says a girl.

'Ad-ven-tyor,' tries another.

'Appier an-D sto-n-gerr,' says the man.

Gosh, I'm so touched, I cling hard to either side of my chair, so that the g-force of emotion doesn't knock me down.

As they all up and leave I notice one girl giving Rocco two jars. I wait until she's out of sight and peer at them.

'Ah, she pay me in jars of food,' Rocco explains. 'Ey, you wanna come to my last class? It's in town so we ave to cycle. I can see you're tired but I ave an idea.'

Rocco ties my bike to his electric bike and we whizz into town, laughing pretty much the whole way there.

We're late, but that's okay because Rocco's last student of the day is even more late (Italians, despite being in a constant state of impatience, are always late).

'Ah, you are such a traveller,' says Rocco as I crunch the second half of the mint from earlier. 'I remember what it's like. Something as smoll as a sweet suddenly becomes special. I saw you tuck it in your purse earlier and save it.'

Rocco's student turns up and the lesson commences.

'I am a ta-x-ee dri-verr and a wri-terr,' he says, hunched over his special exercise book, writing each word in his very best handwriting as though there were never a more important task. He looks up to Rocco, who looks at me.

'Perfect,' I reassure.

At the end of the lesson the taxi driver turns to me 'Dis is for you. To ...learne... Italiano.' He hands me a book, the first page signed. The words on the front read "*Il vita in un sofio*", or 'life goes in a blow'.

Poor Rocco, he's spent all day on a frantic mission, rescuing those poor women and teaching that he'd no time, or light, left to do any shopping, or get his solar battery fixed. Between us we manage to choreograph a dinner of sorts. Rocco presents a bag of dried up, boat-shaped bread things. I've seen these in English supermarkets, but only in a very discreet way, shamed and neglected, tucked below the oatcakes and Ryvita. I have a little food of my own: some rice cakes, some peanuts and something I've never eaten before called *lupins*. Turns out, there was a reason for that: they have the sour, stale taste of long car journeys.

'Ah! An I ave dese. My payment!' Rocco puts two small jars on the table: one of courgette, one of pumpkin, preserved in olive oil.

We munch away, in happy, hungry silence save for the snap of rice cake and squelch of the jar-matter while the bike light struggles on, making everything appear as though coated in blood. Then something bright and white, glowing like a loose ember lands on the wall. Rocco says it's a firefly and I feel as though I might cry. This is the stuff of fairy tales.

'EEEERRRKKK!'

We freeze.

'Oh. Sheet,' says Rocco.

A thump of hoofs shoots up from our toes and fizzes in our heads.

'Sheet!' Rocco hisses, 'Iz wild boar.'

Another zombie-like screech.

'Oh fuck dis,' says Rocco, his panicked face drenched in red, 'Lez go inside. Now. Quick.'

The next morning Rocco shows me a text from one of his students. It reads, 'So, how did it go? ;-)'

We laugh about it all morning, finishing off the breasty biscuits of yesterday, then Rocco says while pouring coffee, 'You wanna to come to a party tonight? Stay ere one more night?'

I pull the coffee cup impatiently to my lip, extinguishing an acute headache, hot as fire, with the very first sip.

'Perché no!' I reply.

Rocco giggles, holding his phone to his ear. 'You always say "perché no!",' he says

A pacing Rocco chats down the phone, describing me as 'a pretty English girl'. A smile grows in my heart.

The atmosphere of the party is tight with the static energy of waiting. There are about a hundred of us, squashed on the back patio like sardines.

Rocco nudges me. 'It's tradition. De Bride will come soon,' he says.

A very cross man swats the air angrily, 'SHH!' he hisses.

This is a miracle: I have never seen so many Italians in one place behaving themselves. Squashed two to a chair, many to a ledge, everybody shuts the hell up and waits around a man who stands in the centre of the patio, swaying nervously on the spot, his shaky breath filling the silence.

Then a cross-looking woman in high heels appears around the corner, blindfolded and stumbling, hissing at her girly crew who pull her about. One of them begins peeling off the blindfold.

'NO! NO! NO!' the crowd insists.

The blindfold is slapped back on the bride, who flinches and opens her mouth to swear but quickly closes it as her shaking fiancé starts to read from a sheet of paper, made limp by his sweaty palms.

"Meet", "beautiful", "love", "life", I manage to understand but the rest of his speech is too trembling to follow. The two fiancés, now both crying, collapse together hysterically. Everybody stands, exploding in every way possible: roaring, whooping, clapping and crying as though it was the end of a war. So the party commences.

For the most part, I'm ignored. Which is absolutely delightful, a great opportunity to eat mushrooms, melon, bread and whatever other vegan-looking things I could find hiding behind the salami and anchovies. This invisibility lasts about ten minutes, after which my curly blonde hair, like the fluorescent stain of a highlighter, attracts all sorts of attention. Rocco introduces me to each inquiring face, all of them enormously impressed. Except for one: a very long man wearing a chequered shirt that makes him look like an enormous piece of graph paper. He just says 'I cycle too', all cross for some reason.

The music is now blaring, pizza circulating, and the guests dancing. Everybody but us who remain disabled by shyness and stay seated, twiddling our thumbs until one by one we are plucked and forced to conjure up some moves. Even eating isn't an excuse to sit: many of these Italians are managing to incorporate pizza into their dance moves. Eventually, I too am plucked and I make a mental note to add 'overcome fear of dancing' to my 'to-do list' as I watch my limbs make the same motions I've seen my Dad attempt. To my enormous relief, some saintly individual starts a conga. Very good, something with a format. I kick and whoop extra hard, one blonde mop in a slinky of Italians.

Inevitably, the conga starts to clot and over-stretch and ends with a dissatisfying dissolve, leaving just me and a hand full of others suddenly feeling stupid with our hands still around someone else's waist. Before I'd even the time to blush though, Rocco grabs me ballroom-style and leads me under a bridge of raised arms, which we join at the end, the tips of our fingers meeting in an upside-down 'V'. What a hoot! I've just about gotten used to the sequence then it ends, and another ritual commences. Buffering me about, a jumping clump of men clap and yell and roar. One of them is wearing a traffic cone on his head, another is drinking from a horn, a horn that is passed around the jumbling clump until it is offered to a very confused me. The raucous men goad and, victimised by my English politeness, I take a sip. It tasted like rotten acid that had been set on fire then infused with farts. The men laugh as I take my shivering stomach away and look for Rocco.

'Hey Rocco,' I ask, 'what was that disgusting liquid in that horn?'

'YOU ACTUALLY DRANK DAT?' Rocco chokes.

I was about to quite frantically insist he tell me what was in the horn, worried it might have been the blood of some poor animal, but the DJ begins yelling at everyone to shut up.

With the shut up finally achieved, a little boy (about four-years-old) in enormous square glasses takes the microphone from the DJ who flicks some switches and nods.

The little boy raps, 'sabato, sabato, É sempre sabato.'

I poke Rocco and ask what the lyrics mean.

'It means, "Saturday, Saturday, it's always Saturday",' he says.

After the miniature human in massive glasses finishes rapping his wee heart out he hands the microphone back to the DJ as if it was burning his fingers, then scuttles off to play with his friends.

'Rocco?' I ask. 'How do I say *you are a great singer* in Italian?'

Rocco smiles with his whole body. 'Sei un grande cantante,' he says.

I approach the little boy and poke his chequered shirt. Peeling himself from his Gameboy, he looks at me with those massive eyes, magnetised beyond the boundaries of his square spectacles.

'Um...' I begin, looking behind me at Rocco, who nods. I clear my throat. 'Sei un grande cantante.'

'Grazie,' says the tiny boy in a voice as delicately soft and fleeting as a snowflake.

He gestures me to come closer then plants a delicate kiss on my cheek. My heart breaks.

Rocco is extremely quiet this morning. And seeing as my jittery chat has gone unreciprocated, so am I. Only the crackle of Rocco's cigarette, the slosh of poured tea and slurps of coffee to soften the brittle tension. Somebody say something! Rocco's not even lamenting about how good his coffee and cigarette tasted, which he always did. '*Iz de best combination in de world*', he would always say. But not this morning.

'Now I am sad.' he says, finally.

I squeak something stupid in response – I can't even remember what – and pedal away.

'*Now I am sad*' rings in my head like the last bell.

22

Holy pizza and sticky loneliness

I'd left Rocco's this morning feeling tough. Tough enough to endure the army attacks of mosquitoes surfing the wind (which of course is blowing in my face), and the blasting heat. It should not surprise me that South Italy is this hot but Christ, it does. With no shops, no people, no cars, no trees to dilute the weather, you'd think I'd be lamenting. Instead I sing because, hallelujah praise the lord, there are also *no dogs*. Just ochre hill after ochre hill, lapping into the distance like a big yellow duvet. It's as deserted as, well, the desert. Maybe it is: it has cacti after all.

It was all going swimmingly, until now. Even wearing this Lara Croft top, I couldn't make the leap across this gap between the snapped halves of concrete. I look around: no other roads, just more ochre. There is though, a thin wall running alongside the imploded bridge. A fall from which would mean a ten-metre shock of broken bones and then a slow, painful death as the mosquitoes suck what they can from my withering body. So I make sure to not fall as I move as slowly as necessary along the wall, taking three trips to shift The Insect, my panniers and my tent to the other side. How very Casino Royale, Goldfinger, Bruce Willis, or whatever. The wind did not help.

After all that wind, precipice, sun and lynch mobs of mosquitoes, safe to say I'm disheartened to arrive in what I'd been warned was *'de best, most beautiful, culturally rich city in Italy,'* The city of Matera . This is what happens when something is titled 'capital of culture 2019': guidebook-wielding blobs tromp through with their screaming children, the price of ice-cream doubles and the city's 'culture' is throttled. Of course, there's the beautiful bit: the golden jumble-tumble of crumbling historical buildings. This might've impressed me a little more if it wasn't dawning on me, as the flip-flopped footfall bangs in my ears, that there is nowhere to camp.

'Posso auitare?' asks a voice.

I pull my head out of my pannier (I was searching for snack debris. Some nuts or crumbs, perhaps) and look up from the kerb at a man who looks to me a little pink, a little... eager.

'Que disastro, niente posto per campegio,' I say.

The pink man says I should stay at his house, that he'll cook for me and let me kip on the sofa and though the thought makes my innards curl up like a nervous woodlouse, I accept. This triggers the man who starts scooping up the stuff I had just decanted, dumping them back in my panniers with awful excitement. Faster and faster, shoving my things about until there are no more things to shove apart from the notebook in my hands which he lunges for.

'NO!' I shriek, pulling it toward my chest.

As much to my surprise as his, I burst into tears. Muttering under his breath, the pink man scurries away, humiliated, leaving me to cuddle my notebook and sob my heart out. But I am less cross with him and more so with the tourists. What the hell are they gawping at? Don't they have trip advisor reviews to read? Fuck it: let's get pizza.

If I'm eating pizza, I'm all right. And once the pizza's finished? Well that's later's problem and later never comes, we can only ever count on a different now. Besides, the boys at the pizza shop are unlawfully cute. They even give me a pizza for free! You wouldn't believe the size of it, not to mention the generosity of olives. I share it with some ants outside a church, basking in the sermon bleeding out of the open door.

Following the boom of the last sacred word, a stampede of suits and dresses floods out of the church, leaving in their wake a concoction of perfume and impatient sweat which lingers inside with the ghostly echo of footfall now gone. I look up at the far-away ceiling, like a sky of sorts, barely containing the hollow, enigmatic breath of I-don't-know-what. Churches: I just can't explain them.

'Scuze?' I ask.

'Sì?' asks the priest, turning to face me.

'Uh,' I stall, frightened by the sincerity in his owlish eyes, magnetised by his huge round glasses.

One quick chat later, the priest escorts me to a room full of tables and chairs, the room the kids go into to be brainwashed by felt tip pens and crackers. There is a mattress on the floor sheathed in plastic and a crucifix where a clock should be. Fwar! Even with that woebegone look, Jesus looks quite dishy. Then again, I've always had a thing for men with long hair.

The priest leaves me to it for a while but returns with a chicken Kiev and some very spicy pasta. I hide the Kiev under one of the tables (RIP), char every taste bud with the lava-pasta and settle down on the mattress, lulled by a ridiculous amount of carbs. You know, a girl could get used to this; perhaps this whole *Christianity* malarkey was maybe worth a go. NO, Alice. This is *exactly* what they want you to think.

Two euros given, one slice of pizza, a coffee and fifty cents returned. This has to be cheapest breakfast ever and totally worth the glares of gambling men obviously not used to girls, or indeed young English ones, or indeed one who has the audacity to eat *sitting down*. What the Italians put chairs in bars for, I've yet to discover.

Two and a half cappuccinos later, Joel rings.

'HEY!' I shout down the line, dashing out the café, abandoning my cappuccino and croissant.

'Hey Alice, how are you doing? What's it like in Italy?'

'Oh my God! It's so good to hear from you! Italy is so great. The food, the people, It's JUST CRAZY. Phew, sorry if I'm talking too quickly, I've had too much coffee! Three cappuccinos! Which was the *worst* idea. Oh! And a croissant, except they call them *cornettos* here, Anyway, how are you?'

'Oh yeah, fine,' he laughs.

I try not to yelp at him, God I do, but like a shaken up can of lemonade, I fizz all over the place, sentences brittle and excited. Thing is, I *love* my brothers. Joel is the youngest of us four, impressively kind for an almost-17-year-old and though he doesn't know this, behind his back I often refer to him as 'the shining beacon of hope in the family'.

'Thanks so much for calling, man,' I say, figuring he might be tiring of my galloping voice. 'I suppose I'll see you in Greece!'

'I know, it's crazy.' he says, 'When's your ferry leaving?'

'Oh, thanks for reminding me, really must book it. I think it leaves on Friday?'

'Woah, amazing. I'll see ya later Alice.'

After the call ends, I polish off my salty cappuccino (of course I'm crying! My little brother just rang!) and *cornetto* and zig-zag euphorically to Puglia, high on sentiment, sugary pastry and too much caffeine.

One thing to bear in mind about the region of Puglia, is that it is not a place for vegans. Pizza, pasta, sandwiches, salad: you name it, they'll give it a carnivorous twist. Even the bread has slithery anchovy corpses all over it. My hosts too are not pleased with my herbivore pretences.

'Vegans are oll sick und weak,' says my host's husband, a very fat Frenchman whose name I do not remember. 'Every vegan we get ere is oll pale and cannut zink fast like normol peepol. Zey tell lies. Zey say meat geeves you cancer but zis is wrong.'

'Leave er alone!' says his wife Meg (I remembered her name because she is nice).

The awful man grunts and drags his unpleasant weight into another room.

'I'm sorry about im,' says Meg, rolling her massive eyes.

'I really don't mind,' I laugh. 'But um, how did you meet?'

'You mean, why am I wit such a grumpy, fat arse-hole?'

'Uh...!'

She laughs, and says, 'Well, I can't explain it. I am away travelling in America, and I see dis great fat man on de orizon. He walk towards me and I see im and I just stop...And I am like, *wow*.' Meg's face opens with bewilderment, 'I see him and I'm in love. I do not understand it.'

'Wow...that's *beautiful*,' I say.

'Yeah...' she sighs. 'Anyway, den dis fat French man say to me, "wanna come on my boat?" So we sail to America and nearly die in a hurricane. Den we get married.'

Somehow, I'm two days early for the ferry. This is great: two days of head-to-sand restoration. Today (day one of ferry-waiting) I will make Italian bruschetta like a true local. This is all I will do. This, and sleep.

After picking it up and putting it back thrice in a nervous supermarket dance, I am buying something I've never bought before: olive oil. See, by the time I was old enough to buy my own food, I knew too much, and oil was not allowed. I almost bought it once, after Kitty said it would give me a shiny coat like a dog, but it felt so wrong next to my usual things (apple, spinach, soup, oat milk) that I dropped my basket and bolted out of Tesco's without buying anything. Anyway, today is the day and I leave triumphantly with a 20ml bottle of greenish-gold liberation and some of those weird dried up bread boats only the locals buy. Tourists don't touch these because they look like dried cow pats. Now for Italian Bruschetta! So, the recipe goes as follows:

Pour water over dried up bread thing (also called bruschetta), enough so it gains the consistency of a just-milked Weetabix.

Pour olive oil over bread thing (be liberal, this is an Italian recipe).

Sprinkle magic red powder over the bruschetta given to you by some hilltop woman in Potenza (fresh tomatoes will also do).

Eat too much.

Fall asleep.

My eyes peel open. Propped up on my elbows I squint at the rosy sky and lilac sea. Suddenly, a bunch of fish leap out of the water in a great arch, flapping in the air like birds. Flying fish! What a life. I eat two more bruschetta, then fall back asleep.

I wake again, disturbed by full bladder. Drunk on sleep and desperate, I crouch behind a well-pruned bush, stooping low enough so it covers up to my shoulders and then (pretending the footfall of tourists isn't happening) the gush commences. Going in the sea would've been a good idea. Why the hell didn't I think of that? Hindsight is a wonderful thing.

Twilight has fallen, bringing with it coolness and respite. Respite, utterly negated by the buzz of tourists and mosquito clouds. Though 'mosquito' is a little too tame a classification: these buggers have the violent blood thirst of little anaemic Draculas. I fall sleep with their tiny little bodies crawling in my eyebrows.

Last night's toxic baptism of mosquito spray, soap, antibacterial gel and shampoo I'd slathered over my face had proved futile. Those malicious little Draculas! Fourteen volcanic bites on my eyebrows, cheeks, chin, nose, forehead cooking themselves up an itch. I plod stiffly inland, the worst side of crusty and the wrong side of moist, twitching at the thought of my own bitten face. This is the most unattractive I've ever been in my life, and the urge for coffee, toothpaste and a shower is inexplicable. Stepping onto The Insect's handle bars, I peer over the wall of a garden. A lady stares back, amused.

'Dentifrigo?' I ask, thrusting my toothbrush in the air.

The woman bathes me in smiles, lends me toothpaste, makes me a coffee, lets me take a shower and then sits me down to breakfast of Taralli.

Bloody ferry companies. You'd think having paid for your ticket, they might actually give you one. Oh no, don't be so naive: this is not the Polar express and you won't be getting an embossed, silky strip, complete with iridescent holograms, nope, you won't even get a receipt. For the bargain price of £90 all you will get is an email alluding to an 'almost' ticket. Never mind, after a bit of a fuss I manage to find a host on couchsurfing.com who says he has my printed 'ticket reference' and a spare sofa bed awaiting.

'Hey welcome!' he says, opening his front door.

Pick an eye — any eye, left or right — and stick to it.

'Hey!' I say to his left eye which was off on an opposite tangent to his right.

'Come on in Alice. I can see you're a traveller like me. I work for the Red Cross.'

'Wow, that's—' I start.

'Yeeeah,' he exhales, 'It's pretty dangerous.'

Two blonde girls titter in the background, rummaging through their suitcase, holding each low-cut outfit to their chins then tossing them on the bed.

'They're from Australia,' says my host, throwing his thumb over his shoulder.

Because he has lazy eyes pointing in either directions like opposing magnets, because he works for the Red Cross, because he printed off and laminated my ferry not-quite-ticket, I really ought to like this guy. But I don't.

'So,' he says. 'Where have you been then, on your journey? Here, sit. I want to hear all about it.'

'Well...' I sit down then pause, waiting for him to butt-in. 'France, Sp—'

'You know, I nearly got blown up once,' he says.

'Shit! That's—'

'Yeeeah, two of my friends got blown to bits. But I survived. My job is *really* dangerous.'

There is something extremely exhausting about being talked at, even if it does involve explosions. In fact, I find myself more interested in the scraping and clanging of outfitted hangers and girlish whooping going on in the background, though I'm still not sure who those Australian girls are or why they're here.

'Yeah!' says one of them, 'let's go pardy!'

My host (sometimes names just escape me) excuses himself immediately and joins the party-girls. I think (though I can't be sure) they're going to have a threesome and though not one inch of me wants to join I do feel a bit cross I wasn't invited.

Twenty-six minutes. I have *twenty-six minutes* to get to the ferry port this morning. A port which I thought I had arrived at, a port which according to the locals *'az not been ere for ten years.'*

'Que disastro! *Que disastro!'* I say, flapping my arms about.

'Not worries,' says the barman, 'Iz maybe five, six kilometri dat way? Maybe you stay an ave a coffee ere firz, ey?'

As if trying to find the *actual* ferry port wasn't stressful enough my left pannier has suddenly decided to fall to pieces. I grunt the remaining three miles to the port swerving all over the place, my right arm aching with the weight of my broken pannier tucked under it like a rugby ball.

On the ferry, I do as the scary ferry man demands and tie The Insect to an oily pipe right at the back, behind the massive lorries.

'Sorry, pal,' I say leaving my trusty steed in the company of mean lorries.

Not only does £90 not buy you a ticket, but it doesn't buy you a seat either. For that privilege, you'd have to have paid a few extra quid, which I, like these many others banished to the deck, did not do. I sit on the deck amidst them with my broken pannier and begin taking everything out: money, rice cakes, nuts, ants, marzipan, a French pocket dictionary, dirty socks, dirtier socks, a dress, a gas cooker — Jesus I'm like Mary Poppins — a pan, some cables, a portable charger, my trusty notebook, passport, sleeping bag, pyjamas, wallet, a soya yogurt, some cable ties and two toothbrushes.

Ten minutes later and thanks to a toothbrush and a cable tie, I have completely fixed my broken pannier.

'Sono intelligente!' I announce to my fellow cheapskate deck-mates.

Nobody, not even that nice mum of four I was talking to a minute ago, gives a hoot. So I do as I was taught in primary school and give my back a little pat. Note to self: put 'problem solving' on CV when home.

What to do on a ferry? For a while I stare at the swashing foam stirring at the sides of the ship, but this makes me nauseous, so I lie on the cool blue steel of the deck and let the sea breeze lull me to sleep. Then I wake, eat lunch, go to the toilet, push the green 'thumbs-up' button to confirm my satisfaction with the toilet facilities, do it thrice more (maybe the cleaners will get a raise), return to deck, read my Italian dictionary, text Mum with updates and then go watch the young boys with tatty guitars fill the deck with music (don't get that in first class, eh?).

'Non via in Corfu?' asks the mum of four, rudely interrupting the flow of our small talk.

'Sì,' I say.

She looks at me like I'm an idiot, 'CORFU È ADDESO!' she shouts. 'DOPPO È ALBANIA!'

'OH! GRAZIE!' I say.

I clumsy my way to the exit just in time. Thank God too, if I'd have missed my stop (since when did ferries have stops?) and been shipped to Albania Mum would've killed me.

Me and The Insect roll into a magically indigo Corfu, its bars and restaurants glowing amber, its streets busy with the new energy hot countries get in their cooler hours. From the first breath of surprisingly cool twilight air I fall in love with the purple hills, the bubbling accents, the barefoot frolicking of kids who should really be in bed.

I make it to the family meeting point at 2am, then lie on a sun bed, staring at the luminous words 'Fresh octopus, scampi, bass... Fresh octopus, scampi, bass...' scrolling on the LED screen. Until it happens: a torch light and five lanky Scooby-doo silhouettes appear in the distance.

'OH MY GOD!' I shout, bolting towards them.

Which familiar face to look at first, Mum's relief? Dad's pride? Billy's dark eyes and L'Oreal head of jet-black hair? Louis, bleach-blonde, fashionably disinterested and clad in loose denim? Joel, olive skinned and kind-looking as always? They open their arms and wrap my laughing self into a group hug, something we have never, ever done before. I wonder to myself whether a bridge has been built, whether I won't be so intimidated by my three towering and gorgeous brothers, who have always surpassed me in dignity and grace. Yeah I'm blonde and tanned, but that's about it.

It's 3am and we trudge through the sand, to the apartment,

deciding in quick whispers who gets which room (Mum and Dad share, Billy and Louis share, and Joel and I share). Then bed.

Day one:

A sickly fatigue comes over me as I wake early to the evil air conditioning, whirring in the room, sucking the moisture from my brain. Air should not be conditioned; it should have its own free will to be as hot and humid as it likes. Throwing back the crisp white sheets before they have the chance to give me grazes, I pour myself a bowl of muesli and wait for the others to stir. They eventually do, coerced by the smell of bacon.

'Want me to cook you some mushrooms, kiddo?' says Dad.

'Nah, that's okay Dad, I ate a couple of hours ago. Hey, what are we gunna do today?'

'Dunno! I think the boys are planning a night out later. You're invited too.'

I laugh, assuming Dad must be mistaken.

Turns out I am invited. And the day becomes a build up to it, which mostly involves Billy and Louis topping up their tans and Joely boy doing lengths in the pool. Times like these, it's hard to believe I'm from the same womb as these gorgeous creatures.

10pm rolls around and Billy, Louis, Joel and I hit 'the strip': a dystopic parade of sweaty bars throbbing with strobe lights and terrible music, intermitted by the odd knockoff 'AZDA' or 'TESKO's. The perfect habitat for boys with less sense than sun cream (which clearly, they didn't have much of) to roar like baboons and for girls to stumble in their high heels acting both boisterous and provocative all in one confusing go. I wonder how Mum and Dad would feel knowing that we'd blown our pocket money on laughing gas?

Two hours later Billy and Louis pack me and Joely boy off in a taxi because, apparently, we are 'too drunk'.

'It's so stupid. They're only sending us home so they can hit on girls,' says Joel.

'YEAH!' I slur, 'And Louis and Silly–'

'Silly? SILLY?' Joel squeaks. 'WHAT KIND OF A NAME IS SILLY?'

Me and Joel explode, laughing all the way back to the apartment.

'Thaaaanks!' I sing, jumping out the taxi.

'Yeah THANKS!' Joel giggles.

'EY!' says the taxi driver, 'PAY THE TAXI.'

We gather our split sides enough to pay him then stumble into the sea slurring 'PAY THE TAXI' over and over. Then we climb aboard an empty tugboat and pretend we're on Grand Theft Auto.

Joel is sick all night.

Day two:

Apartment: what an apt word. I indeed feel apart. *'We'll just go us three boys next time,'* that's what I'd overheard over in the next room along this afternoon. I never wanted to go to that stupid, sickly string of trashy clubs. What a waste of twenty euros, imagine all the tins of beans I could've bought with that pocket money splurged on NOS, booze and 'bonding' that never happened.

A great gnawing loneliness is carving a hole in my chest. I miss my sleep-like-a-caterpillar, fly-like-a-bird, eat-like-a-dog, lifestyle. And Italy. God how I miss Italy. So I order an espresso, just for a little taste of it. But alas, this 'espresso' is no real espresso, it has the same hacking coarseness as the cry of an angry goose. Change of tactics: baklava. Sticky and cultural enough to earn me a sense of belonging? Apparently not. Now I'm lonely *and* sticky.

Day three:

More and more tired. The brilliant sun mocks me, the lapping of the sea like a very slight and very cruel laugh. My soul is a great rot of depression.

Billy, Louis and Joel are having fun looking good and jumping off rocks. Mum and Dad are happy too, doing whatever parents do together in their spare time (deciding what to put in the boy's sandwiches, probably). So that just leaves me. And what should I do? I slog about like a pathetic wet sock, listening to Jacques 'ne me quitte pas' over and over. This makes me think of Loic. Then I listen to 'Sempre sabato' and think of Rocco. Aaron comes to mind too and guilt drives through me like a nail through my sternum.

Day four:

A shower would be a good idea; Mum and Dad have been making comments about it. Even Louis said I was developing dreadlocks which by the way *I wasn't*. Only thing is, this thin layer of filth —

who am I kidding, this cake of filth — it's the only thing left of the me I knew last week. But because we're going out today, I sit under the shower and let the water fall over me like sad rain, wishing I had the strength to cry.

Mum and Dad have paid for us to go on the inflatables. We hand over an unmentionable amount of money to the bored looking man, pull on the life jackets and jump about on the rash-inducing lump out at sea. For a while I keep up the morale, frolicking about like a stunt double, not even minding the wedgies induced by each leap and splash. But that has worn off. So I just let myself drift in the life jacket, looking as dead as I feel.

Day five:

Today we're going on a boat ride. On the boat, the commentator talks in four languages: the French one makes my heart flutter, the Spanish one makes me a little sad, the Italian one breaks my heart.

I go to bed early.

Day six:

I have decided to go on a diet.

Day seven:

For lunch I am eating a tomato sandwich but I feel very guilty about it. I should probably wash my hair. You know, I am the worst daughter and the worst sister to ever live.

Day eight:

One more day.

Day nine:

Today is the day! And my energy has rushed back so thick and fast, it occurs to me I might have the strength to try this holiday again. Be better, nicer, cleaner, less pathetically depressive. Maybe it's that same feeling one gets when leaving school or a job, that old 'if I could do it again' lie we tell ourselves.

'Can I take a picture of you before you head off?' asks Dad.

I oblige, then rush off, embers of freedom sparkling in my hasty toes.

'BYE!' I shout, a little too cheerfully.

On the way over to the ferry, I stop by the 'everything' shop. From overpriced fruit to under-priced t-shirts, pasta, Heinz baked beans, some very oily Greek baked beans, lighters with sexy women on them, inflatable doughnuts, bottles of water large enough to resolve Africa and...

'F-caristo' I thank, placing a baklava on the counter (the diet idea was stupid).

'F-caristo,' returns the shopman. The same shopman of yesterday and the day before and the day before. I don't think he ever takes a day off. He points behind me and asks, 'Is that your bike?'

'Yes!' I beam.

'What? No.' The man rubs his head with his forearm. 'You cycled here?'

'Yes.'

'From England?'

'Yes.'

'No!'

'Yes!' I laugh.

'But de Engleesh no like to do things that are not easy.'

I laugh. 'I know.'

He smiles at me and ruffles my hair. Just like that, everything is good again. And now to the ferry.

23

Homeward bound

It's midnight and the ferry is still delayed. But it's okay because I've spent the last two hours in the waiting room wisely. Firstly, I checked out the limited supply of cellophane-wrapped beige in the optimistically titled 'canteen'. Next, I tested the comfiness of the waiting room chairs (padded, mysteriously warm) and then I had a wash. A challenge, given that the tap and soap dispenser were automatic and the sink was one of those free-for-all troughs. Having done all that, I've nothing left to do but let the air conditioning slowly corrode my brain. Ugh, screw this.

I park my bum on a kerb outside, where I belong amidst the grit and insects, and start waving at people on their way in and out of the waiting room.

'Hello!' reply a cereal-box family of freckled Brits, stepping out of a taxi.

Middle-class. So obviously middle-class: the matching, bought-especially suitcases and the emphasis on the 'H' of 'hello' give them away. They go into the waiting room glossy-eyed, bouncy-haired, clean as whistles. Twenty minutes later they come out haggard, frazzled, dirty as used whistles, the Dad flopping a flaccid hand at me, an attempt at a wave. Poor fella, just another victim of that goddamn air conditioning.

But I am not the only one avoiding the air conditioning. Just ahead, under the lazy light thrown by a lamppost, a motorbike gang are talking loudly, their elongated shadows gesticulating. A homely rush fizzes in my blood, prickles on my goose-bumped arms: I stare at them and they at me. One of the crew, a woman with black, wind-tousled hair, shouts to me, 'DOVE SEI?'

'INGHILTERRA!' I return.

She looks at me, stunned, and asks in passionate lashings of Italian, if I came all the way here from England, all alone, by bicycle? When I tell her yes, from England, just me, she yells the news back to her gang, who close in on me asking question after question. How old? How many months am I travelling? How did I learn Italian? All alone, *really*?

'Hey, Alice,' says another member of the crew: a tall, bald man, eyes half-open with lazy coolness. 'I'm Nico, from New Yawrk. And that woman you talk too, she's Connie. Where are yuh gowin kid?'

'Bari, then along the East coast, maybe the Alps, France, then, well...home, I guess?' I say.

'Are yuh on yuh own?' asks Nico.

'Yeah!'

'Yuh comin' with us,' Nico winks.

A blown whistle cuts through the air and the conductor with thin, brisk arms points to a gate that hums its way open. A mass of engines let rip.

'FOLLOW US!' shouts Nico, revving excessively.

I nod, and convoy the roar of Nico, Connie and six other engines feeling like a rock star. Then I cycle beyond. Beyond the motorbike gang, the ferry passengers, beyond the waiting gazebo, way down the length of the pier.

'Excuse me!' yells a voice. 'Miss! MISS!'

I stop, turn around and watch the brisk-armed man bolt towards me.

'Can you please go back an wait with the rest of the passengers?' he asks, panting.

I look to where he points, at the hundred-person cluster on the horizon, apologise, then slow-walk back to the waiting line. Embarrassing, but not the *most* embarrassing moment of my life. Nothing, I don't reckon, will ever beat the time a sixteen-year-old me was caught by a boy I fancied, slowly inserting a pecan up my nose (I wanted to know how it felt).

Finally, at 2am, we board the ferry. And the relief of it, of knowing Italy waited on the other side, soothes me to a limping daze. All that anxious excitement, melted into a cool, sleepy pool.

'Sei stanca?' asks Connie, squeezing my shoulder.

'Sì,' I rub my eyes 'molto, molto...'

'Vieni con noi. Puoi dormire con noi nella nostra cabina.'

I gasp at this.

'Connie says you can sleep in thaya cabin. They have a spaya room,' Nico translates, even though I understood Connie's Italian a little better than his New Yorkian.

Connie opens the cabin door and pats the top of bunk bed number two.

'Per me?' I ask.

'Per te,' she says, smiling with motherly warmth, 'Buona notte.'

Connie walks off with the rest of the crew, I assume to eat ice cream (the Italians, I've discovered are partial to late-night gelato) while I am left to the cabin. I clamber into bed fully clothed, delight in the swell of the sea for a whole minute, then plunge into a coma.

'Aleechay?' says a voice.

I can feel a hand on my shoulder.

'Aaa-leeeeee-chay?'

The hand gently tugs my shoulder as the sound of suitcase zips and gulls gradually dawn on me.

'Aleechay, dobbiamo andare!' says Connie, smiling that motherly smile.

'Buongiorno,' I mumble.

The gentle rocking had lulled me into such a dense sleep, it was like a lovely sort of drowning. Coming to, feeling the ocean's swell, the swing of my body as Connie shakes my shoulder, the blue light of the cabin, the sound of gulls, it occurs to me that I might have died and gone to heaven. Connie asks if I slept well. I laugh and tell her it was the best sleep of my life.

'PLEASE VACATE THE CABIN FOR THE REMAINING HOUR OF THE JOURNEY' crackles an assertive voice through the speakers.

Connie gives me a fierce squeeze and promises, should I pass Brindisi, I'd have a friend to see, a bed to sleep in.

'Yeah, and you can stay with me and Nicola,' adds Nico. 'If ya like. It's prabably a three-day ride. Good luck, kid.'

Finally, my tyres touch Italian tarmac. With all the frantic impatience of a real Italian, I dash into the first bar I see and order an espresso. A proper Italian one, barely a quarter full in its tiny thimble cup, dense with the promise of bitter-sweet revival. I sip it slow, eyes closed then down the shot of sparkly water next to it. Off I go, now on the homeward stretch.

Oh Italy, look at your figs! Weighing down the trees, dripping all over the place in a dreamy, jammy mess. Of course, I think of Loic. *'I eat oll zee fig.'* His lovely fluffy hair, his tangy version of English, his neat folding, his belly-laughs, the feel of his arms. So I have decided to have barbeque figs for dinner.

Cooked figs aren't quite the same as fresh figs. As they char and bruise under the flame, their tang mellows, their floral notes die (not to mention they're prickling up a weird kind of rash in my mouth). I watch as molten fig number five falls off the end of my stick into the sand. I bury it, sighing thoughtfully. And you wouldn't believe who has decided to text me right in this very fig-burying moment:

'Hi Alice! I hope all is ok for you and you feel great. I think about you in this moment. Where are you? You often come back from Italie to England?' it reads.

I sit there, mouth full of fig, and stare stupidly at the screen. Fucking hell Loic! Are the invisible wires of our spirits subliminally signalling to one another?

I swallow my mouthful and reply: 'Now I am crying because I don't know why, but I've been thinking of you all day and I cook figs.'

Loic replies: 'I think to you this morning, I do my bath on a lake on lake district' and then sends me a photo of him naked and glistening from a recent swim.

Staring at his toned butt glimmering in the English sun, it all comes back in a flood: *'Oh Aleece, you ah zo funny', 'you are so cute', 'Our children will ask us ow we meet'.* But then also: *'I can't believe you.' 'I feel like you ah my child', 'You're over dramatique, just like my last girlfriend', 'I want to travel alone.'* Have I forgotten how I'd wished him away? How it felt when he left me in the desert like a sad prune with no water or food or charge on my phone? And what the hell was he doing in my country anyway? This pisses me off most of all, those are *my* hills, my awkward people, *my* unpredictable weathers. Maybe he'll meet a pretty blonde girl. Oh fuck you Loic, fuck the figs, fuck it all. In a spree of hurt I – with utmost maturity – spin off a text to Loic.

It starts 'Okay, here's the thing.', and continues: 'Panic attack', 'That bloody mattress', 'Nearly fainted', 'Never told me', 'Totally unsympathetic', 'I didn't realise', 'Grumpy with me', 'Upsets me', 'delete', 'continue my journey.'.

I delete Loic's number then start playing with clods of seaweed piled 15ft high on the sand. I pick one up, considering the possibility of flambé seaweed for pudding. But I quickly toss it, realising it was actually dung.

Well how about that for a punch in the gut, twist in the stomach, heart plummeting disaster: I've fallen out with Dad, big time. And of course, here we go again: lost in a city with nowhere to sleep. I ask a silver-haired fella for help and he says, 'Ah! Yez! I know a place you can sleep! An tonight iz de festival for pasta! So you not go ungry.'

Pasta is my favourite. Dad used to make me pasta.

The man leads me through the city and down some steps to a paradise of hippies. Great herds of them, wafting about with their tofu, lighting incense, talking in slow, lazy sentences on a patio bedecked with chalkings, fairy lights and tasselled cushions. Soya products sizzle on a grill and a guitar band is playing, around which the hippies flock, flourishing their tattooed limbs about, doing figures of eight with their dreadlocked heads.

There are sun beds too, in an irregular row. The man points to one of them overlooking the steep drop out to the port and tells me this bed is just for me, and was it all right? I thank him and sit with the hippies a while, thinking about Dad all blurry-eyed. It's simply all too much.

I heave my bicycle with all its luggage up the steps, and pedal off, away from the nice hippies and pasta parties.

Everything about my camp spot is wrong: it's the wrong sort of quiet, the sort that carries invisible echoes of what were once shouts; it smells wrong, like stale litter, pollution and fish, and the cut-glass pebbles make exactly the wrong surface to camp. Even the lighthouse whose red and white stripes are faded and peeled, and whose windows are too filthy to see through, looks wrong. Lighthouses are supposed to be charming, this one looks like the end scene of a horror movie.

As I eat my tear-seasoned rice cakes on a very uncomfortable rock, I look up at the dreamy haze of the hippie place I had been at just an hour ago. If I listen really carefully, I can hear the odd joyful cry, softened by distance. Bedtime.

A shrill scream followed immediately by the smell of smoke startle me awake. My spirit and tent collapse simultaneously, as I am met face-to-face with plastic that flashes bright red with each explosion. Between the giant bangs, a gang of teenagers whisper and laugh, tugging at my fallen-down tent. I stay inside, crying myself to sleep.

This morning, a text arrives from Dad (some ridiculous joke about vegetables) and me (the girl who once ate some noodles found in lost property) and he (the guy who once ate a jacket potato he'd found in a hedge) are friends once more. It's a good job too, because I need as much morale and spirit as I can get to battle through this headwind. A headwind that does no favours to my delicate ears which have been shot to pieces by last night's firework extravaganza.

Forty windy miles down I stop. The porous rock of the coast (there is not a speck of sand here), though sore on bare feet, makes the water look bluer somehow. Perhaps, because held in by the rocks, it's immediately deep so you can jump straight into the bottomless tunnel of electric blue. I was about to do exactly this, when a little boy yelled at me, 'Go ere, go ere!'

Heeding his advice, I run off the rock he was pointing at, fully clothed, and crash feet-first into a blue relief.

'GOOD!' he yells, jumping in after me. 'I'm Jackamo. Iz dat your bike, wit de solar?'

'YES! Do you like it?' I ask.

'Very much,' says Jackamo, pulling himself out the water. He drips his way over to my bike 'Dis,' he taps my solar panel 'Dis is il futoro: de future.'

'YES! You are so clever Jackamo. If you ever visit England, you stay with me, yeah?'

'Oh yez!' he says, 'I alwayz wan to go Lon-don,'

As I drag myself out of the water, clothes dripping great puddles by my feet, I realise in the time it had taken me to swim, meet Jackamo, and heave onto land, I have become a celebrity.

'Ello! You English gorl! Your prime minister Boris Johnson! Iz very bad!' says a woman, throwing down her glossy magazine and grapes, rising to her feet.

'Oh no, no, he's n-not–' I stutter and start laughing. Then I eventually re-gather and continue, 'no, he's just the mayor of London.'

Imagine that, Boris as prime minister!

'No, iz true! Dey elect!' she says, 'He very bad. Conservateeves oll bad. Ere, ave some fruit.'

I eat the fruit and pedal off. Boris as prime minister? Surely not. When I left England, Theresa May was doing just fine bopping with the Africans.

I had an inkling Nico might be rich when his posh watch first glinted at me a couple of days ago in Corfu. And now, as I utter a shivering 'wow' (the air-conditioning here is positively arctic) gawping at the fully grown tree centred in his house, I realise Nico is a bit more than rich.

'I turned the air-can right up to max. Hey, ya take a shower then we go out fowa dinner.'

After one quick ride in Nico's sub-zero car, we dine, all nine of us, bunched hip-to-hip on a table made for five.

'ANTIPASTI!' says the waiter, adorning the table with nuts and olives.

We thank him and eat.

'PRIMI PIATTI,' says the waiter, frolicking about with plates of pasta, glistening with oil.

We thank him and eat and chat. Nico's friends are wildly impressed with my Italian.

'SECONDI PIATTI.' The waiter sets down dishes of fish and meat.

I deflate back into my seat with a long sigh and look out at the harbour. The clatter of plates, the table-shaking exclamations of Nico's friends, the many piattis, dissolve for a moment as I imagine the line between me and home. One of Nico's friends must have noticed because he nudges me firmly and tells me a joke.

'CONTORNI.' Relentlessly enthused, the waiter swaps the plates of meat for ones of char-grilled vegetables and bread.

Nico hoards the plates and insists them towards my end of the table and says, 'Eat as much as ya can, I think alat of this food ain't gunna be vegan.'

'Thanks, but it's okay. I'm stuffed,' I say, cautiously selecting a grilled mushroom.

'Ya barely eatin' kid. Ey, eat as much as ya can.' Says Nico.

'DOLCI!' the waiter lays down plates of panacottas and pastries.

Nico slouches towards me, slackened by food but still going, and with a hint of apology says, 'It's tradition.'

'DIGESTIF!' A few glasses of slushy lemon sorbet land: the finale.

A great symphony of exhales commences around the table, a vain effort to lighten their loaded stomachs. One of Nico's friends, the one who had nudged me earlier, is staring at me, concerned.

'What arr tose on your arms?' he asks, pointing at my shoulder.

I look at my shoulder and startle a little. I'd forgotten all about them. Again I'm reminded, with the same sting of stepping into air too cold, of home. Of what I'd done, what I was.

'Oh! Um, I dived head-first into a bush!' I stare at the six faces, do they believe it? 'It was a really spiky bush!'

The table shakes with laughter and the guy who had asked says, 'You crazy.'

'An aggressive cat', 'Dived into a bush', 'A clumsy baking session', 'Oh my God! I don't know!' Really must find some new material.

I fall asleep with a heavy heart.

Checkpointed by lunch invites from men with hungry stomachs and ravenous loins, I pedal to Brindisi, to Connie's.

Connie is an angel if ever I did see one. When I'd met her in Corfu, wearing a baggy T-shirt and baseball cap, hair tossed about by motorbike rides, Connie looked so wild. But here in her own home, gingham dress flowing around her curves, black hair falling in lashes, she looks so motherly. And she is as happy to see me as a mother too, immediately feeding and watering me, asking me if I'm tired, driving me by my shoulders into the shower. She swifts away, leaving me to watery relief for a whole four minutes before she storms back into the bathroom and says, 'TUTTO BENE?', whipping the shower curtain to one side.

I stand naked and confused, and return, 'SI MOLTO BENE! GRAZIE!'

After the shower she throws a load of clothes at me, then sits me on the sofa and photographs me. Then we go out for pizza and ice-cream with her friends. One of them keeps calling me 'Ay-lis in wonderland.' The other says I am cute and brave.

Today I got lost in an all-inclusive resort. Then I buy some vegan cream cheese from a corner shop. I eat the entire tub in a cave.

This morning I wake up on the sand to a voice.

'Ello? Beautifol girl, can I buy you a coffee?'

I nod, too sleepy and too keen on coffee to decline. But things quickly escalate and he's soon dragging me to a nudist beach. That is the fourth time this year I've been invited to a nudist beach. What the hell kinda vibes am I giving off?

Hard to believe only a week ago I was slogging about in Corfu feeling like a wet sock when now I am whizzing away like a caffeinated Lance Armstrong. Maybe because I have a trajectory, a deadline, a focus. And an allergic reaction tingling in my mouth. Perhaps this is my body's way of telling me to lay off the figs, but I ignore it: a bit of mouth rash isn't going to kill a girl who has survived a cycle down the motorway, a precipice roly-poly, a near crushing from a bin lorry and thunderstorms. Not to mention all that I survived back in England. Death is not made for me. Not just yet.

Never take a short cut. With September's academic demands looming I've decided to cut across the coastal lump of Vieste (shaving a nice fifty miles off). This is a mistake: coastal lumps are the best a country will ever offer you. Like the crustiest, greasiest chip you save till the end: the piece de la resistance. Whereas this 'shortcut' is the sour green chip you spurn, then accidentally eat a little later.

First thing to note: everything here is burnt. Black trees in black fields gradually dissolving into the wind. It's not even really a shortcut thanks to the spiteful 65mph beast that howls in my ears, flicks charcoal dust in my eyes and beats at my legs trying so earnestly to pedal.

Two hours later the wind is beginning to take its toll on my appearance, fixing my face in a grimace and giving my lips a nice black crust. Wanting to make light of accidentally ending up in hell I decide, like an absolute millennial twat, to take a selfie. But just as I raise my phone something hot and sharp stabs my arm. I scream as the searing pain throws me to the floor in shivering agony. Nausea surges in dizzying, goose-bumped waves and my head prickles. This is not good. Breathing heavily through gritted teeth, I inspect the source of the pain: a bright red splash shape (like a blob of paint dropped from a height) inside a raised button of white skin on the underside of my left arm. Is this it, is this the end? I try to stand, but another stab of pain and flush of nausea seize. I shriek as my limbs fizz, full of fever.

After round six of quivering, shrieking, nauseous pain, I yell at myself to pull it together, hop on the bike and continue. 'She died doing what she loved,' they'd sniff at my funeral. I've always quite liked imagining my funeral, the hordes (I'd hope for at least a horde) of anguished faces, the nice things people would say about me.

If this really is the end, what do I want to spend it on? Release. With love in mind, I invent a game.

'J***, you were the first boy I ever loved. I was only fourteen, but I knew it was love. I knew it from the moment I caught your cheeky face on year eight camp. That was it. One moment and my world fell apart. I hated the summer holidays because I missed you and I used to fantasise that someone would lock us in a room together so I could get to know you more.

'Then, M***, I loved you. I really did. You were my first everything! And we had so much fun, didn't we? Sitting on your lap as you rode my bicycle, watching that stupid animated film about that Turbo snail, having blackberry fights, our special erotic club dance. Even though it wasn't meant to be, I loved you then. I'm sorry for the stress of hospital. And I forgive you for running off with that other girl because I know I wasn't even really a person back then. Maybe one day we can be friends? Actually no, I'd rather drink my own piss. Hm, who's next?

'Ah yes, G***. I remember the exact moment I fell in love with you. It came in a flash of that cheeky triangle smile of yours. A secret one, thrown just for me at a staff meeting. God, it shot straight to my soul and put me in a daze. I loved you. Goddammit you were annoying, but after that secret smile I really, really, loved you. Remember how you wrote "you was the highlight of my weekends" in my leaving card? Did you mean that? I hope so.'

Five-long in-love list completed, I move on to confessions of the worst kind, which was going well until I spot something odd and button my dusty black lip in an instant. There is a woman by the roadside, propped on a white garden chair, staring beyond the fringes of a parasol, beyond the road, the scorched fields, to nothing. A dead stare behind make-upped eyes. Spooked, hungry and quite sick of this creepy road, I shake her glassy eyes out of my head and pedal faster.

Again, another girl clutching a frilly, white parasol, staring blankly.

'HEY!' I yell, 'POSSO AIUTARE?'

The girl jolts, as though yanked from a trance, then anxiously shoos me away, her eyes flashing with warning. My initial thought was right: these are prostitutes.

Snip, snip, snip goes each heartstring as I pass three, four, five more prostitutes. Dispersed an even mile or so away from the last it's as if they'd been copied and pasted: the same parasol, plastic chair, bottle of water (put there to keep them just the right degree of dead), the same vacant stare. They're either drugged, or exhausted. Maybe both. Somebody owns them and the thought makes my stomach twist and flip like a beached fish. Suddenly the stabbing pain in my arm doesn't seem like so big a deal.

The prostitute road must've affected me because I have chosen not to sleep on the beach tonight (the beaches here are full of men). Instead, I wander into the carpeted atrium of a church and ask the lanyard acclaimed 'church manager' (what's a priest to the 21st century) if I can camp among the gravestones.

'Ah, no sorry. Iz nut allowed,' he says, 'But I get you peanuts.' He punches some buttons on the church vending machine and hands me a packet of nuts (bread and wine are *so* BC).

Gravestones denied, I continue on my quest for a place to camp, finding myself bumping up a hilltop to a restaurant. The staff in black aprons are busying themselves placing silverware and candles on white tablecloths. Overseeing them, a man with folded arms storms up to me both cross and endeared all at once and demands to see my passport. So I dive head-first into my panniers, throwing its non-passport contents out behind me: toilet roll, rice, herbs, knickers.

'TROVATO!' I cry, foisting that old red booklet of freedom into the air triumphantly.

The manager squirts out a tiny laugh, studies my passport with one eyebrow raised and nods.

'Okay. I elp you. You can campeggio ere, but only in de car park. Watch out for de wild animols. Ere, you go put your tent up, an I get de chef to cook you pizza. What you like on it?'

After a desperate thanks and admitting I am vegan (in Italy this feels, just about every time, like *coming out*), I put my tent up in the far corner of the car park.

'What iz dis?!' Says the manager, pointing at my handiwork: my wonky tent, held up by guy ropes stabbed into a large pile of dung, 'È rotto? Iz...Broke?'

'Naaah, no rotto,' I laugh. 'I like it wonky.'

'No, no, no,' says the manager, barging me out of the way. 'You can't sleep in dat.'

Well, what do ya know: apparently it *is* possible to stick a tent peg into hard concrete.

'Dere,' he exhales, stepping back from my tent. 'Now come. De chef make-ed you pizza.'

Awaiting me on a clothed table sits a pizza, some rice, grilled aubergine and a glass of sparkly water. Behind it stand row of girls in pencil skirts and men in shirts, hands clasped politely behind their backs, watching me. I've always hated being watched eating but today it doesn't bother me at all.

My tent! I'd never gotten around to putting it up properly and with its newfound tautness it's like I've traded in a sack for the Albert Hall. No plastic draped over my face as per, no slack bits. Certainly, I sleep like a baby. Except of course for the odd minor interruption from a herd of rams and the frantic argument I have with a horse who made a valiant effort to eat my bike at the black hour of 2am.

The shortening days are whizzing by, a little too quick so that it feels home is gaining on me, rather than I on home. Sleep, pedal, sand, repeat. A blue line of sea blurring to my right, the hustle of cars to my left. I've made it back to North Italy a little too quickly. September is looming, university is waiting.

Abruzzo. Al dente pasta, dangerous roads, standing lines of espresso drinkers: these are symptoms of the impatient nature of the Italians. My host Marco is the perfect epitome. He talks insatiably fast and when I talk, he pants and twitches, furious for me to get to the damn point. I'm not sure he's listening but God he is just so lovely.

'We can get takeaway,' he says, whipping my not even half-eaten pizza from under my nose, hustling it into a box. 'Lez go ride, you sure dose shoes okay?' he asks, a laugh spreading across his face.

I look down at the two buses stuck to my size five feet (Marco lent me his shoes so I could put mine in his washing machine).

'Perché no!' I say.

'Non stanca?' he asks.

'Sì. Stanca, ma, felice.'

A great smile stretches across his face, 'Dat iz de forst thing you said when I meet you. *Stanca ma felice.*'

Turns out, he was listening all along. I think I love him, a bit.

Another day, another espresso. I eat twenty-eight figs, much to the pain of my mouth. Red ones, purple ones, white ones, green ones: who knew figs came in so many flavours! If you're real smart, and pick the ones that have shrivelled a bit in the sun, you are in for a special treat. These babies taste like a caramel dream of flowers and toast. Oh also, if like me you're allergic to figs, these ones seem to bite less.

Shopping trolleys, broken glass, Barbie dolls, tissue paper: the litter here by the coastal town of someplace north is very diverse. However, there is a church (albeit derelict and smelling of piss) and churches like fathers of concrete make me feel safe, so I set up camp. Just as I bang the last tent peg in, I realise I'm being watched by a girl, about fourteen years old, teasing her hair shyly. I wave and she skips over, dooming what would've been a pleasant evening spent with sweetcorn.

Firstly, she drags me into her house, throws me in her shower, drags me out the shower, does my hair, dresses me in her clothes (being twenty-two and still fitting into age fourteen clothes should not be a mark of pride. But it is). Then we hit the town and she promenade me around the block over and over, showing me to all her friends, taking selfie after selfie stroking my curly blonde mop like I was a show dog. I never asked for fame, I just wanted to eat my sweetcorn in the dark.

Le Marche. The coastline seems to be getting busier and busier the further north I go, heaving with skinny Italian babes with neat hair and hips that twist. All too aware of my three mini bushes, need of shower and scraped legs, I pedal inland, away from the pedigree girls. Olive trees, I want to camp among the olive trees.

Luigi, whose neat apron and twangable moustache make him look brilliantly like Mario's bezzie, is letting me camp on his olive grove, right at the tip-top of the hill. Can't get more Italian than that. The sky is magenta, the sea lilac and the coastline a crust of amber city lights. Am I becoming a hermit? Solitude is my very best friend these days.

Dinner: I discard the ant-infected crust on my marzipan and paste it onto a block of tofu. Yum. Now for a shower. A metallic sink outside Luigi's house winks at me: yes, that'll do.

Well, the worst that could happen is that I'm caught naked and it wouldn't be the first time. Besides, it looks like nobody's home. The metal basin holds me fine, although it does creak a little and smells undeniably of raw meat. I slather myself in nuclear-orange (and nuclear-smelling) washing up liquid and hose myself.

Rimini. This is the last time I'll see the sea, until France, until I'm aboard the ferry home. A grieving thought. As a cheer-up measure, I pluck a carbohydrate pearl from my leftover pizza and plant it on the ground, for my good friends, the ants.

'Good job guys,' I say, impressed by their teamwork as they heft it into their crevice for later, 'Hey, you want another one?' I plant another crumb.

People are so cruel to insects. *'Why can't I squash them, they're pointless? All they do is scamper around, brainwashed by the hive mind.'* Don't they see? Zoom out on us humans, speed us up, we'd look exactly the same: flittering about anxiously, trying to get things done or (more commonly) trying not to get things done.

'Hey!' says a bouncy voice, interrupting my ant-thropology.

I lift my head up. A boy my age stands in front of me, suspiciously clean-looking. Mind you, everybody looks clean next to the cataclysm of filth that is, I.

'Can you elp me?' he asks, putting down his briefcase so that he can hold his hands in begging prayer, 'I am Italian boy. I av no mama, no papa. Tey both die. An I sell Art so I can av monay for a pizza an a coffee. Can you elp, please?'

'Oh goodness, I'm so sorry. And of course, let me just find some change...' While riffling through my panniers I ask, 'Where do you live, if you have no mama or papa?'

'My friend let me stay in an otel. Ere, which one you like?' He opens up his briefcase and proudly shows me a whole glossy catalogue of cat pictures, fresh from the internet. 'Tey are my art.'

'Oh! Nice! You keep your, um, art? It'll only get crumpled in my bag. Here, that'll buy you your pizza and a coffee.'

'Oh my Gud!' he gasps and takes the note. 'Tank you. You are so kind. Ere, take my pen. Take two pens!'

'No. It's okay, you keep them.'

'Please! Please, take them.' He drops two pens in my lap and swishes off.

I watch him repeat the charade, word-for-word, to a couple of polished tourists. One can't help but wonder what a poor orphan boy was doing with a briefcase like that. Weird. Anyway, fate has been kind to me because I really needed a pen (my pencil is getting very blunt). And, get this, it's got a calendar rolled up inside it: you just pull the metal strip on its shaft, and out scrolls twelve months of the year: one side for 2019, the other for 2020. Genius. And I have two!

— charlie

24

One last week in Italy

I've been robbed. Of course I've been robbed! What kind of an orphan carries around a briefcase full of cat pictures? The whole thing could not have been more obvious a con if he'd tip-toed creepily towards me in striped black and white overalls with a dollar-signed sack slung across his back. I slump on the supermarket's kerb, panniers turned inside-out to no avail other than €4.30 in change and a few neglected snacks, sugared with a few hitch-hiking ants. I smile at the tarnished coins, – that's four espressos and a tin of chickpeas – stash them in my sock, then call the bank.

'Okay Miss Lushington, we will have someone from the bank call you tomorrow to work out a money transfer, for you to pick up in Bologna, okay? Can you reach the city centre by tomorrow evening Miss Lushington?' asks the bank man.

'I CAN. There's loads of figs here so I won't starve.'

'Great,' he says buoyantly, nearly laughing. He clears his throat and continues, 'We'll be in touch with the address and instructions by tomorrow morning. Make sure you have your phone on.'

I take a quick glance at my phone screen, now 70% obscured by an ever-growing black splodge (since I dropped it in Imperia, it's been getting progressively worse).

'Yep! Will do!' I chirp.

'Good luck.' says the bank man.

And I know he means it.

So, I go to see my Warmshowers host Guglielmo, dragging The Insect and my feet. Because Guglielmo says he won't be home until dark, so don't wait up. Because he says he doesn't do vegan food and I'll have to provide for myself. I text back, that I have raw tofu, that he needn't worry. He texts back 'fine'. When is fine ever fine? We all know what 'fine' stands for: Furious Inside, Not Expressing.

On my begrudging wander over to Guglielmo's house I spot a

decrepit thing weighed down by two very light shopping bags. She accepts my help gratefully and I tell her about being robbed.

'QUE BRUTO! QUE BRUTO!' she shouts, voice quivering with anger.

Then she stops, suddenly confused, takes her shopping bags and shuffles off. I ask her again if she wants help and with the same gratefulness of the first time, she hands the bags back over. Aha! Dementia. Before she died, my Granny Lush had dementia, though we all pretended otherwise, blaming her mad ramblings about having 'gone to China last night' on 'dreams', 'old age', 'tiredness' or 'diabetes'. Classic British denial.

Forty minutes and one hundred metres later, we make it to the old lady's house.

'Grazie,' she says, taking her shopping bags. She stops half way up her path, turns around in slow-motion, 'Grazie' she repeats.

Outside Guglielmo's, a man who had seen the whole dementia shopping-bag charade approaches me and thanks me for helping the old woman, who he says is called Evlyn. I shrug, and tell him about the boy who robbed me. The good thing about being robbed is it makes a fun story. Then another man storms out of the dark, shoulders as tight as a cat about to lunge, neck chain spitting light at me.

'I told you not to wait!' Guglielmo snaps. 'I told you I be late!'

'Ah! Guglielmo!' Guglielmo's neighbour butts in, 'Lei auitare Evlyn!'

'You helped Evlyn?' Guglielmo asks me.

I nod.

All the anger in Guglielmo's face dissolves, 'Come inside, welcome, take a shower, I cook.'

While showering, I can hear Guglielmo shout, so I turn it off.

'VIENNI! È PRONTO!' he yells, above the sizzling of something.

'COMING!' I return, hopping out the shower, into my 'A team' dress, pulling my dirty socks back on. Pants! Where the hell are my pants!

'PRONTO!' shouts Guglielmo.

'COMING!' I repeat, skipping downstairs, full-commando,

'Graz- JEEZ!'

Guglielmo had taken the sweaty, beaten, gritty tofu out of my pannier, and turned it into a dream: two glossy fillets, griddled, studded with peppercorns, stacked artfully, a rust-coloured dressing swirled around the plate. Guglielmo laughs, tells me it's no bother, that he's a chef anyway.

'Let's get ice-cream!' says Guglielmo, taking our empty plates into the kitchen, 'NO WORRY ABOUT MONAY. I PAY.'

I have learned in my time in Italy, not to be too polite, to dither with 'you shouldn't have's and 'are you sures'. So I follow Guglielmo out the front door remembering a little too late, as the cool night air swoops between my legs, I am without pants.

What a thrill! So long as I pedal with my knees brushing, so long as the night is black, nobody can see my...*thing*. Then we enter the city. Then we stop. Damn this crossbar.

'Oh, wow!' I announce, looking over Guglielmo's shoulder.

My plan works a treat, Guglielmo turns around and in a flash of personal foliage, seen by some but not Guglielmo, I whip my leg over the saddle.

Oh God the ice-cream! There are three, yes *three* vegan flavours to choose from. So I choose all. The rich seduction of chocolate, the flirty zing of lemon and then pistachio, glazing my tongue in a nutty, creamy climax of –fuck! Look at what I'm becoming without pants!

The next day, Guglielmo sends me away with sugared almonds to keep me going until I can replenish my cash in Bologna. By 9.40am, the almonds are gone. However, I still have €4.20 sagging in my sock and the trees are heavy enough with figs to ensure my survival (though I am, aforementioned, allergic to them).

The phone rings but as phone was going through one of its 'not working phases' the screen is completely black. I try my usual trick of sticking a licked finger in the smashed hole, but no such luck. It continues to ring and I bang on the screen frantically until finally, 'HELLO?' I gasp, 'Is this the bank?'

'Alice!' cries an exasperated mum.

'Oh, Mum. Really sorry, I can't talk right now.' I say.

'Could you please tell me what's going on! You've been robbed?!'

'Yeah, I'll explain later. I really have to go,' I say, then hang up.

In the next few seconds, the bank rings. And despite my desperate banging on the screen, I cannot answer the call. I can't help but feel that it's Mum's fault.

Feeling quite exhausted by it all, I flop in a bar and order an espresso, which arrives on the end of a tweezering thumb and forefinger, courtesy of a cringing barwoman. I yell at her defensively that I've been robbed, as if an excuse for my usual appearance, but this does not satisfy her. She looks at me like I'm scum. That may be so, but don't forget: scum rises to the top! At least I get my money's worth: I bathe in the toilet sink, charge and sort of fix my phone, and then wave at the clique of dodgy men who'd been staring at me throughout.

A while later, I spend two more euros: spaghetti, chickpeas and a peach. So far, I've only eaten figs. Nineteen to be exact. But thanks to *my allergy* (I always a wanted an allergy as a kid, I thought it would make me special) my poor mouth looks and feels like a sore cave of tenderised meat. I draw my peach close to my 'O' shaped mouth but stop, and noticing his sad eyes, give it to a beggar.

'Yeah...Tanks,' he says.

You wouldn't believe what I saw just as I pulled onto the road: the cheeky git has only gone at thrown my freaking peach in the bin!

'ARRRGGG YOU CHEEKY DICK HEAD!' I shout, 'YOU FU–' – My phone rings. –'Hello?'

'Is this Miss Alice Lushington?' asks the bank man.

'Yes! Are you going to sort out my empty pockets? I've been surviving off figs and I'M ALLERGIC TO FIGS!'

'Yes Miss Lushington. Do you have a pen? You'll need to write this down.'

I rummage in my panniers frantically, 'A pen, a pen, a pen... hold on...'

'Miss Lushington?'

'Yes,' I say, smiling at my lucky calendar pen given to me by the conman, 'I do have a pen.'

Three hours later and I arrive at *Star communications*. Or in other words, a stuffy office full of desperate foreign faces, their foreheads entrenched with worry-lines that carry streams of anxious sweat away from their bloodshot eyes. All of them seem to be after some kind of money, or paperwork to get them some money, or paperwork excusing them from paying someone else.

I stand in front of the depressed receptionist, trying to look as much like my passport photo as possible. He glares, hard, deciding my fate then says, 'Ere we goh Mizz Lashington,' handing me an envelope.

I tear it open, shuffle the stacks of euros and yell, shaking my fists of cash, 'OH MY GOD! WOO-HOO! MONEY, MONEY, MONEY!'

Laughter breaks through the depressing room.

Now to enjoy Bologna, which is so easy to do because it is apocalyptically quiet. There are actually more birds than people, swooping about the traffic free roads, meeting up in gangs, singing in a great overlap of squeaky song.

'Ah, dis is becowse dis time of year, de Italians lika go to de beach, coz iz too ot' explains Frederico, a friend of one of my Italian friend's who has a sofa for me to kip on.

'Look! I get vegan pasta especially for you! I check especially,' he pulls a bag of pasta out the fridge, then in a light-bulb moment, dives back into the fridge and says 'Ah! Dis is good for vegan too!' showing me a tomato.

It was all going so well what with olive oil, the pasta, the tomatoes right up until a jar of pesto flops onto the pasta in a sad, lactose splat. Shoot.

'Dere! Pasta alla Genova' says Frederico, holding a plate out to me, 'It az something colled *Pesto* in it. Iz made from basil. I tink you like it.'

'Grazie.' I say, gulping hard.

For the first time in seven years, I knowingly break my vegan streak. The taste, offensively soured by what had once belonged to a cow, is at first difficult to endure. But my visceral reaction eases as I remind myself of the hurt feelings and wasted pasta I'm sparing. As my knife and fork meet on my empty plate and I thank Fredrico, who has absolutely no idea of the gravity of the dinner he'd just made me, I feel a little uplifted by my self-sacrifice. Humbled, in a good way. And though I know how cruel the dairy industry is, corrupting my inner compost bin with cheese felt like exactly the right thing to do, the kind thing to do. Call it, moral re-calibration.

Cycling without the guide of the sea is strange. At the best of times it's an adventure of plazas, fruit trees, churches, supermarkets and lunch invitations. And at the worst, it's a nightmare of perilous roundabouts, thumping heat and great swarms of tiger mosquitoes that seem to magic out of thin air should you stop for more than two point five seconds. One of them has bitten me so hard in fact, my shin is now missing a small chunk of flesh.

Today's road, without towns or trees or anything tallish to bathe shade over my burning skin, is cooking me into delirium: good news for the mosquitoes who have developed a taste for my Mediterranean caramelisation. Upon spotting a church, I eject from the saddle – CRASH. Sorry The Insect! – and run inside. A rush of cool relief soothes me for about five seconds and then in come the mosquitoes. I break dance to keep them off.

It is getting late and I'm still going, on a beeline for home.

'EY!' shouts an shirtless old man, waving from his balcony.

'CIAO!' I shout back.

'YOU ARE ENGLISH!'

'YES! AND I'M JUST LOOKING FOR SOMEWHERE TO CAMP!' I return.

'EY! COME UP! I MAKE YOU DINNER!'

Thin and gnarled, Charlie trembles with all the fragile extremes of an old tree in a storm. It seems to get worse when he is trying. Which makes me especially nervous as he tries to pour fusilli into a pan of boiling water. My heart reels with the want to help him, but I don't because I know he wants to cook for me. The pasta rattles into the pan and I finally stop holding my breath.

'Grazie, Charlie. How come you speak such good English?'

'I can spek English cawse I travell de world, look!' says Charlie, thumping his gnarled, wobbling finger on the photos pasted on the walls: Charlie in England, Charlie in America, Charlie up a mountain.

'I am a traveller, like you!' he beams.

'Yes!' I say, 'just like me!'

'Tell me where you go, tell me oll.' he says.

Charlie's eye sparkle like wet pebbles as I tell him about France, the Pyrenees, Spain, Italy, the Appenini, Greece. About dogs, lightning, men, flies, pizza, focaccia, gelato, happy accidents, sad accidents, all the beaches I'd kipped on, taralli, sunburn, Loic, Aaron, Eric, Rocco. Charlie listens intently, drinking a cup of wine with his wrists. When I stop talking to eat the pasta he'd made me, he smiles a trembling smile, silenced by something. Maybe I'm boring him.

'Mm, la pasta è deliziosa!' I announce, foisting a spiral of fusilli in the air.

'I am so appy!' Charlie bursts, voice choked, 'So appy to meet such a fanastico ragazza. Tank you, Aleechay. For I meet a girl like you, I so appy. I so, *SO* appy!'

Only now do I notice, the only thing about Charlie that doesn't wobble is his voice. It is as though I was the best thing to ever happen to him in his long and adventurous life. And I laugh, to stop myself from weeping.

After dinner and many rounds of cigarettes Charlie says 'Aleechay, you sleep in my bed tonight.'

I look at him, shocked.

'An I sleep dere, on de sofa,' Charlie points to his tiny sofa.

I really could've cried, right there and then.

Today I was supposed to be staying with a guy called Sandro, but Sandro (my Warmshowers host) has cycled off on a spontaneous beer and cheese adventure and left me a flat all to myself. This, I think as I dive, head-first, onto the sofa, is *way* bigger than a tent. Not only that, but Sandro has left a gift for me: a purse, made from an old carton of juice. How absolutely brilliantly perfect! I transfer the wad of cash from my sock into my new purse, then do a few joyful jumps. Then the doorbell rings. On the other side of the door stand Sandro's neighbours, wild-eyed with excitement.

'Sono Delia,' says the woman.

'Ciao,' says the cheeky looking bald guy, waving behind Delia.

And that was all it took.

Over pasta (cooked by Delia), my two new bezzies convince me to stay tomorrow night too so we can hang out more. I gleefully agree and we celebrate by joining the clots stood outside noisy gelato parlours. It doesn't matter that 11pm is too late for a child to slurp sugar, or that OAPs are too old for the noise and crowds: one is never too *anything* for gelato here. Not even too vegan: they've always got an unblemished vat of soya shamed to the corner. Delia's fella, Delia and I exit with ridiculously top-heavy ice creams whose cones cripple and whose sagging mounds creep stickiness all over our hands. We eat them in silent concentration.

The next day, Delia and Delia's fella burst in for coffee. After which we go shopping, spending a laughing hour stamping our bums on a variety of deck chairs until Delia decides on the nice blue one. Next on the agenda is lunch (pasta again, cooked by Delia) then we watch Pavarotti on Sandro's plasma TV. Having learned enough Italian, I manage to point at the scorched face of the singer and say, 'Pavarotti has a big voice because he has a big heart. But he is dead.' Delia and her fella are very impressed. Pavarotti finished, we drive through the mountains to a lake flume. Delia says if you stand under the torrent, the waterfall will give you a massage. I try this, and find quite horribly that she was right. The damn thing nearly lost me my new bikini.

What a shining example of how to spend unemployment! Though Delia says she has a job coming up working in what she calls 'chicken logistics'. She explains this as we pull into the 'fiesta di patatas', a party celebrating all things potato held in the mountains. Mash, gnocchi, croquettes, Spanish omelettes, chips.

Mum would be so proud.

'They're going to make you better,' says Mum, more to herself than me.

I look out the window and shuffle in the car seat, which after one hour is already killing what's left of an arse. How has it come to this? It's humiliating, and kind of exciting too. But a little trip to the loony bin shouldn't surprise me, not really. I am actually their perfect candidate. But note to self: do not let them know this.

'Alice,' says Mum, her voice is sounding more Irish, as it always does when any kind of strong emotion effervesces. 'Y're not eating enough potatoes,' she says.

With bellies congested with all things patata, a disco commences. 'Pensale male', 'Ostio lido', 'Dove quando': familiar songs that walk me through all the bars, parties, supermarkets and kitchens of my Italian saga. A great flourish of nostalgia colours my brain and my heartstrings tug (though that might be the chips).

Even though I've known Delia and her fella just a shave off two days and even though our chats had been limited to my sketchy Italian lexicon, the atmosphere in Sandro's flat as we share our goodbye morning coffee is one of great sadness. Delia runs back and forth from her flat to Sandro's giving me things for the Alps: a baseball cap for the sun, and a jumper for the cold. The agony of leaving them is almost enough to tempt me to stay another night, or forever, even. But the bell of September is poised above my head, ready to chime its sad, mournful note. Life as I left it, my friends, my final year at university awaits. I only hope this time I'm different, better. I do feel better. But thinking of home reminds me of screaming, panic, throwing up, and terror so vividly, maybe I'm not better at all.

The sky must've also known September is looming because it's bawling it's heart out in a blinding torrent this afternoon. And with the ground hard-baked from a very dry summer, everything floods. Including the river Po of Turin which gushes so deafeningly to my right I don't even hear the smash noise of the glass bottle, exploding beneath my tire. Check for punctures: all clear. God bless those

Ultra-Marathon Plus tyres courtesy of Cycle Revival: when they say 'punctureless' they sure as hell mean it. But I barely make it ten feet from the shrapnel when a shrill crack noise splits in my head. I turn. A brick has fallen off the bridge-tunnel, just one second away from crushing my smaller than average head (that's cat life number five, gone). God, is that you? What are you trying to tell me?

As I reach Susa, the rain stops as though it had never started, the mountains and trees vibrant and sparkling as the sun blasts away. A focacceria ahead glistens too. Painfully aware of my dwindling focaccia-eating days I buy a piece the size of a laptop before going to meet my Couchsurfing host. Did I say buy? A man in the queue is so charmed by my blonde curly mop he buys it for me.

'Hey! Aleechay!' says my host Gabriel, hopping out of a car.

'HEY!' says a girl, leaping out the passenger seat, 'I'm Vivian!'

Gabriel is a tall boy with kind eyes and artist's hands. He speaks gently, on the few occasions Vivian is not talking. Vivian loves to chat and I *love* Vivian.

'People don't hunderstand vhy I choose zis fegetarian lifestyle. Oh, *Grazie*,' says Vivian, beaming as the waiter lays a pizza in front of her. She studies the pizza, then chooses the most bacon-heavy of the meat-feast slices and continues, 'People don't hunderstand, Iz zomezing important to me. Oh yum, dis is *so* good!'

Me and Gabriel (both actual vegetarians) smile lovingly at Vivian as she, between lustful mouthfuls of wine and pizza, tells us the most vulgar jokes. Dicey ones, spicy ones, even Jewish ones. Which make me quite uncomfortable. Wasn't it too soon?

'Oh und hey! I have another one! Ahem, a blind guy walks into a fishmongers und he says "*well hellooo ladies!*"

'Oh! Yuck!' Says Gabriel.

'Do you get it? You get it, don't you?' says Vivian.

'Yes but none of my ladies have ever smelled like dat,' says Gabriel.

Vivian's secret to boundless energy, is sleep. Long, deep, unflinching sleep that continues into late morning as Gabriel and I share a jittery feast of jam and mud-thick coffee.

'Yeah,' Gabriel sighs sadly, applying jam to bread with the delicate touch of a flower in the breeze, 'I just sometimes get zo sad.

Iz like de world is doomed. When I think, so many bad people, so much suffering. It make me tired.'

'No!' I insist, 'It might seem that way, but the world is good and most people are nice and–'

'MORNING!' Vivian bounds in and flumps down on the chair next to me. 'Oh yah, ze world is real bad. When I went to China, zey keep eferybody in zese massife, massife apartments in little box rooms und no one iz allowed to leave ze city.'

'Jeez, that's awful!' I say.

Poor Gabriel seems to wilt in his chair.

'Alice, I zink you should stay another night' says Vivian, slashing jam across a slice of bread. 'We can go exploring!'

There are many reasons to say yes. Firstly, Vivian is fun, secondly, she won't let me go anyway, thirdly, I could do with a day off and fourth, only one day's pedalling stands between me and France and I'm not ready to leave Italy behind. There is only one reason to say no to Vivian: September is lurking dangerously close.

'Sure!' I say.

Vivian bursts into a great mess of delight, downs her coffee then pulls me outside, shouting to Gabriel, 'WE'RE GOING OUT! SEE YA' as she closes the door behind her.

We wander, past the mountains, the train station, down the high street and then across the bridge, where we bump into an old lady who claws at our t-shirts, drawing mine and Vivian's faces close. She tries to kiss us but her loose dentures get there first, hanging off her face like a horse. We wait until the woman is out of sight then shudder, wiping our wet cheeks.

'Well that was WEIRD. Hey look, a church!' says Vivian.

We creak open the enormous wooden door and duck inside.

'WOW,' my exclamation swells through the church.

'HEY!' Vivian yells, and the sound carries on a long while.

Then she swallows a lungful of air and lets out a whopping beast of a burp, which recurs alongside our manic laughter. This is pretty much how we spend the next hour.

Lunchtime: a ham and cheese sandwich for Vivian the vegetarian, and a piece of wholemeal focaccia for me. After lunch, we drink coffee and play cards.

'Zis game is called slam and...' Vivian goes on explaining while I zone out.

It's supervision and me and Summer lie on our backs, staring at the mural on the ceiling.

'That one can be called Zach,' says Summer, pointing at one of the many naked cherubs.

'Oh yeah and that one there, that one with the face like this,' I cringe at Summer, 'she is Maria. Her and Zach are having an affair.'

'What about her?' asks Summer, pointing again.

'Oh, that's...Claire! She's a bitch,' I say.

Summer explodes with laughter. Times like these are good times, times that almost make irrelevant of the fact that I am actually locked up in a mental hospital. Games keep all us girls going here and we needed a new one after 'wool fight' had landed us all in a whole heap of trouble, 'jumping down the stairs' landed us in even more trouble and 'slow racing' is not really a game but another way of pursuing our eating disorders at mealtimes. And don't even get me started on the naked dares.

'Hey, Alice!' says Ruby, crawling towards me and Summer (in supervision, standing is not allowed).

I roll my head to one side and look at her dainty teenage face. 'Yeah?' I ask.

'Wanna play slam? I'll teach you!' she says.

So that was that, 'slam' became 'the thing', and we spent the next few weeks in a cross-legged factory of shuffling, slamming, and explosions of victory and commiserations. Sometimes, it's like a big old sleepover here. And sometimes (well, always), when the doctors let me go home for 48hr leave, the hollow carve of not being in the unit makes me sick with grief.

Vivian zips about with cards, roaring when she wins, roaring even more when she loses. Meanwhile I think of hospital, my soul churning with a confusing mixture of loss and relief.

Back at Gabriel's and Vivian is rummaging gleefully through her yellow suitcase, showing me her high heels, clutch bags, lipsticks.

'Zis is for ze concert,' she says, reaching an elegant ash-rose gown away from her, smiling at it. 'Hey, do you vant me to play?'

'Would you? I'd *love* that,' I say.

Vivian rests her violin on her shoulder, her volcanic boisterousness melting away as she drags her bow and pierces the room with the first, flawless, shrieking note. Then more passionately, her whole body swerving as she saws at her violin, jittery tunes filling the room. From mournful whines to prancing song, Vivian fills the room, shatters it to pieces, then fills it again. After the last sad whimper resonates, Vivian peels away from the violin, her face once again filling with mischief.

'Wow... Jesus. You have... I can't even tell you. You're so talented!' I say.

'Well, tank you, tank you,' she says, bowing theatrically.

After dinner (chickpeas mashed with beer for me), Vivian and Gabriel play music: Vivian on violin, Gabriel on acoustic guitar. Every now and then, their rhythms synchronize and this sparks an electrical current in the room that gives me prickly goose bumps. Lovely, achingly lovely, the perfect nightcap to my final hours in Italy.

I dream of hospital, of screaming, 'I WANT TO GO HOME, JUST LET ME OUT, JUST LET ME OUT!' I dream of the unrelenting itch of wanting to be outside the sickly orbit of madness and pills and weigh-ins and locked windows. I wake up with a jolt and leave without saying goodbye to Vivian and Gabriel.

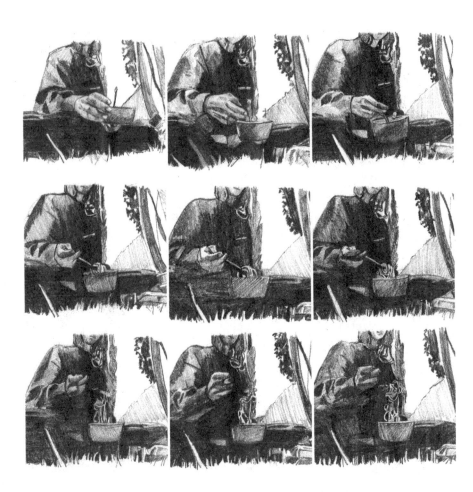

25

The Alps

'Un cappuccino con latte di soia, grazie. E una focaccia dolce. Questa.' I point at a sugary slice of focaccia, punctured with raisins, for the last time.

The lady hands me my final supper, cross for some reason. Women: you just never know what's the matter with them.

I flap open an Italian paper and run my index finger across lines of pretty words, tapping furiously on the ones I recognise: 'prima', 'nonostante', 'Pericoloso', 'adesso', 'bambini', 'gia', 'volta' and my personal favourite *'morto'*.

One final dribble of coffee, one last bite of focaccia; I take a wide, lung-stretching breath and turn to face the Alps.

'LET'S DO THIS SHIT!' I yell.

Everyone in the street stares at me. Turns out 'shit' is universally understood.

Houses become shapes, then blots, dots, flecks, and now I can't see them at all: all I can see is dramatic carves of land pocketed with the odd village or town. The air is thin, the drop on the other side of the crash barrier, deadly. Delicate clouds pour around me, cold and sweet. That's it, isn't it? I belong in the sky! Why haven't I ever known that I've *always* belonged in the sky?

'I'M FLYING!' I yell, cycling at the amazing speed of 2.5mph.

A whirring noise buzzes in my ear and I turn to face the head-down-bum-up lycra package gaining on me. I yell pleasantries at him but he remains unsmiling, lest it interfere with his razor-sharp, streamlined aerodynamics.

An hour later, I see Mr lycra again, slurping a sachet of green glucose jelly by the roadside. Seems ridiculous to me that at the same rate we avoid sugar like the plague, there's a whole industry dedicated on ways to inhale it. Get over yourself and eat some fucking raisins.

'Ciao!' I wave.

Poor fella almost chokes on his alien jelly as I overtake. Nice to meet you Hare, I am the Tortoise.

7000ft up. The Alps thunder around me, piercing through cushions of cloud, stinging on my soul. Because I never knew beauty could be so violent. More violent than the razor-sharp, HD, over-saturated, blare of them portrayed in a desktop screensaver, even. The air is snappable and magically chilly, each breath like an Airwaves advert. I suck the welling tears back in, saying aloud 'No crying until you reach the summit'.

It dawns on me as the ground falls yet further away, that there was once a time I'd wince heaving up the thirteen shallow stairs of the unit (we counted them, we were always counting). That miserable pain, thighs burning, knees shattering as though knocked again and again with a hammer, doesn't seem so long ago. I think of this as my legs, a little jellied but still strong, carry me towards a sign that blurs.

'FRANCE'

I burst into a seizure of hysterical tears, ignoring Mr. Lycra who zips past again. That's it: Italy over. And here are the stats:

Travel mates: 2 (Aaron and Eric)

Times I was inappropriately touched: 4.5

Free pizzas: 12

Mosquito bites: Lost count at 43

Lunch invites: Countless

Cat's lives lost: -4 (the roly-poly, the rubbish truck, the lightning, the brick)

Money gifted: €20

Money stolen: €85

Miles travelled: 2,500

Figs eaten: At least 400

I exhaust away the last of the tears, then strike down on the pedal, holding my breath as if expecting a camembert-yielding, beret-wearing Frenchman to gallop at me, his garlic garland banging against a striped shirt. No such thing occurs. Mountains ahead, mountains behind: the only difference being a sobering change of my heart.

At the summit (which was curiously a mile on from the border), I stand on a rock at the precipice. A cold, thin wind swooping in and out of my lungs. Look at how high I am, how free I am, how better I am. Great thumping sobs lunge in my chest again. Good legs, strong legs. I've made it, in all sorts of ways.

I hug my knees tight, my nails piercing crescents into my arms. The shaking and rocking are uncontrollable, but I don't mind. I don't even mind the slamming of my spine against the wall over and over. Besides, I like bruises. Along with the thunder of my screams and lightning strikes on my arms, these perfect little storm clouds relieve some of my mind's weather. Here in the unit, we all have bruises (headbanging – not the concert kind – is very on trend at the moment). Half of us have purple foreheads.

What I do mind is the screaming because it has prompted the heavy footsteps of Nurse Christina who opens the door and says 'Alice?' She walks over and stands above me, 'ALICE?' she repeats.

The staff here usually kneel down, rest a palm on your back, tell you it will all be all right, prise open your fist, place a tiny blue pill in it 'take it, it'll calm you' they say, usually. Nurse Christina does no such thing.

Instead, she says with a bored sigh, 'You're never going home.'

'Excuse me?' says a freckled lady, approaching nervously, 'Are you... are you alright?'

'Huh?' I sniff. 'Yes. Oh my God, sorry. I'm just overwhelmed... It's so...There's Italy and...I am free. It's so beautiful! I'm free!'

'Oh, bless you!' she exhales, 'I have to admit I was a little worried about you.'

'...You thought I was going to jump?!'

'Well, yeah, a bit!' She says.

We laugh our English heads off and share lunch. It's all (quite literally) downhill from here.

My original plan was to camp here, right at the summit. It had seemed like a wicked idea, only the angry black marbling of clouds spinning overhead is reminding me of what Vivian had said to me,

'You can't camp up the mountains! You'll be struck by lightning!' And after that night of the creepy binman, I'm keen to avoid lightning at all costs.

So the plummet begins in a whoosh of wind that flicks away the concoction of euphoria and sadness melting out of my eyeballs. Peeling over the other side, snowy mountains barbed with ski lifts rise around me. I cry all the way to Termignon: a little Alpine village comprising of fairy-tale wooden cabins.

'Fuck!' I hiss to an aisle of tins.

How have I forgotten how *expensive* France is? There is nothing in this shop, not even an apple or tin of beans, for less than 50 cents. But never mind at all because I am leaving €1.50 lighter, carrying a bar of dark chocolate, a packet of spaghetti and a really wicked grin.

This village, Termignon, has all the stereotypes of heaven: bakeries, low clouds, a babbling brook, grass so green it makes one envy the sheep, one perfect looking church (God I love a church), outdoor plug sockets, Alpine huts and a *free* campsite with real toilets and hot showers and everything. I pick a spot, far away from all the other proper campers, and set up my wee plastic house.

'EY!' says a man, raising a mallet above my head.

'AH! Oh! Graz– Merci!' I drop my pink trainer and bang the last tent peg in with his mallet. 'Voila!' I announce, handing his mallet back to him.

'Non, non, non!' says the man, shooing me out of the way, undoing my wonky guy ropes.

With a few grunts and bangs, he fixes up my crooked tent then returns to his caravan, his wife, and their postponed cheese.

Ah, the smell of bubbling pasta, the shine of it when doused in olive oil, the seductiveness of it as lumps of chocolate melt in: what a luscious dinner! I guzzle, moan, slurp away, nestled among mountains, bum to Alpine grass, mountains keeping me company. And just as I finish the last silky ribbon, a drop of rain lands in my bowl, as though it'd been politely waiting for me to finish my dinner. The sky rumbles too, a livid indigo colour. I tilt back my head and sure enough, the heavens open. Thunder roaring, flashes of lightning pulsing, rain clattering on the roof of my tent and a little me tucked away in my sleeping bag in *the Alps*.

I wake and gasp. Is it true? I unzip my tent and take a peep. It *is* true! I am in the Alps! I draw in a long breath. France smells pretty great this morning: a fairy-tale perfume of wet grass, baked dough and that whiff of cheese that mysteriously haunts every last French corner. I'd forgotten (suppose because I'd been so taken with focaccia) the joy of French bread but it all comes flooding back in a soft, buttery plume of steam as I crack open a warm baguette. The barman, who had determinedly disliked me when I'd first burst in asking for bread, smiles warmly at me as I pick the last few golden flakes off the bar with a licked finger. How could I have forgotten the charm of throaty accents, brasseries, sexily pissed off men and tidy streets? I *love* France.

With the first of many baguettes downloaded, I whiz down the mountains, like a fly caught in a stream, pulling along with no effort. Most people rave about downhill cycling. But actually, the uphills are way more fun: the chug and effort, the deepening precipice, the quiet, are much more gratifying than the greedy whiz of tumbling back down. I actually laugh with joy as I find myself at the mercy of a climb. Then I laugh yet more as a man shout to me, 'HEY! ENGLISH GIRL! BRAVO YOU CYCLE THE SAME ROUTE AZ DE TOUR DE FRANCE'.

Another mostly downhill hour passes and the Alpine magic seems to be ever diminishing. Roads become more industrial, the trees less springy looking, the air warming with each passed mile, and perhaps the worst of all, I cycle past a McDonalds. But oh! Look! A stick insect on a lamppost! Sacrebleu!

This morning I have found myself in a bit of desperate rush because I've suddenly realised, whispering a 'fuck' to the gargantuan bell of the church I'd camped next to, that it is Sunday.

I'm so happy, just so unbelievably, toe-wrigglingly, butt-twitchingly, hysterically, HAPPY! What a life. The Alps are behind me now, yet still their bigness remains, somewhere in my chest, as courage. And camping is great. Who needs walls and bricks and mortgages when you can have your own little portable den? And who needs to strive for such petty things as good looks and good money? Eh? Freedom is the real gold. More and more, it seems, we've all gotten life wrong. All but me! Who has solved the great puzzle of unhappiness in just four months! It might just be okay, maybe I'm better and ready to go home.

Tip-tap. I open Komoot. My heart sinks. I'm getting closer. Which is good, surely? The morning air is notably sharpening, the leaves of the trees slowly losing their waxiness and, glittering in the bushes, I even spot a couple of blackberries. Autumn is beginning to whisper on things.

For lunch I am cooking sweetcorn, pinched for free from a field absolutely heaving with it. Only it's taking an age to cook: it's been an hour so far and the damn stuff still looks unpleasantly pale.

'EY!' shouts a man, 'DAT IS NOT CORN FOR UMANS, DAT IZ CORN FOR ANIMALES!'

'OH! SACREBLUE!' I shout back. Then, 'MAIS NE PAS GRAVE! JE SUIS UN ANIMEAUX AUSSI!'

The corn sits in my stomach like cement all day.

I camp by a lake and wear Delia's jumper to bed, saddened by the absence of my nemesis: the mosquito. Summer is dying.

In Chalon-sur-Saône, I knock on Judith's (my host's) door. Judith is a tall and crazy Dutch woman, talks as she walks, in floaty, nonsensical wafts that don't seem to lead anywhere.

'He, yes, I see, very good,' she mutters, still wafting in a slightly revealing nightie. 'Sit.'

And I do.

'And why?' she says, 'Why are you here doing this travel, there is a reason...'

Something about Judith's question has disturbed me so I say, 'Oh yeah, dunno. For freedom, adventure. But what about you? What do you do?'

'I get tribeswomen with big hats on and women in Burkas to ride bicycles in the city.'

'Oh! Wow!' I say, wondering if she was maybe speaking in metaphors again.

'Yes. But no one pays me. Dinner?'

Judith swifts off to make dinner for her family who have not spoken a word since I arrived and still do not speak as we sit down to... Spaghetti and ketchup. I have mine plain, but the smell of that disgusting sauce seems to climb down my throat anyway.

The next morning Judith tells me my fortune, though it was so ethereal, and my brain is so static with caffeine (Judith makes very strong coffee), I can't make head or toe of it. But she does mention that I have a purpose to help people. She says this quite seriously while handing me some rather phallic looking dried bananas and a badge that reads 'YOU ARE ON THE JOURNEY'.

Oh the rain! The dark, shivery, rain. My clothes weigh down on me and my fingers lose all their gear-changing strength. So I make up a song, *en Français,* and it carries me thirty sodden miles until the clouds are fully wrung out. I stop to snack on bread, and stare at the fluorescent scars in the evening sky, a sky that is already darkening even though it's only eight o'clock. Then a boy on a BMX whizzes past me. Then he whizzes by again, this time doing wheelies. He does this a few times before finally mustering the courage to cup my ear with his hand and whisper, 'I LOVE YOU,' into it.

26

I am French

Shaken by the first school bell, the trees all at once shrug away their caramelised leaves: a clatter of yellows, reds, oranges and browns coating the cool gravel in an autumnal carpet. September has arrived and if you pay enough attention, you can feel the brilliant energy of nervous students of all ages, pulsing through the air. Students who will rise early this morning, unlike the sun that seems to be slackening with each passing day: late for work in the mornings and resigning too early in the evening, but making up for it with the most heartbreaking sunsets and rises. And the night air has lost its softness, making camping a chilly nightmare as my Mediterranean marination (tanned skin, blonde hair, freckle plethora) has me equipped only for heat. Anything below 25° makes me simply cross.

So no camping. Tonight, I'm staying in a barn with a goat farmer. A very strange goat farmer called Thomas who stares at me in a very particular way I haven't yet worked out. It's like he's on some kind of internal rollercoaster: his face filling with thrill, then humour, then utter daze. I ramble on at him nervously and he just stands there, saying basically nothing. He even starts to laugh at me. Perhaps 'goat' is a euphemism for drugs.

'Oh my God,' he says, finally.

I stand panicked, wondering what faux pas I might've achieved.

'You are so beautiful,' he says.

I laugh, heat blooming in my cheeks. Thomas just stares, amazed.

Eventually he comes to, and gives me a cheese-tour, wafting his arms about proudly at the many white lumps in his basement. I wish he wouldn't waft, it's making the smell even worse. This is not an enjoyable bad smell like manure or one's own fart, but a vicious lung-curdling pong; even the tablecloth of Thomas's kitchen looks limper for it.

A girl, Thomas's cheese apprentice, joins us in the kitchen to help with dinner. She's a pretty thing with neat hair and a good set of teeth and this puts me at ease for a moment. Until I realise that to Thomas, she may well be invisible. God! He won't stop staring at me! Even as I mash blackberries into my rice, even as I refuse his wine, even as I add more weird ingredients to my rice (chocolate, olive oil, salt, pepper). No luck, he's still transfixed.

'One day we should go cycol togezer' he says, blatantly ignoring his poor cheese girl.

'Oh! Pourquois pas!' I say.

'Ey Aleece, you zon't mind if we share a room tonight? I usually sleep in my caravan but today I wunt to try ze spare room, I nut no why, but I juz wunt to try out de spare bed.'

'Oh!' I say.

'Zere are two beds.'

'Pourquois pas!'

'Great. I never sleep in zis room. Could be fun.'

I think for a moment then say, 'Pourquois pas!'

I instantly regret it.

Something is stopping me from falling asleep. Maybe the brittle urgency of the atmosphere, of somehow knowing that Thomas's bright blue eyes were open and glimmering in the dark. A gentle patter on the floorboard moves towards me, then the duvet tugs a little. And would you believe it Thomas is sliding into bed with me, his cheese odour following swiftly behind. I let out a little nervous laugh. Thomas giggles and starts to nuzzle.

'What the hell are you doing?!' I whisper.

'I am French!' he whispers back.

I cross my arms defensively, trying to ignore the humidity of his breath on my neck.

'You don't wunt me?' he asks.

'No!' I say.

'But you zay *pourquois pas*. You zay I can sleep ere.'

'YES, but there are TWO beds in this room,' I say this to the ceiling because his sad, shiny eyes are killing me. 'One for you, one for me.'

'But I'm *culd*, I ave no duvet.'

I gather the damp duvet (I blame the cheese) and dump it on top of him. 'Take mine,' I say.

'Oh...Okay.'

Thomas crawls back into his own bed, stiffening the cheesy air with his disappointed sighs. The cheese smell is suddenly weighing as heavy on me as a wet blanket.

'Aleece?' he whispers.

I ignore him, trying to keep my pretend snore as believable and unattractive as possible.

'Aleece!' he pleads, 'Aleece, can I sleep with you? I'm culd. Aleece? Please? Please Aleece!'

A full night's sleep would have been great, but instead I am leaving with a tiny fracture of sleep and an aura of cheese: warm and sour clinging to my clothes, my skin, my hair. I just couldn't bring myself to use Thomas's shower, because I felt sure that if I'd turned the dial, a glut of liquid cheese would pour out.

'Au revoir!' I call, pedalling away from the fromage hemisphere.

Thomas is too sad to speak, or wave.

Maybe I should've just slept with the guy.

I hadn't felt so bad earlier, but two hours in and my brain feels hot and stuffy, despite the fact the rest of me is cold. A feeling that intensifies considerably after a tinned ravioli lunch break. All I want to do is sleep. I'm *thirsty* for it.

'UGH! I CAN'T DO IT!' I yell at the hill rising in front of me, 'NO Alice...Keep going...Keep....GOING. I can't, I can't, you can, I can't. Come on legs, COME ON LEGS!' I yell.

But it's all too much. The sun slices my retinas, blares like noise in my feverish brain and, UGH, the wind. Such unnecessarily windy, wind.

Then a mysterious message hums in my head, it says 'at the top of the hill, there's a place to sleep'.

So I say it aloud, 'At the top of the hill there's a place to sleep.' It feels nice so again, 'At the top of the hill, there's a place to sleep. At-the-top-of-the-hill-there's-a-place-to-sleep-at-the-top-of-the-hill-there's-a-place-to-sleep'

Finally I reach the top of the hill and waiting for me at the exact tip-top is a bird of prey, sitting on a post. Well thanks a lot *universe,* what the hell am I supposed to do? Sleep in his nest? I stop to stare at him angrily and he shouts back, 'HEY!'

I stare open mouthed at the miracle bird.

'HEY! OVER HERE!'

I turn around and on the opposite side of the road a small, mad-scientist looking fella flaps at me. I skip across the road, waving.

'You are Anglaise!' he says. 'An where you go?'

'Back to England. I'm actually looking for a place to sleep. It's so cold and *ugh*, I'm so TIRED. I didn't sleep last night because a goat farmer tried to jump into bed with me. But anyway, never mind. Sorry, am I making sense? I'm just so, *so* sleepy.'

He laughs, and says, 'Come, I have a place you can sleep. A *wwoofing* farm. Iz half hour dis way.'

'My gosh, and I can sleep? Really?'

'Yes. Oh, by de way, I'm George. I am a Mexican how you say... a shrink? Come. Let's go.' George pedals on.

For a moment, the word 'shrink' pulses in my head like an injury. But George's big rainbow jumper and mischievous grin are so far detached from the ironed trousers, clicky-pens and long, judgemental silences of Dr Julia.

So I catch up behind him and say 'Thanks so much. I'm Alice.'

George throws a dangerous smile over his shoulder.

'What's in there?' I ask, pointing at the cardboard box bound to his bike.

'Here, I show you,' says George slowing down so we are cycling double-file.

He begins pulling things out of his box: out of date bread, a couple of bruised bell peppers, beaten up pastries. 'I get dem from a bin,' he says proudly.

'OH! I've *always* wanted to jump into a bin!' I say.

George laughs, because that was a stupid thing for me to say.

Cycling parallel, I get a better look at George and come to the conclusion he looks just like an elf. His ears are wider at the top and exaggerated in shape, his curly black hair springs in every direction possible, and his moustache and goatee, draw around a cheeky grin: all that wrapped in a rainbow jumper too big for his small body.

Our bikes crunch into the farm's drive. And with the earth shattering wallop of a didgeridoo against a sheepskin gong (both of which exist here), the w*woofing* farm hits just about every hippie stereotype.

'Here, I show you around...Dis is where de boss sleeps,' says George, pointing at a cosy looking stone cottage.

Three large stones rest against the cottage, painted with the slightly insistent words 'SMILE', 'HARMONY', and 'BE HAPPY'.

'And this is the sound therapy room,' says George as we pass an enormous yurt. 'And come, under ere,' George ducks into an underground cave. I follow him. 'This is a room for massage.'

I stare at the suspended bed hanging from the ceiling, circled by glassy trinkets. The wind chimes jangle and chink outside. I actually shudder.

'Nice,' I say.

We continue the tour passing the allotment, the caravan (where George sleeps), a zip wire, George's 'meditation and thinking' zone (a sheet of metal laid on top of a rock). And just as George is explaining the complicated dos and don'ts of the compost toilet a very beautiful but very sick looking girl in ratty clothes staggers towards us, barefooted. Her skin has the greenish tinge of a pale bruise and I almost flinch, thinking she might be a zombie.

'Hey' she says, giving George a flaccid hug. 'Hey,' she repeats to me.

Before she has the chance to infect me her new boyfriend joins her side: a bearded fella who looks markedly fresher that her, but still a little clammy. Then another, healthier looking girl strides up to us: a Spanish babe of mellow blonde waves and again not as poorly looking, but getting there. It then occurs to me that you can tell exactly how long each 'w*woofer*' has been here based on how ill they look. I make a game of this: standing them in an imaginary anaemic line with the German zombie girl at one end and George at the other. Then a man who doesn't look poorly at all marches towards us authoritatively, commanding silence on the parting group with his presence. He looks clean, too clean given how filthy his servants are, and I can't help but find the neatness of his white beard suspicious. Everybody calls him 'the boss' and I dislike him immediately for it. But like George, the German girl, her boyfriend and the Spanish chick, I follow his orders and enter the sound therapy yurt. We remove our shoes, and lie amidst the beaten cushions and tattered rugs.

It all begins with the Spanish girl, stirring chiming notes into the sound bowls. Next, the boss' starts bonging his gong (*not like that*) enjoying the power of it way too much. Then a didgeridoo: gurgling and groaning right in my fucking ear like an upset stomach. Tired ears do not appreciate such demonic sounds.

At the end of the noise the boss asks us each how we found the experience. Everybody has something inspired to say, 'emotional', 'spiritual', 'peace', 'searching', 'soul': these are all words I manage to translate. And then it is my turn. Fuck.

'Et Alice, Comment avez-vouz trouvé l'expérience?' asks the boss.

'Ur...C'est bizarre!' I say, 'Un nouveau experience pour moi.'

The whole group 'Mmm' in agreement.

Dinner tonight is to be couscous, potatoes and salad, made by me and George. I chop, he fries. But just as George and I dig our spoons into the couscous, the boss interrupts, calling George outside with a single motion, as if he were a dog.

After their secret chat, George pokes his head through the door and says, 'Alice, we ave to do a jub. It won't take long. We will be back by nine an den we can eat. Yez? Iz okay?'

There is something deeply unsettling about how much authority 'the boss' has over these anaemic youth-slaves. I do not want to be an anaemic-youth slave, I do not want to go and do a job with George, I want to eat my fucking couscous! But I like George, so I hop in the passenger seat and we bump along until we reach a house with no lights on, in search of a man named 'Luke'.

'Why are we looking for this guy, Luke?' I ask, as we scour the empty farm.

'I don't know. Maybe to help him mobe something?' says George.

'LUKE!' I scream, 'LUUUKKEEE?... Ah well, we tried.'

George howls with laughter.

We search and search, poking about with a weak torch.

'Peut-être...' I narrow my eyes at George, *Luke est mort.*

George laughs in great squeals then says, 'Yeah. LUKE EST MORT.'

'LUKE EST MORT! LUKE AS UN MALADIE!' I yell.

George laughs louder then says, 'Alice, let's go get beer.'

'Sure!' I hop back in the passenger seat.

'Alice, it very important you *not* to tell de boss we get beer. If e ask, we say we spend ages looking for Luke.' he says steering us into town with all the control of a five-year-old in a go kart. I'm not actually sure George has a license.

'Bien sûr! Nous chercher pour Luke!' I say.

'Exactament.'

We sing the whole way there, slapping our thighs, 'LUKE EST MORT LUKE EST MORT LUKE E CUISINÉ DANS LE FEUR!' we roar over and over, finding new ways to kill Luke with each verse.

Beer in George's glass, water in mine.

George turns to me and says 'So why are you trabel all alone like dis? It is nut normal to want to be so alone.'

'Well, I like it best on my own. Besides, I'm getting a bit sick of men touching me all the time. Like the goat farmer jumping into my bed and I guess a few times in Italy... and I just- I just like being on my own.'

George deflates a little, then says, 'Well, personally I don't understand dis. I dink you are a really beautiful girl, but it has to be both ways. If you didn't want dis sort of thing, neither would I.'

'Ah well, it's okay... I feel safe with you because I know you won't grab me,' I hint, staring at my shoes.

George knocks back the last dreg of beer. 'Let's go,' he says.

By the time we've made it back, everyone is fast asleep in their yurts and all that remains under the meek amber light in the kitchen are some speckled remains of couscous and some stale bread. George and I eat them and wander back to the caravan.

'You can sleep in my bet tonight, if you like?' George whispers.

'I think I'll be happy just on the sofa' I whisper.

'You sure? It's warmer? You'll get bery colt on your own.'

'I'm sure.'

'Okay,' he says softly, 'But come join me if you get colt, I won't touch you if you don't want. Goodnight...' he flicks out the light.

Should I do it? Crawl into his bed? I don't want to. But I want to want to. And I know it's what he wants. I could, I really could. If only I could move beyond the fear of not wanting to, I'd do it, I swear I'd do it.

Morning feels very awkward.

'Let me gibe you a massage before you go,' says George.

'Ah, that's so kind but I don't like massages. Sorry... I had a bad experience...In Italy...He touched me. I didn't like it.'

'I won't touch you.'

'I know...But I still don't like massages. But thanks.'

'Okay, I understand. But can I gibe you something before you go?'

Not a kiss, please not a kiss.

George turns around, takes something out from a drawer, 'I made it. For you,' he says, dropping a pile of green beads into my hands.

'My goodness. Uh– Thank you so much, it's beautiful,' I say, draping the necklace over my chest.

George grips both my forearms and leans in for a kiss which, with an awkward resist, I turn into a hug. Time to leave, I think.

With each passing day, the mornings are starkly colder, the sort that makes one's eyes water and one's breath puff out clouds. I put my hand on my chest: warm. Really warm. That must be the fire in my belly: a long burning fire that must've started a long while ago but that I hadn't noticed. Perhaps because the cooler weather has given it contrast, or maybe I only notice now because I'm nearly there. I'll be in Paris soon – tomorrow, perhaps – and after Paris is Normandy and after Normandy... home. I cry hot tears and sing 'Maybe Tomorrow' by the Stereophonics.

Paris is rising up around me in great high-rises, billboards and oh, there she is, just like four months ago: that scrawny LED Julia Roberts, still trying to sell her perfume. There's something so thrillingly coarse about a city's outskirts: an urban crust of grit and survival. Tomorrow I will pass through the poncy culture of the city centre, but for tonight I stay in this urban crust, with Patrice: a strange chap who speaks no English and apparently no French either. He just points at things nervously. I guess he must be shy.

Patrice feeds me avocado then insists that I sleep in his double bed and that he take the camping mat on the floor because I need to be strong, to get a good rest. I try to argue, but towards a man who speaks so seldom, my efforts are useless. *Incroyable*, I stay in rural nowhere and men leap into bed with me and then I stay in the roughest high rise of nowhere and the guy sleeps on the floor so I can have a whole room to myself. Magic. Absolute magic.

27

Dead

My alarm shrieks at me from underneath my pillow. It's 5am. I haven't woken up this early since May the 17th (the day me and Dad set off) and the slap of a day too raw, followed immediately by the strain of gravity too dense, renders me nauseous.

'Uggghh,' I moan, heaving myself from the plush depths of a fluffy duvet.

Nobody should enter the day when the sky is still black and cold: it's a crime against nature, jarring to a body otherwise so warm and safe. So even though Patrice had let me stay in his house, filled my bones with organic avocado, taken the blooming floor so I could have his double bed all to myself, in these first few moments of uncooked day, I *hate* him. I hate him and his stupid bus driver job.

'Bon matin,' says Patrice, an apologetic lilt to his voice. 'Café?'

'Oh, *oui*,' I say reaching out for a cup of offensively strong black coffee. 'Merci, Merci, *Merci*.'

It grates down my throat, black and acrid like the early morning air. One sip and my hatred towards Patrice and the ache for sleep is extinguished. I step outside into the hollow chill, caffeinated and excited: watch out big city, I'm good to go.

Chasing the blueish haze of my feeble bike light, I parallel the river Seine. It. looks so black and cruel this morning, like it actually wants you to fall it, to suck you under, to drown you with no one but the odd mangle-footed pigeon to witness it. And it's so deathly cold. I have no memories of cities being quiet and cold, and this makes me suspicious of every sparse suit, cyclist, pedestrian: what do they think they are doing being out in such a sinister morning?

The first blue light creeps in. A mottling of purple cloud stretches across the sky, starkly toothed by a black horizon of high rises and the river Seine develops a very slight silver glaze. I stare up at the sparse lit windows of the many-windowed high rises and imagine behind them perhaps cleaners, couriers, new mothers. It really seems cruel we call them 'high rises' when it is the most poor who end up there. And then I look ahead, at the smoke billowing from an open manhole. I have no idea what that's about.

I'm approaching the city centre now and save for the amber glow of the odd cosy bakery, everything is cast in cruel blue light. I think about stopping, about dashing into that yellow haven of fresh dough just across the road, but still my legs continue, not wanting to miss the recovery of morning. Also, I want to know what's going on a few metres ahead, what those three policemen are doing and what is that thing, that lump, on the ground between them? Between the columns of their legs I see a jacket. Time buffers as I near the scene. A body?

A man is lying in the recovery position, his fingers unfurled on the ends of splayed arms, his blueish face on coarse gravel and worst of all his eyes: as still as beads but without any shine, staring straight through me. Dead.

No, he can't be dead: there's no blood, or injury. Young people don't just drop dead in the streets, they don't. I stand staring at his slack face, his black hair, his vacant eyes. He must be about thirty. Or...was. No, that's ridiculous, I'm being a drama queen, he's fine, he's *fine*. Just watch, just watch his chest: any second now it'll move, rise, twitch at least. But the many awful seconds spend themselves and the man does not move. Everything remains cold and calm. A new calm, stiller than ice and more quiet than any quiet I'd known despite the fact this is Paris city centre. I pull my eyes away and pedal on with robotic steadiness, in desperate need of a cup of tea.

Starbucks: trashy, American gentrification in a convenient hub of overpriced coffees. Something about its hollowness, its lack of humanity has brought me here, puncturing a messy, quivering hole in a queue of yuppies. My turn comes, and glassy tuts go on behind me as I dither about, asking how much a soya hot chocolate would cost. The barista, who I think I may be in love with, hands me a tank of hot chocolate then uses his other hand to push my money away.

'Zon't worry,' he says.

'Th– thanks...So much,' I say, rattling away.

I burn my hands with hot chocolate and fall off the high chair, twice. Again, the tuts and scorns go on around me because I am ruining the synthetic vibe of the flat whites with their flat whites. Well, fuck 'em. Fuck 'em all, they don't know what I've seen, the trauma of 6.45am and I will cry into my hot chocolate as much as I want.

Grandpa rings.

'Hey kid, are you nearly home?' he asks.

'Uh...Yeah, I'm in...Paris,' I reply.

'What's up buzzbomb?' he ask, 'You sound different. Has something happened?'

'Sorry,' I sob.

'Take your time, tell me what's happened.'

'Well, um. I'm in Paris. And I've just seen a guy...On the ground...Dead.'

'Oh my God...' says Grandpa, quietly. 'Wow...My, God. Sweetie, you can cry if you like. Just imagine I am there with you with an arm on your sh– hold on a minute... YEAH? WHAT? SHE SAYS SHE'S SEEN A DEAD MAN THIS MORNING...YEAH... OH, OKAY I'LL TELL HER. Ahem, Jannie says you'll never get over it for the rest of your life.'

Typical Jannie. Also, I have realised I *detest* Paris.

After a Russian-roulette spin around the L'Arc de Triomphe (somebody really needs to sort out that roundabout), after an endless series of traffic lights, after blaring horn after blaring horn, finally me and The Insect crawl out of the vortex of chaos that is Paris. At the first sight of green (true green, not limp grey trees), my lungs unfold in a great 'Haaaahhhh' and my stomach unknots and starts to crunch. Oh yeah, food!

I skip into Carrefour, curiously upbeat, laughing at the swoosh of automatic doors. Then I laugh at the beans, the dried bananas, the tofu. Everything is just so funny, and why hadn't I noticed before, how utterly hilarious life is? I laugh, I skip, I sing, I smile a great smile of Stilton cheese and then I snap. Shielding behind a packet of linguini, great wracking sobs retch out of me like vomit.

After a session of crying, eating, laughing, eating, crying, I pedal onward feeling again curiously happy. Dad rings, having heard the news from Grandpa.

'Gosh, that's tough stuff,' he says, 'even I haven't ever seen a dead person. In a way, it's a kind of privilege!'

I laugh. 'Well, yeah! I guess you're right! Only...I wish he hadn't been so young.'

'Shit,' he says.

The rest of the day is a blur of tears. Alice crying in a health food shop, Alice crying through villages, Alice crying into a cup of tea, Alice crying on a dual carriage way (whoops), Alice crying until she finally arrives in Vigny, quite dehydrated.

'Ello Aleece, welcome!' says Oliver, gesturing me through the enormous door of his enormous house. 'Oh! An you Vegan, maybe you come an meet my chickens!'

We wander through the house, out into the back garden which is gently bubbling with the clucking of chickens.

'Awh, they're so *cute!*'

'And delicious,' he winks, 'sorry. An tell me Aleece, ow was your day?'

'Today was...Difficile. I saw a dead guy on the ground, in Paris. I saw his eyes too, they were empty and very dead.'

'Oh!' says Oliver, trying and failing to keep the corners of his mouth down.

'Yeah, *quelle dommage,*' I say.

'Waz it you? Did you keel im? Like zis–' Oliver pretends to kick his chicken, 'PSH, PSH, PSH!'

Suddenly the traumatic event at 6.45am seems like the most hillarious thing in the entire world. Oliver and I laugh all the way to dinner (pasta and raisins). I sleep like a baby.

Only one more pit stop between me and the Channel now and the blackberries are twinkling in the bushes. They've become my new figs, only without the horrible allergic reaction. I miss figs: the hot adrenaline, the mouth pain, the one-too-many regret, the stickiness of them. Blackberries are about right though: as each juicy autumnal cluster bursts in my mouth their mellow sweetness and slightly iron-y flavour of rain reminds me of home, of picking them with Mum, straining our backs and tipped toes, trying to get that fat one just out of reach. And of the inevitable crumble: warm and buttery on a Sunday. Nostalgia can be so wonderfully painful sometimes. Anyway, the berries are good, free fuel and I eat them vigorously, saving the best ones for my couchsurfing hosts, Bernadette and Paul.

'Salut Aleece!' says Bernadette, emerging from her overgrown garden. She has a homely face, and a silver bob fluffed up like she was falling from a height.

'Salut! Exchanté! Oh, um.' I hand her a small box of blackberries which look a little gory from the journey. 'I picked them for you!'

'Aleece!' she gasps, 'Zank you! Zese look délicieuse. My favorot! Oh, an zis is Paul.'

A man approaches dusting his hands. He stops and gasps.

'Oh my gush!' he says, 'but you are zo zin! We muz feed you!'

We eat dinner outside, the setting sun throwing a rosy light over everything, the steam from our lentils catching the peachy light.

'We like to sing togezer,' says Bernadette, staring lovingly at Paul.

'All ze time,' he agrees, returning the look.

'Go on then!' I say.

And they do, their honey-sweet voices humming together in the muffled damp of late evening. Perhaps it is this, or the warm belly of lentils, or the crooked wood of the cabin, or the enormous weight of all these quilts, or this little mouse gnawing at the peanuts in my bags, whatever it is, as my eyelids drag down and the beginnings of dreams flutter in my head, I know the best sleep of my life is swallowing me up.

Deep sleep and plenty of lentils can only mean one thing: poor, poor compost toilet.

'Goodbye Aleece!' calls Bernadette, waving.

'Ave a safe journey home!' says Paul.

'BYE!' I yell, blushing with guilt.

Home. I'm going home. And something about that fact finds me spinning ahead faster than necessary on that same liquid-smooth bike path of day one. Passing those cute-gothic houses and the Barbie catalogue château Dad had photographed me in front of four months ago, I think about stopping to send him a photo, to let him know I'll be home tonight. But I do not stop. Not for coffee, not for red lights, not for any other reason than to replenish my buckling legs with handfuls of scoffed blackberries. Until fifty miles later, there she is: the Channel.

'Un ticket pour Angleterre? S'il vous plait?' I ask.

'Yez...' The receptionist tip-taps exaggeratedly, waits for the chug of the printer then says, 'Zirty euro, please.'

I slide the cash under the glass window, the lady replaces it with a small blue ticket. I stare at the wobbling, watery word 'Newhaven', and then look up at the bored ticket lady.

'Thirty euros,' I mumble. 'Thirty euros...for home.'

Outside the air is bright and fresh. I stare out to the infinity of sea and sky, imagining the face of home only a watery blue jump away. But then something familiar distracts me, a voice, an accent.

I look over my shoulder at the woman, hands tucked firmly into the pockets of her gilet, storming towards the empty seat opposite her friend.

'Av you sin the size of those fackin toilets? I fawt I might've had too much Stella,' she says, slumping in the chair. I nearly pissed me self just lookin' at 'em!'

Hunched over an unyielding lighter her friend takes out her unlit cigarette and rasps, as much a laugh as her smoker's lung will allow.

'You twatt!' says the friend, 'That was the kids toilet! You absolute twatt!'

'Oh. Well I didn't know, did I? My arse barely fitted on the seat. Oi, gis one of those would cha?' The gilet woman reaches out for a cigarette. 'Fackin ell.'

Home... I'm going home.

Never eat an avocado as a snack on a ship: you never know how rough it might be, how sick you might feel. Having turned the same green as that of my lunch, I go outside for some fresh air and the wind – my goodness! – it blows my mouth right open. Bellows to my newfound belly-fire, fuel for the soul, winds of change! I'm going home, browner, blonder and better.

It's dark now. And having spent three hours furiously excited, giggling at the plastic thimbles of UHT milk, pacing up and down the ship, trying out all the windy decks, I am now curled up like a sleepy cat on a musty arm chair, drifting towards dreams. But they jolt away, as the ferry judders and an incoherent message crackles through the tannoy.

'Yep, you go on ahead there love,' says the high-vis ferry man.

And so I push on the pedals, rolling onto the grey, grey concrete of home.

I'd never missed England, not for one baguette-tearing, gazpacho-glugging, espresso-sipping second. Could you explain then, why am I crying so aggressively as my meek bicycle light feebly illuminates red bricks, tunnels of trees and familiar names '*Eastbourne, Brighton, Lewes*'. Even the wrist-shattering judder of surprise potholes fills me with nostalgic euphoria.

But that wild ecstasy lasts only an hour, and now I'm sick with fatigue, as though those 4,475 miles behind me had finally let themselves be known to my quivering legs. Seven *measly* miles left to go, after all that I'd been through surely seven miles was nothing. Yet, here I am: slumped in the dark eating a pot of cold soya custard, resisting the lunge of tears.

'Alice,' I whisper, 'fuck's sake, pull yourself together. Let's finish what we started. Come *on*.'

Twitching with exhaustion, I return to the saddle and heave the last of the 4,482 miles.

I stumble, I sway, I shake, I twitch my way around the back of my house and open the door. Everything looks exactly as I left it: those non-working pens still at the same spot on the windowsill, all six of our mobile numbers still jotted above the curly-wired telephone, the note I wrote on the whiteboard just before I was taken to hospital, still in its same unblemished space. It reads 'I will really miss my lovely family. You guys are my favourite people on earth. xox' I meant it then, five years ago, and I mean it now.

The same old ticking clock in the kitchen reads 1am. Will anyone be awake? I creak open the living room door and stare at Dad and Billy who reluctantly prise their eyes from the telly.

'Oh, hi Alice,' says Billy.

Dad takes a swig of beer then says, 'Hey kiddo.'

I fall into the armchair and collapse into a fit of tears. Billy and Dad look at one another awkwardly, then resume sipping beer and watching Family Guy. It's good to be back.

Epilogue

Mrs Edmonds enters the classroom and hushes the class.

'I have an announcement!' she says, clasping her hands together purposefully.

I know it has something to do with me: I saw her eye flicker in my direction. Though maybe that's just because we've been spending lots of time together recently.

'Okay, go LEFT, Alice. Yes? NOT right. Yes? Okay, go, go! Yep, that's it, THAT'S IT!' she'd said.

And bless her, for doing the whole bloody thing again in the vain hope of rectifying a useless cyclist such as me. Just me, Mrs Edmonds and that cycling proficiency lady who looks at me with such sickening sympathy, out in the cold twice a week like three losers. I'm not sure that I wanted a second chance because you know what? I don't think cycling is really my thing.

'ALICE...' Mrs Edmonds begins, voice husky with fervour.

The class goes silent. Uh-oh. This can't be good. Was it that constipation joke I made earlier? Well if it is, that's unfair: I've already done my time for that. The entire class stare at Mrs Edmonds, waiting for her to finish her sentence.

'...HAS PASSED!' she shouts, bursting her palms open.

'YEEAAAHHH!' screams the entire classroom, smacking their palms, rising from their chairs.

I sit amidst my standing ovation, basking in every roar and whoop.

About the author

Alice is a 25-year-old disaster, currently living in Sussex. She wrote this book to prove that craziness need not stand in the way of a full and happy life: quite the contrary. One day, she hopes to be a cyclist, an artist and a writer. Perhaps this is what she has naively attempted with this book.

She likes to chat so please do get in touch.

alicelushington@hotmail.co.uk
Instagram: @alicelushington